Voices from Iran

Gender, Culture, and Politics in the Middle East

Leila Ahmed, miriam cooke, Simona Sharoni, *and* Suad Joseph, *Series Editors*

Voices from Iran

THE CHANGING LIVES
OF IRANIAN WOMEN

Mahnaz Kousha

Syracuse University Press

First Edition 2002

03   04   05   06   07   6   5   4   3   2

The paper used in this publication meets the minimum requirements of
American National Standard for Information Sciences—Permanence
of Paper for Printed Library Materials, ANSI Z39.48–1984.∞™

Library of Congress Cataloging-in-Publication Data

Kousha, Mahnaz.
   Voices from Iran : the changing lives of Iranian women / Mahnaz
Kousha.—1st ed.
      p. cm.—(Gender, culture, and politics in the Middle East)
Includes bibliographical references.
   ISBN 0-8156-2962-1 (hardcover : alk. paper)—ISBN 0-8156-2981-8
(pbk. : alk. paper)
1. Women—Iran. 2. Women—Iran—Family relationships. 3.
Women—Iran—Social conditions. I. Title. II. Series.
HQ1735.2 .K68 2002
305.4'0955—dc21   2002013874

Manufactured in the United States of America

To my parents, Ahmed Kousha and Toktam Aghevli

Mahnaz Kousha is an associate professor of sociology at Macalester College, Saint Paul, Minnesota. She studied art at the College of Fine Arts in Tehran, Iran. Her graduate work was conducted at the University of Kentucky, where she received her master's degree in art education and her Ph.D. in sociology.

Contents

Acknowledgments

WRITING A BOOK always involves more people than one can adequately and justly thank. Life is about conversations. Family gatherings attended at the age of twelve or thirty-five, a long or short taxi drive in Tehran, a lively discussion over the dinner table—any of these mundane activities may contribute to the beginning of a chapter or the end of another; any may rekindle diminishing interest in an old issue and the desire to pursue it. This is a book of conversations, but the forces that have brought it into existence go beyond those that I can acknowledge specifically. I am indebted to all who contributed to this book, formally or informally.

I give endless thanks to the many women who contributed to the writing of this book, whose words, in fact, form the body of this work. Without their willingness to share their thoughts, this project would not have been possible. In a culture unfamiliar with the notion of interviewing as a research methodology, their permission to tape-record the interviews was extremely valuable; it helped create a much more accurate picture of the worlds they live in, the thoughts they harbor, and their reasons for taking different paths in their lives.

Thank you also to my sisters, Mehrvash and Mahvash Kousha, who provided channels for me to meet the women. I also appreciate the assistance they gave me when I was in Iran; the map for everyday life in Iran has changed dramatically over the last two decades, and my sisters never tire of showing me new routes to take and the various paths I might explore. I am very fortunate to still have these links.

Many thanks to my partner for being a source of balance in my life, for always searching for a flicker of light in the sea of darkness, for seeing shades of color in the dark blue sky of Minnesota nights.

I would also like to acknowledge my endless debt to Eric Hooglund for his continuing support, enthusiasm, and guidance. Eric's words of wisdom have been with me every step of the way, encouraging me to move forward. His enthusiasm, profound knowledge of Iran and the Middle East, dedication to representing the region in all its complexity and humanity, and courage in presenting an alternative perspective have always been a source of inspiration for those studying the Middle East. Many thanks also to Mary Selden Evans, executive editor at Syracuse University Press, for her interest in and devotion to seeing this work published.

My thanks go to my father-in-law, Aziz Mohseni, whose early interest in my writing letters home when my husband and I first moved to the United States as foreign students inspired a desire to write more, allowing me to leave behind the idea that writing essays was drudgery. His desire, or perhaps his parental need, to know more about our lives in the United States during those early days of upheaval and change inspired in me the desire to write. Once I had a captive reader, it was hard to stop writing.

I would like to express my appreciation for the Wallace Travel Grants awarded me by Macalester College. Their support facilitated the completion of this research.

Voices from Iran

1

Introduction

THE CUSTODIAN WAS HELPING ME move to a more spacious office; we talked about the usual topics; perhaps more important than all was the January weather in Minnesota. I guess most conversations in Minnesota refer to the weather at least once—that is, if this topic does not overshadow all other subjects. We had plenty of time; there were many stacks of books to be relocated to the new office. We talked about her children, their ages, what time she gets up to be at work so early in the morning to ensure that the crew is finished before classes start and the faculty members start arriving. We talked about work, retirement, and more, until that eventual and inevitable question came up. "So, where are you from?" Long pause. There we go again. Am I ready for this? How deeply do I want to get into this discussion? "I am from Iran." "Oh, that country where that guy, . . .what is his name?" I did not volunteer any names. "You are from the country where all women are veiled and have no rights? How do women manage there? It's a mystery to me. Why don't they do something about it?"

This question can come up at any point, at any location, and when you are least ready for it. It comes up on a regular basis, almost every time you meet somebody at a conference or at friendly gatherings, at the grocery store or the antique shop, in Target or Macy's, in the plane when you are having a casual conversation with the person sitting next to you, to name a few places. Any new encounter potentially leads to this ultimate question. And this in a land where all the citizens, with the exception of American Indians, can trace their roots to some other country. Some remember their past while many have lost their ties to their ancestral heritage. More than twenty years of living in the United States have not eased the difficulty of answering this question. The decision to respond correctly and comfortably—and to face the consequent awkward inquiries—is a personal choice rooted in the need to speak a version of truth. That is, my version, placed against the dominant images presented in the media.[1]

As an Iranian and a college professor who has been teaching a class on women in the Middle East, I have faced this multilayered question too many times to count. The question is pregnant with a multitude of inquiries about women's lives. "Are all women veiled in your country?" "Do they all wear black veils?" "Can women choose their own husbands?" Once in a while, a sneaky question is hidden among a number of other inquiries. "Did you choose your husband?" "Do you practice child marriage in your country?" "What would women do if they were given the same level of freedom we have in the West?" "Is there any feminist consciousness?" "Can women divorce if they are unhappy in their marriage?" "Are men allowed to have more than one wife?" "Can women travel by themselves?" "Can women date?" "Who gets child custody in case of divorce?" "Is abortion legal?"

A never-ending series of questions follows, each demanding clarification while revealing the depth of enigma surrounding women's lives in Iran—and, I should add, in other countries in the Middle East. The 1979 Iranian Revolution brought the country into the world's spotlight. From an obscure country with which only a limited number of academicians and scholars of the region were familiar, Iran moved straight into American living rooms, occupying the television screen. This occupation has not ended. A generation of American children grew up remembering the hostage crisis and praying in their classrooms for the hostages' safety. Their parents, on the other hand, started seeing Iran and other countries in the Middle East as a major threat to America and to their own lifestyle. More importantly, they saw the emergence and solidification in Iran of a government that embodied anger, hostility, and anti-American sentiments. The mere mention of Iran invokes suspicion and a sense of backwardness, fundamentalism, and terrorism. The name brings to mind conflicting images of men—bearded, militant, hostile, and not least of all chauvinist—and women—veiled, oppressed, and submissive. Shrouded in their black *chadors* (the ultimate symbol of their oppression), women on the television screen are angry, holding their hands up and chanting anti-American slogans. The women are more than willing to fight Westernization and U.S. domination in the region, yet they contribute in the process to their own oppression. What is the truth behind these images? Is there one single truth? Are most so-called truths only media images created for political expediency, food for an anxious public mind that meets the needs of policymakers? Are some images manufactured collages that deprive millions of people of their humanity, denying them their voice and the right to a decent, proud existence?

Who is the woman, the individual, behind these images? Her appearance typifies the ultimate inferiority and oppression of the "second sex" in the region. She is oppressed yet rebellious. She is subjugated yet unruly. She is controlled yet defiant. She is hushed and subservient. She is a religious fanatic living a secluded life. She is a revolutionary, a fighter, yet segregated and oppressed. Willing to die for her nation, she is a mother and a wife. The images contradict, with each emerging to deconstruct the others. Outsiders, foreigners, and bystanders, however, tend to hold onto certain characteristics of these images, unaware of the role the West itself has played in the creation and perpetuation of a certain branch of Islamic revivalism. For them, these stereotypical attributes contain momentous significance because they remain resistant to the passage of time, oblivious to the change of governments, and blind to the dramatic socioeconomic changes that have swept the country during the twentieth century. The undue loyalty to the convoluted images—perhaps even the psychological, political, and economic need to view these differences through the lens of inferiority—has induced many a viewer to avoid questioning the validity of such images, to avoid inquiring about the politics of the region, and to avoid acknowledging the complete humanity of those who live there. The mere fact of difference signifies to the outsider a lack of change, transformation, and movement through time. The outsider is perplexed because of the extremity of these images. The difference testifies to the all-encompassing superiority of anything Western.

These images, while extremely contradictory, have proven most resilient; they have enshrouded reality. A thick white fog has fallen. It is a beautiful and mysterious fog, but because of it we have lost our vision. Image and reality, dream and nightmare, illusion and everyday life all become one. A true understanding of the humanity embedded in these convoluted pictures is denied.

No single image adequately can reveal the complexity of the lives that Iranian women live. To expect a manufactured image to explain amply the existence of more than thirty million women is unrealistic; no single image adequately can reveal the totality of any one person, let alone millions of people. The diversity of individual lives defies such confinement. The reduction of the lives of millions of women to a single familiar picture that appeals to the gaze of outsiders gravely distorts reality and minimizes the complexity of cultures and of individual lives.

Do all Iranian women share a history and culture that uniformly shape women's lives and their experiences? Judith Tucker, speaking of women throughout the Arab world, points out that the diversity of the region warns against trafficking in generalizations.[2] However, this diversity is colored by a common regional understanding of how gender is constructed. Issues of concern to women (as well as to men) emerge out of this shared understanding of their gender. Recurring themes emerge that address the experiences of women (and men) in the Middle East. However, Tucker goes beyond the specificity of women's experiences in the region to call attention to the similarity of experiences among women in the world as a whole. Instead of emphasizing the difference, the otherness, and the specificity of experiences, Tucker offers another perspective, that of inclusion and similarity arising from socially constructed gender roles.

Pointing to differences in order to signify a perpetual "otherness" or highlighting similarities to foster understanding on the basis of shared experiences are both significant attempts to comprehend women's lives. However, in these grand moves the individual and her voice are lost. With the loss of the individual goes the complexity of her experiences along with her daily life and struggles. The individual biography is rendered inconsequential because a grand picture is supposed to posit all the dimensions, presenting the ideal type with all its complexity. However, the disappearance of the individual buries her biography deep in the historical memory, buries her as deeply as if she had never existed.

While most studies on Iran have focused on the macro level of analysis and the impact of economic domination and Western influence and intervention, I have chosen to focus on the micro level, to reveal the individual voices in all the complexities and simplicities that they embody. Such a return to the individual is valuable because it allows a close look at how women themselves see their lives and how they make sense of their worlds. This approach allows the reader to join the speaker throughout her life, to accompany her in her attempt to establish an identity as a daughter, a woman, a mother, a wife, and as a person within the larger social context.

Unlike many books on women in the Middle East in which the authors move from place to place, from individual to individual, from country to country, I have stayed with the same women throughout this work.[3] The book starts and ends with the fifteen women I have interviewed. This technique provides a large picture of the women's lives instead of rendering snapshots of individual women. This small-scale study has its own merits for exploring in detail the women's diverse experiences. The interviews offer a deeper insight into the tensions and conflicts that exist in women's lives; the reader can follow the speaker from childhood to later stages in life, understanding the circumstances that led, for example, to a particular career or an early marriage.

While the grand picture is constructive in providing a general idea, the individual portraits sketched in this book allow the viewer to pause and consider the brushwork, the combination of colors, the contrasting hues, and the unpredictable results that emerge from mixing all possible colors and shades. Thus, my aim is to highlight the individual lives experienced behind the all-powerful images that have been manufactured to define the existence of Iranian women.

Even more, my aim is to move from these pictures to one- or two-story houses, to private households, to the places where individual women live their everyday lives. Therefore, this study is not about the generic title "Iranian women." To the degree that the label "American women" is problematic because it overlooks racial, ethnic, and class differences, the title "Iranian women" also presents its own problems. Such general terms deny women their personal qualities, obscuring their diverse backgrounds and various lifestyles.

To achieve the goal of exploring individual lives, this work focuses on the words of fifteen women who happened to be born in Iran. I primarily wished to hear from the women themselves and to record their words. However, to assume that fifteen women can represent a nation would be to award them enormous power and authority over women's issues. To generalize their experiences to a total population of more than thirty million women would be seriously misleading. The women in this work stand for themselves and no others. While one reader may find experiences or obstacles in common with these women, another may find no personal echo in the stories the women share. Like Tucker, I believe that the problems, the experiences, and the feelings voiced by the women in this study cut across classes, cultures, and nationalities.

This book is not an attempt to travel in search of Islamic feminism or feminism in Iran. Neither is it an attempt to explore the possibility of cohabitation among feminism, Islam, and cultural traditions. Women's lives and rights in Iran have received considerable attention since the early 1980s. The dramatic changes introduced by the Islamic Republic only a few years after its ascent to power prompted many scholars and students of Iran to delve into a thorough examination of the position of women in Iran during the nineteenth and twentieth centuries. While such scholarship has unearthed women's veiled but volatile presence in sociopolitical domains, it has also exposed the fragile and nascent nature of modernization attempts initiated during the Pahlavi regime. Historical studies on Iranian women, for example, have recorded the lives and travails of individual women who tried to introduce the first schools for girls in Tehran (1907) or in other cities.[4] The founders of these schools were denounced, attacked, and harassed by the authorities. At times, the founders were even harassed by members of their own families. Ostracized and isolated, these women nevertheless paved the way for the opening of the first public schools for girls by 1918. Their veiling had not crushed their desire to push forward for change.

A few years before these initial attempts to introduce public education for girls, a small but courageous group of women from upper- and upper-middle-class families became politically active, playing a noteworthy role on the side of Constitutionalists.[5] Condemning the Russian government's intervention in Iran's affairs in 1911, these women formed secret societies; using their veils, they transferred messages and arms to various parties involved. Finally, they gathered one thousand women to protest Russia's interference. In a country and at a historical conjuncture where society condemned as immoral any kind of women's activity outside the house, these veiled women managed to express their opinion on the future of their country. The gathering of more than one thousand veiled women outside the parliament on November 29, 1911, to reprimand the men for yielding to Russia's ultimatum is a historical image never to be forgotten.

The Iranian Revolution prompted many scholars to unearth the frighteningly limited and oppressive lives women lived around the turn of the twentieth century. It also laid bare the courage and bravery the women demonstrated in pushing forward for social change and political integrity. While defeat, harassment, and loss were a perennial part of their struggles in any path they chose, the women's efforts were not in vain. It was only a matter of time before they spurred change—gradual and slow, perhaps, but steady. If women were beaten and imprisoned at the turn of century for opening schools for girls, by the end of the century higher education became an ideal goal for the majority of girls regardless of their class backgrounds. While in the past it was traditional values and conservative ideas that stopped young women from pursuing their higher education, now it is their class and financial assets, along with the extremely difficult entrance examinations and the limited number of universities, that inhibit some young women from attending university.

Historically, the veil created mystery; gender segregation brought seclusion, isolation, and perhaps a narrow and limited world view. Regressive laws and cultural traditions hindered women's mobility and their civic rights. But women in twentieth-century Iran showed tremendous initiative in shaping their lives. If the new scholarship on women in Iran testifies to the hardships Iranian women endured, it also brings to light their resilience and determination to change their lives. The women in twentieth-century Iran were pioneers, displaying sparks of genius illuminating education, careers, politics, family life, poetry, and literature. They embodied a new source of energy, and there is no stopping it. Using a metaphor from the much-beloved Arabic tale *One Thousand and One Nights,* the genie is out of the bottle and no force can trick it into returning to confinement.[6] Women, an enormous force of energy and power confined for centuries, now have had ample time to rethink their life courses and to envision a new world.

In addition to exploring women's role in Iran's history, the new scholarship has examined many other aspects of women's lives, including the Islamic Republic's stance on women's position and rights, family planning in pre- and post-Revolutionary Iran, and the emergence of centuries-old institutions such as temporary marriage.[7] Some scholars have inquired into the practice of veiling, exploring its meanings for various groups, in different historical epochs, among different classes, and in different regions.[8]

Because of the proclaimed religious nature of the new government, much of the literature on the position of women in Iran has focused on the dominant interpretation of religious laws as they apply to women. While those supporting the revolutionary government abhorred the secular changes introduced during the Pahlavi regime (1921–79), those critical of the Islamic Republic recorded the deteriorating positions of women in different domains. The 1979 Revolution led to a long and arduous process of gender awakening. Women's lives in both the private and public spheres became topics of inquiry and investigation as the government attempted to undo the secular changes enforced during the twentieth century, to control educational opportunities and career options, and instead to introduce a new image of the Muslim woman. The government was set to Islamicize the country and to create an ideal Muslim image for all women to emulate. A discourse began that oscillated between two ideological camps, the first based on Islamic tenets that abhorred the secular changes made during the pre-Revolutionary era and the second critical of the series of changes introduced since the onset of the Revolution.

However, since those public affairs related to women's positions have been at the forefront of most investigations, the private aspects of women's lives and intimate family dynamics affecting them have received limited attention. The intimate aspects of family life and women's views of their relationships within the family and in the larger society were left unexplored. While laws, whether secular or religiously based, affect women's lives, their opportunities in terms of education, family life, and career opportunities, and even their choice of dress style and color, women live their lives both within and beyond the laws enacted by the government in power. The women's words in this study show the complex nature of everyday life and reveal a layer of reality that transcends what any government does and does not do.

Inasmuch as this work is not an attempt to search for feminism, one cannot help but wonder about the degree of feminist consciousness that exists among the fifteen women— highly diverse in terms of economic, educational, and family backgrounds—speaking here. A recurring theme throughout the chapters is a strong belief in women's innate power. The women in this study have shown an extraordinary desire to stand against all sources of oppression, be they restrictive parents, regressive laws, limited work opportunities, or uncooperative husbands. In the end, after all the discrimination the women have suffered at the hands of loved ones (family members) and in the larger society, it is extraordinary to see that many still claim that it is women who have power to shape their families, to influence their husbands, and to lead their lives. Some may try openly to exert a level of control; others may resort to more diplomatic means. Whatever strategy these women choose, the result is that many still see women as the ultimate source of power and change; perhaps as long as one has cause to struggle, the fountains of energy will continue to generate the power to overcome.

While their own voices are crucial, the interpretations following these women's words are also important. I have not shied away from inserting my own analysis of women's accounts in early chapters, but I also have tried to let each woman speak for herself. Although I asked each woman the same set of questions, I left the decision as to how much to talk about a certain topic or what issues to elaborate on to each individual. Many women tended to restructure the direction of the questions and elaborate on those issues that were more appropriate to their lives.

My goal was not to conduct a comparative research study on women in Iran and the United States. However, I could not resist the temptation to refer to relevant studies conducted in the West. While I do not engage in a comparative analysis, I believe that minimal references to literature on, for example, the mother–daughter relationship, the interaction between fathers and children, the division of household labor, or the issue of child care do provide a larger framework for interpretation. Without these minimal references, the women's accounts might be read as the predicament of Iranian women alone, while I contend that the tensions and conflicts explored here are much more universal than they are specific.

As the voices rise and fall, as the images take shape through the uttered words, full lives come into view. Nevertheless, since no person is willing completely to reveal her complexity, there are still gaps; the speakers share only some experiences and facets of their lives, leaving certain doors shut. Each woman grants only certain glimpses into her life and no more, and each stands for herself and no one else. I am, however, grateful for the glimpses allowed, attentive to the women's attempts to maintain their privacy, and ever aware of the doors that remained shut throughout our exchanges. I respect their privacy and value their openness. Were it not for their willingness to talk to me, this book would not have come into existence.

Like the marginalized and the nonmarginalized in the West, women in Iran come in a variety of classes, religions, and ethnic backgrounds. Some, albeit a limited number, still live a tribal life, while others, again a very small number, live extravagant lives. Most of the women live ordinary lives as daughters, mothers, housewives, and working women. Sometimes leaping forward, sometimes staying put, they only move forward in time. Some women may leave a mark on history to be unearthed by future generations. Most will pass through life leaving only their words as a trail to understanding their individual travails.

This book is divided into nine chapters. In "Starry Nights," I explain the methodology and the personal rationale behind this work. I am an Iranian who left the country a few months before the onset of the 1979 Revolution, right after I graduated from college. During the first part of my life in Iran, I grew up pondering certain questions and ideas that will be considered in this book. Needless to say, the 1979 Revolution and its immediate impact on women's lives and rights generated more questions. I switched my field of study from art to sociology, hoping to better understand the massive changes that were occurring in the country. One outcome of this study is that, while pondering these questions was intellectually stimulating, finding answers for them, I believe, is a challenging and never-ending endeavor. I found that while similarities exist among the women, their life experiences are so diverse that the grand generalizations often made about women in the Middle East could not be sustained. While the tendency to generalize is strong, minor variations demand attention and require a fair hearing. This chapter starts with the questions I grew up with and explains the way I approached this project.

"The Women: Cast of Characters" introduces the individual women who participated in this study. It discusses the women's family backgrounds and provides a measure of information about their level of education, employment, and marital status. To assure anonymity, I have taken liberties with names and with the details of the women's lives. These modifications, I believe, do not distort the authenticity or the reality of their lives or the particular backgrounds they come from. This chapter is important because, I

believe, readers will want to know more about the women's general backgrounds as they proceed from chapter to chapter, reading the women's own
words on diverse issues.

The range of relationships between mothers and daughters is explored in
"Ties that Bind: Mothers and Daughters" and "Cherished Bonds: Mothers
and Daughters Revisited." Together these chapters look into this primordial
relationship and its effects on daughters. When they talk about their relationships with their mothers, the daughters are talking not only about their
own lives but also about the kind of predicaments some mothers experienced and the ways in which they adjusted and adapted to their problems. In
other words, by talking about their relationships with their mothers, the
daughters also are shedding light on the lives their mothers led.

"Fathers and Daughters" examines the roles of fathers and their aspirations and dreams in their daughters' lives, and shows the diverse kinds of relationships existing between daughters and fathers. While some fathers
played nurturing and supportive roles in their daughters' lives, others remained distant authority figures. Still others adhered to strict gender rules,
trying to inhibit their daughters' every move and thwart their desire to advance with time and break away from strictly traditional gender precepts.
Nevertheless, regardless of the particular role each father played, the accounts the women share indicate that their fathers were critical figures in
their lives.

"Marriage and Courtship" looks at courtship practices and explores
how the women came to the decision to marry. What were their reasons
for marriage? Was it a result of family pressure? Did they choose their husbands themselves, or did their parents choose for them? Who were the primary players, the key decision makers in this game of love and lifetime
commitment? Would the women do it again, that is, marry the same man
provided they could start all over? The women's words show that although
most of them were not seriously thinking about marriage, marriage was
awaiting them.

Diverse aspects of women's lives and experiences are explored in

"Women's Lives, Women's Words." These topics include employment—notably how fathers, mothers, and husbands responded to the pioneering generation of women who embarked on employment outside the home on a much larger scale than any generation before. In most cases, the fathers were positive forces who encouraged their daughters' entrance into the labor force, while the husbands played at best a neutral role. While fathers in general took pride in their daughters' careers, most husbands had problems with their wife's employment. This was particularly the case after childbirth. This chapter also looks at how women spend their salaries before and after marriage, revealing that while most of the women felt free to spend their wages on personal needs before marriage, after marriage they began spending their wages on household expenses. These women felt a sense of loss, for they believed that their financial contributions to the family economy did not bring them any higher respect or reward. Furthermore, their careers meant that their needs as wives and as women with their own personal expenses were never recognized or acknowledged. The rest of this chapter explores how the women negotiate housework, child care, and the care of aging parents and in-laws. Housework remains a point of contention in most marriages. Many women did not expect their husbands to help out at the beginning of their marriage, believing that housework was their duty regardless of the fact that they were gainfully employed. Over time, however, this began to change as the women realized that their contributions to their family's economy merited a corresponding shift to a more active role in the house by their husbands. Most of the husbands adamantly refused to take on housework, however, contending that employment was the women's choice and that they did not have to work if housework and child care became too burdensome.

In "A Man or a Woman? Which Is Better Off?" I start with a hypothetical question, one that I have often asked myself and many others throughout the years. Given the incessant problems and challenges women experience on a daily basis, I have always wondered which gender people would choose if they actually could select their own. In response to this question, the majority of the women chose to be female. Their reasons varied and were rooted in different rationales. One woman chose to be female because she believed in women's purity and sacred qualities. Others wanted to be born female because they believed in their potential and yearned for a second chance. A few women made conditional choices; they would choose to be female again only if social conditions were different or if they could live abroad in the West where women had more rights.

"Women's Words" explores the range of problems the women have faced throughout their lifetimes. Each woman chose to talk about those issues most important to her personally. The problems had their roots in social, economic, legal, historical, familial, and religious issues. In this chapter, many women question the invisible social contract that has rendered them powerless. Throughout their lives, these speakers were compelled to question their worth as women and the merits attached to womanhood. Some contrasted their upbringing to that of their brothers. Others questioned the multitude of rights men of any class enjoy. A few critically examined other women, such as mothers who constantly calmed and consoled their daughters while advising further submission and friends who betrayed and undermined those women who enjoyed more rights than they in their marriages. These few acknowledged women's vices and shortcomings and the role of some women in perpetuating the subordination of women as a group. This chapter shows that while some women openly rebel, others resort to silence. Some only harbor the idea of rebellion, dreaming of change and hoping for better days. Many see the younger generation as much more conscious than they of their own rights and believe that their daughters' generation will demand the rights and the privileges they were denied.

A final word of caution: in the West, much of the discourse on women in the Middle East revolves around the issue of veiling. Those who expect the same degree of attention to veiling in this work may be disappointed. Veiling did not emerge as an all-encompassing topic of conversation. While some women referred to it in passing as a nuisance, others bypassed it to address other issues they saw as more critical. There were also those who did not mind the veil. As one woman put it, "Veiling is a problem for those of us who were raised before the Revolution." One might add that, inasmuch as veiling is significant both symbolically and in actuality, the women's personal accounts show that much change is happening both beyond and behind the veil.

2

Starry Nights

SLEEPING ON THE THIRD-FLOOR BALCONY on summer nights felt like an out-of-this world experience. The stars seemed so close I could reach up and hold them in my hands. So close, so real, they were within my reach. The chill of the night had taken over and the hot blazing sun of only a few hours earlier had become a distant memory. Even as a young girl I cherished those nights, knowing too well that they would not last forever. We had those starry nights only in summer months on the third-floor balcony, and I knew that sooner or later all of us, my two sisters and I, would be in different places. It seemed as if those nights were already part of a long-cherished memory.

Lying down on the chilled sheets, watching the universe spread out before us, those nights were our conference time. Relaxed and comfortable, released from the anxiety of daily activities, we talked about everything, excluding no topic. We discussed literature, art, and more. One of my sisters was studying art and the other loved European literature. At times, I fell asleep only to open my eyes a little later to hear my sisters still continuing their conversation. Lying there listening to them, I felt serene and happy to be able to spend many a summer night like that. We talked about books we read in those days, *Crime and Punishment, The Cherry Orchard, Little Women, The Second Sex,* and *Great Expectations.*[1] Each one of us related to some books and not to others, each appreciating one author or book over another. Back then we thought of these books as works of fiction and not serious literature, not knowing that they were taught in literature classes in the West. For us, they were entertainment, a break from the rigid and boring schoolwork. But we talked about more than literature. Our lives, our upbringing, mother and father, women and men, marriage and divorce, and friends and relatives were exciting topics that kept us up way into the night.

Those summer nights came to an abrupt end. One of my sisters married and moved in with her husband. I, the youngest sister who was determined never to marry, married a little later and moved to the United States to pursue my graduate work in art. The year was 1979, the year of the Iranian Revolution. I left a few months before the massive uprisings and dramatic changes shook the country. I still miss those summer nights, those long nights of chatting. I miss the closeness of the stars, the belief that I could reach out and hold them in my hands, the dreamy feeling of being lost in the universe. Fourteen years passed before I was able to go back to Iran to visit my family, to take a peek at the balcony where no one slept any longer, to walk in the back alleys and streets where I grew up. Fourteen years had left their inevitable impact. Although my sisters and I were as close as we had been when we separated, the fact remained that we were no longer the same young, hopeful persons. The passage of time had touched us in too many ways, reaching into the deepest corners of our souls, leaving nothing unmarked. We could not fight against the tyranny of time and its eroding impact, against forces that were stronger than individuals.

My move to the United States made my life both exciting and unsettling. The political turmoil in Iran further exacerbated the situation, cutting ties to my family back home. The Revolution had started and Iran was on the news every night. I remember days of darkness in 1979, living in absolute confusion about what was happening in the country, not knowing if my family or people I knew were all right. All of a sudden, we, the Iranian foreign students, became the enemy, the unwanted aliens in the United States. All of a sudden, our collective identity changed from being an ally and supporter of the United States' politics in the region to that of a hostile adversary. Because of this situation, the past twenty years—especially those early days—have not been easy. Living with an identity not of our own choice, an identity bestowed on us because of political expediency and international relationships, has been problematic if not excessively uncomfortable. But life goes on.

While I was never able to pick up where I left off with my sisters, those topics of conversation remained as poignant as ever. After the Revolution, I had even more reasons to think about men and women, fathers and mothers, marriage and divorce. The Revolution had introduced dramatic changes that affected not only women's civil and family rights but also men's lives. The old topics of conversation and issues related to women's experiences seemed to have gained an enormous significance. These topics and related questions became sources of casual conversation with friends, colleagues, and those interested in the changes happening in Iran. However, these conversations occurred in the United States with men and women who had left Iran some time ago. Obviously, our perspective was different from those who were still living in Iran. Given the upheavals the country was going through, women's lives were a recurring theme of conversation for those of us living abroad. Needless to say, those women were our mothers, sisters, aunts, and friends. However, while we talked about women in Iran, the voices of these women were absent from our conversations. While we talked on their behalf, trying to grasp the depth of their feelings and daily experiences, there was a grave need to hear the voices of women still living in Iran.

A couple of trips to Iran during 1995 and 1997 gave me an excellent opportunity to listen to women directly. I could hear the women themselves talking about their lives instead of engaging in speculation about them. Because it was impossible to leave behind my training as a sociologist and I was as interested as ever in the women's personal accounts, I found the words and the stories that were being exchanged in friendly gatherings too valuable to be deposited only to the memory box. While the stories confirmed some thoughts, they raised questions about others. No sooner was one image constructed to claim the totality of women's experiences in Iran than a smaller whisper demanded the right to be heard, the right to existence. The stories exchanged were diverse; the experiences depicted a multitude of family lives and relationships.

I decided to listen more systematically and to more women. By living away from Iran for so many years, I had lost my contact with the larger community. I had minimal connection to the larger society, to a pool of people I could approach. I talked to friends and relatives to see if the women they knew were willing to talk to me. Although I was not hopeful, a few women, friends of friends, showed interest. Two women actually said that other women had interviewed them on various topics in the past; I was not the first person interested in interviewing them.

This book is the result of all those conversations. Overall, fifteen women agreed to talk to me. I did not know these women in advance; they did not know me either, but we both knew somebody in common. I was a stranger, somebody who had come for a visit for a few weeks, but that knowledge did not stop them from sharing their thoughts and experiences with me. I attribute the women's willingness to open up to me to the third parties involved (the women who had introduced us). I believe their trust in their friends persuaded the women I spoke with to trust me in turn with their life stories and innermost thoughts.

Furthermore, the fact that I was a stranger who was going to leave the country soon may have made me a safe person to talk to. Also, perhaps as a fellow Iranian, I was seen as close enough to understand their lives, their concerns, and the issues they found important. I could easily be in their place had I not left the country years earlier, or if the Revolution had not prolonged my stay in the United States.

The experience of living for years in another country is uprooting for all immigrants. While return to the country of origin poses its own challenges, living in an adoptive country is not free of problems either. I would like to call the first generation of immigrants world citizens. Having this global citizenship means belonging to nowhere; we are like wanderers, wondering where we belong, where we feel at home. No place any longer feels like home; while we have maintained certain ties with the old country, we have also developed new roots. In spite of these tenacious roots, we remain perpetual strangers in both worlds. Visitors in both, we never completely belong to either. Perhaps it was this tacit knowledge of my not belonging, of having breathed different air yet being Iranian and speaking Farsi that enabled the women to open up and to trust me. Perhaps there was enough geographical distance yet enough similar experiences that brought us close. I had no personal connection to their private lives; I did not know their husbands, children, mothers, or fathers. Their stories were safe with me; they were stories in a vacuum. I saw the women once and no more. Obscurity and anonymity were crucial to both of us and to the process of sharing.[2]

Although each interview had its own difficult moments, the women seemed at ease communicating private aspects of their lives. Perhaps for some, it was the first time they openly talked about certain parts of their lives. For others, I was the first person who posed questions about family relationships such as those with their mothers or fathers. I was viewed as a harmless listener, not as a family member or a friend who might betray their trust. There were also those who were happy that their experiences would be part of a research project. While the initial topic of the research, women's daily life experiences, did not seem to be an emotionally charged one, talking about their lives, the relationships with their mothers, fathers, siblings, husbands, or work-related individuals brought deep thoughts and emotions to the surface. The feelings were especially strong in those cases in which women had lost a loving parent or had endured serious emotional hardships in their lives.

Overall, the interviews lasted for about two hours each. I tape-recorded all the interviews with the women who granted their permission; those women who did not grant their permission are not included in this study. For a culture not familiar with the notion of interviewing or being tape-recorded, the women's permission was extremely valuable. In a culture where women do share their life stories with each other, but are at the same time extremely concerned about their privacy, allowing me to record their interviews enabled me to retell their stories more accurately. While I often glanced at the tape recorder to make sure it was working or simply to change the tape at the end of each side, the women hardly paid any attention to the machine that was recording their voices. During two of the interviews I turned the tape recorder off because I felt the stories they were sharing were deeply personal and private. I was concerned about how they were going to feel after they left, after they had time to reflect on their accounts. At times, I was surprised at their openness, their willingness to share their private family stories.

In speaking about their stories, the women perhaps put into words the experiences of many other women. However, while similarities exist, differences demand attention. While strong patterns emerged, there were also enough cases to warrant against trafficking in easy generalizations. As sociologists, and perhaps as lay persons, we need to develop patterns in order to make sense of reality. While there are certainly patterns in this study, the particular nature of each experience should not be overlooked. The complexity of lives, even in one family (the differences between how the eldest daughter is treated versus how the youngest daughter has been treated in the same family, for example), renders facile generalizations meaningless.

The fluidity of women's experiences deserves much attention. The range of experiences calls into question the inclination to view women in Muslim societies with only one lens: that of passivity and subjugation at the hands of men—be they fathers, brothers, husbands, or patriarchal social institutions. While there is much truth in the image of the subjugated and oppressed Middle Eastern woman who is ruled by the laws of the country, religion, and her family, that is only one side of the story. Some women are subjugated but there are also those who have shown tremendous power and resistance. While some women in this study accepted their lot and followed their parents' advice, there were those who steadfastly followed their own calling. While some remained in unhappy marriages, there were those who turned away from an unhappy marriage to work toward their goals. In short, women have fought; they have fought against domineering mothers, tyrannical fathers, demanding husbands, strict work atmospheres, and social conservatism. They also have had supportive fathers, loving mothers, understanding husbands, and fulfilling yet challenging work experiences. If not included in this study, there are certainly women scholars, lawyers, and politicians in the country who continue to challenge women's subjugation from dominating laws and customary practices. These efforts are done in order to create a more egalitarian environment for women and for the country as a whole.

While patterns of behavior, action, and interaction exist, the uniqueness of each person's experiences in this study proved to be of prominent significance. The particularity of each woman's life can be an unsettling experience for those, Western or non-Western, who seek a clear and straightforward answer to their questions regarding women's lives. Similarly, the accounts shared may anger those who believe in the universality of the experiences with which they are especially familiar. Obviously, not all readers will be able to find their own experiences in these accounts. Not all women and men agree with the stories retold here because a) these experiences may differ from their own experiences, and b) doing so may require a critical reevaluation of gender roles within their own families. Most, if not all, men have sisters, mothers, daughters, and wives. Most, if not all, men have brothers and fathers. Most, if not all, men, are brothers, husbands, and fathers. To hear women talking about gender-biased treatment in their families, to hear them expressing frustration about emotional burdens they have experienced due to their gender and unique closeness to their mothers, may be an eye-opening experience for some men and even disturbing for others. To see a world of pain shared among women—to mothers, sisters, and daughters—while it has remained closed shut to men—to sons, brothers, and fathers—may require a new look at the past, at the stable, orderly family portrait many carry with them.

After a close friend of mine read the chapter on mothers and daughters, "Ties that Bind," he recommended that I interview the women in his family, believing that their accounts would render a different picture. Coming from a solid middle-class religious background where mutual respect was the dominant mode of conduct between his parents and family members, he believed that the women in his family would provide a contrasting perspective. I appreciated the offer, always looking for more people who would feel comfortable talking to me. However, before I had the opportunity to travel to Iran, he had made a trip there himself, talking to the women in his family about the relationships between them and their mothers. Having expected to hear a different account, he returned surprised that the women had actually shared similar sentiments. This finding did not stop him from talking to women friends and relatives about their relationship with their mothers in the United States. He continued having casual conversations with friends only to report to me that, much to his surprise, many women expressed similar thoughts.

The realization that those sentiments were shared by more women than my friend had assumed, that even women in his own family shared similar thoughts, demanded a new and immediate look at gender relations in their family. A long-held notion about ideal family relations was questioned. The need was seen for a new notion to be constructed, one that would have ample space for divergent experiences—not only for pleasant and fulfilling relationships but also for difficult and painful ones that demanded the inclusion of different accounts. Instead of loyal adherence to only the accounts with which one is most familiar (whether a rosy picture or a gloomy family portrait), the whole spectrum should be included.

While my friend had to revise his perception of family life, many Iranian women may not find their voice or experiences in any of the accounts retold here. To assume that fifteen people will adequately represent the experiences of all women is an unrealistic expectation. Perhaps this book of stories will enable us to dissect similarities and differences in our own lives, as my friend did. Perhaps this book will enable the reader, Western or non-Western, to appreciate the diversity of experiences in women's lives across cultures— both the challenges they face and the ingenious solutions they devise.

I have tried to show how these women see their own lives in the context of Iranian society. In telling their stories, the women open some windows to their lives. Their answers were obviously limited by the questions I posed and were shaped by their desire to share only certain aspects of their lives and experiences. In opening up to me, in telling their stories, the women only emerged as a bigger mystery to unravel. While some doors were opened, others, I am sure, remained shut. The women shared those accounts they were willing to share and no more. Those accounts obviously neither cover all their lives nor encompass other women's experiences.

The women talk about a range of different topics, from their childhoods to their adult lives. They talk about the desire to be male or female, about mothers and fathers, work, marriage, and divorce. They invite you, the reader, to get acquainted with them, to see why they made certain decisions and how they acted or reacted to certain life events.

The retelling of these stories involves limited analysis throughout the chapters. This book is the story of women's lives and my search for understanding how women, albeit a small number of them, perceive their lives. These women and their words cannot be used as a device for constructing general statements about Iranian women. But the women offer significant insights into their own lives. I do not view the stories shared by these women as being symbolic or representative of Iranian women or Iranian society as a whole. Their number is too small and they are all located in Tehran. Obviously, the experiences of women from cities other than the capital, from tribal women, the very poor, and the very rich are not covered. Therefore, a word of caution regarding generalizations. It should also be appreciated that neither are these women a marginal group in the country. While the reader should avoid the general tendency to develop easy generalizations, he or she should also be open to the insights the women offer.

Maintaining distance or invisibility in order to render an "objective" account was impossible. I was as much part of these women's lives as they became part of mine. Their stories touched me deeply and stayed with me for days after the interviews. The questions I raised were embedded in a personal context; I grew up and came of age thinking about them. I grew up pondering how other women thought about these issues. Living in two worlds, having strong ties to both, I tried to combine two viewpoints while writing this book: that of the outsider and the insider. Which role was stronger? I am an outsider in both worlds. The women knew I was there to research, that I would leave the country soon. While they could relate to me because I am an Iranian, they had minimal information about me, my life, or who I was. I could relate to the difficulties and challenges they faced on a daily basis. I also knew that some aspects of women's lives in Iran have remained a mystery in the West. However, I was hoping to undo some of that mystery and shed some light on their reality. I also believe in maintaining the overall mystery because that is where the beauty of other cultures lies. Respecting the mystery embedded in otherness, in difference, is key to understanding. Unfortunately, this difference, this otherness, is more often than not translated into inferiority, a grave wrong committed time and again.

The women's word portraits follow.

The Women

Cast of Characters

THIS IS THE STORY of fifteen women and their personal lives. It is based on in-depth interviews completed during the summers of 1995 and 1997 in Tehran, Iran. The women ranged in age from thirty-eight to fifty-five years and came from different walks of life. All had finished high school and a few had pursued higher degrees. All the respondents were either working or had work experience before marriage. Their occupations represented a wide range of jobs, including teachers of different grades and ages, bank clerks, government employees, university professors, and physicians.

Following is a brief biography of each respondent. Because ample space is devoted to the women's words throughout the chapters, this section provides minimal information. Simple sketches are drawn to depict the women's backgrounds in terms of education, class background, type of family, number of children, city of origin, marital status, and employment status. Minimal changes in these details have been made in order to protect the anonymity of the respondents. However, as the sketches will show, the women's backgrounds are not unique. Thousands of others share similar characteristics.

Azar

Azar is a vibrant, energetic, forty-four-year-old woman married with one daughter. She comes from a family of six children, four brothers and one sister. She was raised in an economically middle-class but culturally traditional family. Her father was a Bazari and had a conventional attitude about gender roles. "There were always restrictions in my family," Azar recalls. "My family is very religious. Everybody was restricted in her or his own way." However, all the siblings were interested in school and studied hard; that is how they spent their time. While she was a young girl, Azar was particularly close to her brothers, who took care of her, involved her in their activities, and took her out with them. Therefore, while she was raised in a restrictive environment, Azar did not feel many limitations because she was welcomed to join her brothers when they participated in sports such as mountain climbing and walking. However, her oldest sister, being the first daughter in the family, faced severe restrictions.

Azar was a straight-A student in high school and attended one of the most rigorous schools in Tehran. She had no doubt that she would continue her higher education. Although Azar was allowed to pursue higher education, her older sister's education was halted in the middle of high school because her father was against girls' education after a certain grade. He hired a private tutor for her. Furthermore, she was forced into an early arranged marriage and did not benefit from engaging in her younger brothers' activities. But in Iran's fast-changing society, even a few years made a dramatic difference in introducing new ideas and outlooks on life to the family. By the time Azar finished high school, her father's attitude toward education and marriage for girls was different. Although still concerned about the appropriate degree of education for his daughter, he allowed Azar to pursue higher education and to choose her own husband.

After earning her master's degree in chemical engineering, Azar was offered a fellowship to go to England to finish her Ph.D. Instead, she married. She and her husband left Iran to go abroad after a few years. Both were successful and managed to find lucrative jobs, but her husband did not like living outside the country. They returned to Iran, where both continued working. Thus work, research, and accomplishment were Azar's ambitions in life.

Although Azar was highly accomplished, she felt a sense of dissatisfaction, believing that she was hindered in life because of her gender. She believed she could have been more successful had she been a man. "I am a successful person, but I have many unfulfilled dreams and ideals," she said. "I don't have enough time to fulfill my goals." Feeling a sense of deprivation in life, Azar regretted the fact that she could not enjoy even simple things in life. Azar envied those women who were satisfied with their lives and were capable of drawing satisfaction from activities such as housekeeping, flower arranging, or listening to music and dancing. But Azar's life was so consumed by work, family responsibilities, and the desire to do more that it became impossible for her even to enjoy simple activities. Her commitment to work competed with her desire to do her best for her family, especially for her young daughter. Azar felt that her husband not only left all the family responsibilities to her but also erected many barriers for her to overcome. Although she was highly accomplished, her voice rang with a tone of disappointment, her words expressing a strong sense of dissatisfaction and a deep desire to have lived a more fulfilling life.

Jasmin

During my interview with Mina, one of her friends, Jasmin, was also present and joined in our interview. I asked Jasmin to feel free to share her viewpoints whenever she wished. Time constraints, however, did not allow us to schedule a separate meeting. Although she did not answer all the questions, she found them stimulating enough to participate in the interview, throwing in her viewpoints. Because of her presence, this interview was actually more like a discussion that the two friends were having, although they were actually discussing the questions that I raised.

Jasmin was in her mid-forties. Going to college, pursuing higher degrees, and having a career were all expected from Jasmin and her siblings. Her father had high expectations for all his children (boys and girls) and was a major force in encouraging them to pursue their higher education. Furthermore, her mother worked for many years and was among the very limited number of women of her generation who pursued a gainful occupation. Although education and economic success were highly encouraged in the family, Jasmin's father was a strict and stern person. Jasmin, fortunately, was extremely interested in education.

A mother of three children, she had been married for more than twenty years after a rather long engagement of more than three years. She had worked throughout her college years and for a few years after her marriage. Unsuccessful at his own career, her husband did not approve of Jasmin having her own career. Although she had the educational credentials and the talent to be highly successful, she submitted to her husband's will and did not pursue an independent career. Jasmin kept busy by engaging in occupations that did not seriously threaten her husband's pride. This allowed her to make pocket money instead of being completely economically independent. At the time of the interview, she and her husband had separate living arrangements. Although living in an unhappy marriage, Jasmin had not filed for divorce because she was afraid of losing custody of her children. In spite of the marital discontent, she is a dynamic and lively person.

Layla

Perhaps the most cheerful and energetic of the interviewees, Layla is forty years old, married, and has two children (a son and a daughter). She is a rather petite woman; her jovial presence and laughter fill the room. She is extremely easy and comfortable with herself, asking questions and talking about different topics while answering the ones I raise. In a way, she does not wait for the questions.

Layla has four sisters and no brothers. Her mother is a Christian, the first-generation daughter of an immigrant family, married to a Muslim man. Layla cherishes her parents and believes they were (and still are) the best influence in her life. Her father valued education and encouraged all of his daughters to pursue higher education. Living a middle-class lifestyle, her family managed to send the children to various classes such as piano or language lessons. She believes she received the most care from her parents because they thought she was their brightest child. They managed to send her to one of the best schools because of some connections her father had in the army, and they arranged for many extracurricular activities for all their children. Layla is aware of the difficulties her grandparents faced due to their immigrant status in their adopted country. She admires her father's open-mindedness for marrying her mother and acting as a bridge, or mediator, between her family and their new country. Layla believes that her parents made many sacrifices in order to provide the best for the children. As she says, her dream was to return all that her father had done for them and the only way to do that was by studying hard to become a dentist. Layla is, however, the most accomplished child; while the other children finished either high school or at most their bachelor's degrees, she is the only child who pursued her higher education.

Layla had her own dentist's office for years until her back problem and a consequent surgery stopped her from continuing her practice. At the time of the interview, she was still recuperating, but she was also thinking about going back to work. Her marriage had proven to be ruinous, a constant source of tension and conflict. In contrast to her father, who was kind and caring to his wife and daughters, Layla's husband turned out to be authoritative and demanding. Her husband's personality traits completely shocked her because she expected that most, if not all, men would be like her father. She never recovered from this initial shock and their life, therefore, became a constant struggle. Extremely confident and accomplished in her own life and career, she would not submit to her husband's wishes. Layla was not a submissive person; the personality clashes continue. "I am going to divorce him when my children grow up," Layla confided. "I think I am going to save myself then. I gave my youth in order to have my old age to myself. I wouldn't have lived with him if it were not because of the children. After the children are grown, I have to think about myself before I worry about him." Layla and her husband were living separately at the time of the interview.

Mariam

Mariam, age thirty-nine, is the eldest daughter in a family of eight (six boys and two girls). She comes from a poor background. Her father worked for the government at a menial job. Although it was steady, his salary was not enough to provide adequately for his eight children. Her family had moved from a small city to Tehran. Mariam was raised in a rigid and conservative environment. The women did the housework and the men, regardless of their ages, received services. "The boys sat and ate," Mariam said. "We fetched and carried and cleaned up after them." Mariam was against this system and rebelled. "Of course, I didn't accept this. If I have to take my plate to the kitchen, then Ahmed has to pick up his, Abbas, too, and Ali, too. Why do I have to work and they get to sit?" As the eldest daughter, she refused to clean up after her brothers. In her family, the boys were treated differently than the girls. The boys had pocket money while the girls did not. The assumption was something like "the boys go out so their pockets should be full. Where do the girls go? They are always in the house." Mariam grew up challenging her parents from an early age. Interested in school, she did her studying in the kitchen because it was the only available location.

Although she was a good student in high school, her parents were determined to marry her off. She was engaged to her cousin at the age of sixteen. The groom was not present at the engagement ceremony; his mother acted on his behalf. It was only later that Mariam's mother and brother found out through some distant relatives that the groom was a drug addict, and they called off the ceremony. Canceling the ceremony caused a great deal of scandal among relatives and the neighbors. Mariam paid dearly for the breakup; she was taken out of school by her father and was not allowed to finish her education. Furthermore, while her mother supported the breakup she was now after Mariam to marry as soon as possible. Her mother was worried that if Mariam did not marry early enough nobody would marry her. Mariam eventually agreed to marry one of her suitors because he appeared to be the most harmless person.

Having experienced a harsh and unkind childhood, Mariam turned out to be a successful and lively person as an adult. She hardly waited for my questions in order to start speaking. She had her life and was more than willing to share her success and travail. In a way, she took control of the interview and did not sit back until she was almost finished. I just needed to pose certain questions a few times to ensure that everything was covered. As a constructive and energetic person, she saw herself as being in charge of her life instead of allowing her life to control her.

Happily married, Mariam had to struggle against poverty, uncaring parents, alcoholism and criminal tendencies among her in-laws, and a demanding mother-in-law. Marriage brought some distance from her strict parents. It was upon marriage that she discovered her husband suffered from a chronic ailment; that, however, only brought them closer, strengthening their union. Having to live in the poorest parts of Tehran during the early years of their marriage, she had only herself and her husband on whom to rely. Mariam's life was a story of personal triumph against all the odds. Hard work, dedication, cooperation, and wisdom eventually brought stability and success. Economic hardships and anxieties were gone. After twenty years of marriage, Mariam and her husband had managed to provide a decent living standard for their three children. Believing in her strengths, she regarded women as the major source of power in life and marriage.

Mina

Born into a family of five, Mina is the oldest daughter. She has four sisters and one brother, who is the youngest child in the family. Mina is forty-one and has one daughter. Raised in an upper-middle-class family, she had a very liberal upbringing and believed that her parents did not restrict or curtail her activities in any significant way. Mina saw her parents as being two individuals from an older generation who lived separate lives. They did not understand each other and did not seem to have much in common. However, in spite of lack of understanding, her father did not try to limit his wife's activities. She was free to do as she pleased, go where she wished, wear whatever she wanted, and meet friends. These were all the kinds of freedoms that Mina lost when she married.

Mina's mother was a very quiet and accepting person. She never challenged her husband or tried to gain any rights in her marriage. Mina believes that her mother's personality critically shaped all the children in the family. Mina grew up feeling caught between her parents. Her mother opened up to her from a young age and complained about her own life. While Mina's mother talked to her about her problems, Mina loved her father and could not accept her mother's words. It was only after her own marriage that she had a better understanding of her mother. "When she opened up to me it hurt because I could see she was unhappy," Mina recalled. "But my feelings toward men never changed because I loved my father. He was a very good father."

Marrying young, at the age of nineteen, Mina managed to finish her bachelor's degree and worked for many years, even from the beginning of her marriage. She quit working only when her daughter reached an age when she needed more supervision. Quitting her work brought Mina disappointment, making her question the value of her work and her husband's lack of appreciation regarding her economic contributions throughout the years.

Mina is a quiet woman. She was the only person who asked me what my goal was regarding the interview and wondered what I wanted to discover. The rest of the women did not question me regarding the project. Although Mina was quiet, she showed she had a lot to say. While she talked about many sensitive issues, she remained stoic throughout the interview and never lost her poise. She took her time answering the questions, thinking twice about what she said. It seemed as if she had been pondering these issues for a long time.

Minoo

Minoo is forty-five years old and married with two children (a son and a daughter). She lived her childhood as a lonely child; her father divorced her mother after one year of marriage. Minoo's mother had lost her own father when she was only five or six years old; her stepmother did not want her around and arranged an early marriage for her. When that marriage failed, she basically did not allow her to move back. With the help of a relative, Minoo's mother managed to find a job in Tehran and they both moved to the capital. In Tehran, her mother married a second time, but that marriage also lasted only a short time. Minoo knew about this marriage and its duration through her mother's birth certificate; she was too young to remember anything about it. Although there were other men who were willing to marry her mother, Minoo's presence dissuaded them. Her mother did not marry again because, according to Minoo, she was concerned about her daughter. In Tehran, Minoo's mother made a living by working at menial jobs such as a cleaning person in a hospital.

Minoo grew up to be an independent person. She started to work at the age of seventeen, even before her graduation from high school, and managed to advance considerably. As a young, intelligent, and single woman, working in a bank allowed her to accumulate enough money to buy a small house in an affordable neighborhood. Her economic situation was better than that of her father, to the point that she actually housed her father, his children, and his second wife for some time. While her mother stayed in that same house, Minoo moved to a separate apartment, taking the youngest stepbrother with her and raising him. Her mother, however, disliked this arrangement and criticized Minoo for housing the man who years earlier had divorced her and left the two of them to fend for themselves.

Although Minoo sympathized with the hardships her mother experienced in life, she grew weary of her mother. Their relationship deteriorated throughout the years; it seemed as if the hardships her mother experienced were taking their psychological toll on her. Living with her mother was becoming unbearable for Minoo. While she economically supported her mother she refused to see her for quite a few years. Minoo did not miss not having a father during the early years of her life. It was only later, when she started school, that she felt the lack of a father. The presence of parents, especially the father, was often required at various school functions; thus it was at these times that she realized she had no father who could go to these functions.

Minoo is an exceptionally capable woman. Although she quit working due to motherhood, she was a right hand to her husband, for years managing his business and helping him with his work. She questioned the institution of marriage as a goal for women. "A successful woman is one who keeps her husband satisfied," Minoo said. "Her own feelings don't count." Critically evaluating marriage, she believed that "young couples are experiencing a crisis because they cannot satisfy each other. They have never learned how to please each other. It doesn't matter who is the oppressor, male or female. The result is that they do harm to each other and to the rest of the society."

Pari

At forty-two years of age, Pari looked young and energetic. Married while in her early twenties, she had two children (a son and a daughter). Pari came from a family of five sisters and brothers. As a talented student, she was accepted at the university in Tehran and earned her bachelor's degree. Even before attending university, she managed to find a teaching job in one of the international schools in the city. She worked during her college years, enjoying her economic independence although she did not need the money. She worked after her marriage, but pregnancy and the coming of the Revolution brought an end to her career aspirations.

Looking at her parents, Pari saw them as being a distant couple who did not share much in common. As a child, she missed having her father around more often. He was self-employed and was often working late hours. She felt her parents lacked a sense of intimacy and closeness; as two separate individuals, each one was after his or her own life and work. Her parents traveled often. Pari remembered one trip in particular when they traveled to Japan and did not take the children with them. The children were in their teens and refused to have any other relatives stay with them. This was a great opportunity for Pari and her sister because they made their brothers work at home and do their share. The four kids alone at home had a good time and apparently enjoyed themselves. Pari believed that, while her parents did have fun moments, the children did not share those happy moments. Hearing her parents' arguments, there were times that Pari felt sorry for her father and times that she worried about her mother, but overall, she sensed they had equal power in their relationship. Desiring intimacy and closeness in her marriage, she looked for a partner she could feel close to and relate to like a friend or companion. Forces of circumstances and her mother's insistence combined with perhaps her personal characteristics did not allow the realization of her wish. She married the man her mother had approved, a man she never grew to love. While she had not thought about divorce, she had entertained the idea of living separately.

Once, when visiting her brothers and sister abroad, she had seriously considered the option of not returning to Iran. Although her brother had his own private business and could hire her, he refused to do so because he argued he needed a full-time worker. She was left to explore job options such as working as a sales clerk at department stores. Child care was another problem; what would she do with two children when she went to work? How long would it take for them to adjust? Would they blame her for leaving their father? The inability to find a good job that would adequately provide a decent living standard for her two children made her change her mind. Furthermore, her comfortable middle-class lifestyle in Tehran, along with an awareness of the fact that her children loved their father and that he was a good father to them, made her return.

Pari was a comfortable and curious woman. As we talked more, we realized that we were the same age. This made her curious about my life; she wanted to know about my life choices and whether I was happy with the decisions and the moves I had made in my life. But she patiently waited until I had finished my questions and only then started asking her questions. We had started at the same point in time, in similar families, with comparable educational backgrounds. Why was it that we had ended up at such divergent points forty years later? Our talk was an eye-opening experience, for both of us realized the significance of the forces of circumstances and the role of the individual within the limited range of possibilities available. Resigned to continue living with her husband because her children loved him dearly, she still yearned for a more fulfilling relationship within marriage.

Roya

Forty-two years old, Roya is married with two children. She was raised in a lower-middle-class family. Her father worked in the bazaar. There were three brothers and two sisters. She admired her mother for the positive outlook she maintained in life. Her mother's early attempts to attend adult literacy classes were opposed by her husband, who believed her job was to stay at home with the children. However, at age sixty she eventually gained the right to educate herself. Roya believes she had an easy upbringing because her mother allowed many liberties. She could bring friends home and join others for certain activities such as mountain climbing. Needless to say, these activities included both boys and girls, but her mother knew everybody who partook in these daylong exercises.

Although Roya's parents were kind and loving, she contended that male supremacy was an ever-present situation in her family. Her parents, especially her father, paid tremendous attention to the boys. She believed that if she or her sister had received the same degree of attention, they would have been considerably more successful in their lives. All three of her brothers were sent abroad for their higher education, but the girls were kept in the country. Roya remembered that the daughters were encouraged to make their living in the country. She began working after high school graduation; she enjoyed making money and believed that her family could use another source of income.

She married at the age of twenty-eight, after one and one-half years of engagement. The reason for her relatively late marriage was that she was actually in love with another person, but that relationship fell through. While all the relatives advised her against breaking up the engagement with the first man, the couple eventually broke up. Apparently, her fiancé was under tremendous pressure to marry his cousin and he eventually gave in to his family's demands. It took Roya a few years to recover from her breakup, especially because family gossip and pressure further exacerbated the situation. She, however, loves her present husband and admires his dedication to his family. Roya continued to work after her two children were born, with her mother taking care of them while she worked. Her husband lost his father in childhood. His older brother married and established a separate life for his family. But Roya's husband wanted to stay close to his family and told Roya from the very beginning that when they married he wanted to live close to his mother and sister and that he would be supporting them economically. At the beginning, they rented an apartment in the same building in which his family lived. When Roya's sister-in-law married and moved in with her husband, her mother-in-law moved in with them. They have been living together since then.

Roya appears to be happy, confident, and curious. She is content with her marriage, satisfied with her life partner, and loving with her children. She aspires to achieve a better standard of living for her family. But in this effort, she sees herself as a partner with her husband and does not leave the job of achieving a better economic condition entirely to her husband. She is a partner, a planner, a woman with vision. Trying to provide the best for her children, she, like her mother, keeps an open eye for diverse opportunities for them. For example, while computer classes are quite expensive, she managed to send her two children to such classes and is always looking for what they need to know in order to achieve success.

Sara

Sara is the youngest child in a family of four children. She is forty-four years old and has two children. Her father passed away when she was eight years old. Upon her father's death, her mother found a job through some family connections in order to provide for her family. Sara remembers her father believing in her mother; he saw her as a strong, frugal, hard-working, and diplomatic person. She remembers her father handing his monthly salary over to her mother, telling her she knew how best to spend the money for the family. His last words were, "My children have a strong mother." Sara believed that her father's exceptional qualities had shaped her expectations of men. She used to believe most men were like her father, but accumulating experiences in society, in addition to twenty-two years of marriage, made her change her mind.

Interested in helping their mother out and craving an economically independent life, Sara and her sister started working upon graduation from high school. Sara also managed to get her bachelor's degree. Although she had continued to work against her husband's wishes, it was child care responsibilities that eventually brought an end to her work. Her mother and sister took care of her children when she went to work, but the children needed more care and supervision as they grew older.

Sara highly values women and believes in their hidden, innate powers. She believes women are beautiful and delicate, seeing them as symbols of love, affection, art, and poetry. This beauty and delicate spirit is, however, mixed with an innate sense of power and resilience. For her, it is women who are the driving force in life, leading a family to ultimate happiness or eventual deterioration. "It is women who make a life," Sara contended. "They can change everything. They can even change men." Sara felt she was in control of her life; she believed in her ability to overcome life difficulties and challenges and to bring her husband to work with her even on those issues with which he disagreed. All this was not due to direct frontal challenge and opposition. Rather, she believes it is women's tactfulness, finesse, and cunning that gives them such powers. All a woman must do is to take advantage of these innate sources, to be ever aware of this never-ending source of power. For Sara, her husband was her success story, an ultimate sign to prove woman's innate power and her ability to change, to transform, and to build. "It is the woman's forbearance, brilliance, extreme patience, and genius that enables them to shape the fate of their families and eventually the world," she said.

Sima

The eldest daughter in a family of four children, Sima at the age of fifty-four had remained single and was determined never to marry. She was raised in an economically middle-class family. Sima believes her parents never understood her and her potential. Looking back at her upbringing, she has concluded that she was a talented child but her talents were not in those areas that her parents appreciated. For example, she was interested in studying literature, but her father was adamantly against such a major because he believed it offered no future; the only jobs available were teaching positions with minimal pay. He had bigger dreams for her, but their clash of ideas crippled Sima. As an authoritarian father, he was able to enforce his will but it came at the high cost of Sima quitting school. The damage was done and the path was paved for a lifetime of struggle over everyday issues.

For her, discrimination between boys and girls was a prominent part of her upbringing. Furthermore, as a sensitive child, she found herself responsible for the welfare of everyone in the family. She played mother not only to her own mother but also to her sisters and brothers. She took it upon herself to protect her mother and the children against their authoritarian father. Her mother opened up to her from very early in life; sharing her difficulties is still a continuous part of their relationship. The nature of their relationship, however, has changed over time due to the aging of the parents and their increasing dependence on her. Sima's independence due to age and relative economic autonomy has also allowed her to be more self-reliant. She has, however, remained the main source of emotional support for her parents. Of all the four children, she is the person who tends not only to her elderly parents but also to her siblings and their children.

Sima started working a few years after her high school graduation and is still working. Facing many difficulties at work, she persevered and turned her job into a successful career. Although her pay was minimal, hardly enough to pay for her expenses, she had proven herself, showing extreme talent and dedication. Without much support or guidance at work or at home, Sima managed to find her hidden potential and to succeed. Her accomplishments at work had enabled her to attain a personal sense of self-respect and confidence. While her upbringing had destroyed her sense of self-confidence, her work allowed her to build a new sense of self. Years of perseverance allowed her to gain the respect of a demanding father who expected nothing short of excellence and personal success from all his children, regardless of their gender. Sima came from a middle-class background, but like many other middle-class families, her family's economic situation had deteriorated after the Revolution. Pondering her life and her unique position in her family and society, Sima was a quiet person who had a solemn and dignified presence. The questions did not seem to surprise her, and her answers showed insight from years of reflection and contemplation.

Sousan

Quiet, calm, and poised, Sousan was the youngest daughter among seven sisters and brothers in an upper-class family. She loved her parents and perceived them as being constructive and supportive forces in her life. Although she did not enjoy pursuing higher education, she nevertheless got her bachelor's degree in foreign languages because of her father's constant encouragement. She saw her father as a constant source of support and motivation. He treated his daughters respectfully and had high aspirations for them while being cognizant of their individual capabilities and talents. Even later in life when all the sisters were married, Sousan's father functioned as an economic backbone for they all knew that if something went wrong, if some economic hardship happened, their father would always be there for them. Although he did not impose his wealth on them, he assured them of his support if it were needed; this gave Sousan a strong sense of relief and contentment. Furthermore, work and career were options but were not perceived as economic necessities.

As a member of a religious minority, Sousan got engaged at the age of twenty-one to her cousin, a Muslim man. They married after her college graduation. Having worked for two years before her marriage, she did not find her work experience enjoyable and was glad to quit her job. Agreeing with her husband that the dominant society does not appreciate women's contributions, she did not look for any employment. However, coming from an upper-class background allowed her to take advantage of diverse opportunities such as language, cooking, or art classes.

Sousan faced unique situations because of her religion. There were both difficulties and blessings. For example, on the one hand, the quotas for admittance to college for religious minorities were small. She worried about her children and their future if they did not get accepted at the university. On the other hand, she felt that people paid them more respect; they were perceived as being trustworthy and were believed never to cheat in their dealings. "This belief stops you from cheating," Sousan said. "Even if you want to cheat, this belief unconsciously prevents you. These kinds of attitudes actually encourage you to try to meet people's expectations. I don't feel like a minority. People like us and give us a lot of respect. But there are also some who are defensive against us."

Sousan's children adhered to her faith and not that of her husband. They were, therefore, considered a religious minority. She believed her children were bright enough to achieve their best in life, but their opportunities depended on their educational achievements, which were limited in the country due to their religious status. Perhaps her major source of frustration in life was rooted in the belief that she could not provide the best for her children in order to guarantee their success. Sousan had a calming presence with a content smile.

Tara

Forty-four years old, Tara has three children. She is the eldest daughter among three siblings. Tara is a lively and vivacious person. Free and comfortable with herself, she talks easily and did not wait for me to ask questions.

Tara lived with her parents for the first three or four years of her life while they were studying abroad. However, when her father returned home because of some family-related crisis, her mother remained there to finish her degree. Tara was sent to Tehran to live with her maternal grandparents.

Tara's parents, especially her mother, were highly educated for their generation. There were perhaps only a handful of women in Tara's mother's generation in Iran who had their doctorate from a European university. Upon her mother's return she was offered a highly prestigious position and continued to work until her retirement.

Tara lost her father when she was fourteen years old. Although she did not live long with him, she had pleasant memories of him. When her mother returned to Iran with her Ph.D., she started working full time and Tara continued to live with her grandparents. She visited her parents for two hours each week when her grandparents went for their weekly visits. She eventually moved in with her mother when she was ten years old. Ten years later, she married at the age of twenty. While Tara's parents were highly successful in their careers, they had divergent world views about their goals in life. Tara's father believed in a version of socialism where all people deserved opportunities to improve their life standard, while her mother was not interested in deferred gratification and wanted the best in her own life. That was depicted in the kind of clothing and jewelry that she bought for her daughters from a very young age. Moving in with her parents at the age of ten, Tara could not understand the conflict between her parents.

Tara's unusual upbringing had colored her relationship with her mother; they had serious problems. In spite of her achievement in life, Tara's mother was strict and somewhat traditional. For example, the only kind of leisure activity that was allowed was walking. Tara could not partake in any other form of entertainment with her friends. Having lost her father at the age of fourteen and living with an unkind and strict mother made Tara choose marriage as an escape; she married rather early to get out of the house and away from her mother's constant criticism and surveillance. As the only child who had remained in the country (her two sisters were living abroad), Tara was solely responsible for her mother; they lived in the same house. Respecting her mother, she believed she should not set limits for somebody who was older than herself. In turn, she expected her mother to respect her rights, but apparently that was not the case. Therefore, their relationship was a constant source of tension and conflict. Tara believed that her mother did not feel motherly toward her because she had not really raised her.

Tara had a bachelor's degree in economics and had married while still in college. Her five years of work experience started after she finished her degree. Familial problems and the aging of her in-laws, however, compelled her to quit a lucrative job. But she did not regret quitting her job, nor did she stay at home all the time. Interested in societal issues and in improving her skills, she had taken a variety of classes, always trying to add to her skills. Tara was acutely aware of changes happening in the country for women of different classes. She saw it as her job (although she did not have a paid job) to make trips to different neighborhoods, looking into community centers and exploring new opportunities opening up to women of various classes. If she was curious enough about some of these opportunities, she did not shy away from making weekly trips to these centers to take advantage of what was available. This brought her into close contact with women of different classes and family backgrounds. These activities gave her a new outlook on what the Revolution had brought for women. In appearance and mannerism, Tara was perhaps the most nonconformist among all the women I interviewed. Her nonconformity could be seen in her choice of outfits (mixing tennis shoes with dressy attire) or loving her in-laws more than her own family members.

Zahra

Zahra's mother was married at the young age of eight and sent to live with her mother-in-law. Her husband was twenty-four years old. In her new house, she was treated like a servant, expected to do all the housework in order to learn how to run a house. Zahra believed that her mother was barely given decent clothing or adequate food because her husband had to find work before he could send money for her. The oldest daughter among six siblings, Zahra felt like a mother toward her younger brothers and sisters. Her mother became sick when Zahra was nine years old and that brought a too-early start into adulthood for Zahra.

Upon her mother's illness, Zahra's grandmother, the same woman who had trained Zahra's mother, moved in with them. She was a stern and religiously orthodox woman who tried to severely limit Zahra's movement as a child. Zahra was not even allowed to go to the store to buy things or to accompany her brother; instead her younger brothers were sent. She tried to train Zahra to become a housewife and perform the same duties that her mother could no longer do.

Taking care of the family fell on Zahra's shoulders. Hearing her mother confiding in her friends about bitter experiences with her in-laws and her painful relationship with her husband when Zahra was eight years old critically shaped her mind about marriage and men. She had heard too much at too young an age. Zahra's father was a servant in the military; he believed everything he had was due to the military institution. In the military he was taught that he was nothing and he was therefore teaching the same lesson to his children at home. He believed in breaking their spirits in order to turn them into independent individuals.

Zahra avoided men. "I hated wearing nice clothes or fixing my hair," she said. "I would pass by a mirror as quickly as possible. I intentionally acquired a stooped posture when I walked." Coming from an impoverished and religiously conservative family, Zahra's choice to remain single was not easy. But Zahra managed to stay single in spite of all the familial and societal pressures she experienced. Although she had a number of suitors, she turned all of them away, deciding never to marry because of the kind of relationship she saw between her parents. Zahra loved children; her job was mainly working with children. "When I play with children I feel like I am playing my childhood games," Zahra said. She did not, however, want to have her own children. "I have always been terrified of having children. Because I know if you have children they will be like chains around your neck. I know if I had children I won't be able to do anything because I'll be so tied to them."

Zahra started working upon graduation from high school. Like most single women (and men) in Iran, she is still living with her parents. She was thirty-eight years old at the time of the interview. Zahra always covered her hair with a scarf regardless of whether a man was present. She did this before the Revolution, when veiling was not enforced by the government, and after the Revolution, when veiling became the law of the country. Zahra had a somber look. Her steady job combined with the fact that she was the oldest child in the family had allowed her to assert a certain level of autonomy. She did this within a family that had not been penetrated by modern ideas about women's rights to seek employment or higher education. But Zahra had fought very hard to get where she was; the continual fight seemed to have left little energy for her to smile or to enjoy life as it unfolded. While working with children enabled her to nourish and share her love, the dramatic absence of cheerful or happy facial impressions was certainly noticeable.

Zhaleh

Zhaleh, thirty-nine years old, is the youngest daughter in a family of six. She is a joyful and fun person. Zhaleh listened to the questions carefully and pondered them before answering, thinking twice about what she had to say. She took her time during the interview and was relaxed and comfortable. A tall woman, Zhaleh holds her head up and projects the image of a woman in control, proud and dignified.

Zhaleh was raised in a working-class family. Her life seemed to be a constant struggle against her mother to gain a measure of freedom. Zhaleh's mother was forceful and strong, believing in a strict upbringing for her children. As a young girl, Zhaleh felt sorry for her mother because she saw her as being an oppressed woman in her marriage. But her mother was also the main source of discipline and control in Zhaleh's life, overseeing her every move and not allowing Zhaleh much freedom. To some degree, as the youngest child in the family Zhaleh had a much easier time than did her siblings. Her older sisters and brothers were there to protect her against strict rules of propriety in the family. But she was also a challenging child, never accepting anything at face value.

Zhaleh's parents could not adequately provide for all their children. They had therefore started all of them working early in life, often right after high school graduation. The women embarked on typically female occupations, such as teaching and working with mentally or physically challenged children. Obviously, the boys had more choices. Economic necessity had forced Zhaleh's parents to be more accepting of employment for their daughters. They, however, certainly adhered to strict gender-specific expectations regarding the occupations their daughters chose.

As the youngest child in the family Zhaleh experienced both advantages and disadvantages, benefitting from a certain degree of protection and support while not being left free to do as she pleased. Although having a job was expected from her because her sisters had established careers, divorcing her husband proved to be particularly challenging for the same reasons. Zhaleh's two sisters were both divorced and it was therefore particularly difficult for her parents to see their third daughter divorcing her husband. They did their best to dissuade her, and it took her years to eventually agree to divorce.

Zhaleh's parents were from an ethnic minority, migrating from a different province to the capital city. She was raised biculturally, both as a Turk and as a Tehrani, speaking both languages. Although people in Tehran adhere to codes of appropriate behavior for both men and women, people in other provinces and cities may adhere to more strict gender roles. Zhaleh's parents came from a conservative background and tried to raise her according to their traditional values. She proved to be recalcitrant enough to challenge them every step of the way. Living in Tehran did allow some freedom of movement and Zhaleh was determined to have a share of this freedom.

Ziba

At the time of the interview, Ziba was forty-seven years old and had been married for twenty-two years. She was the mother of two children (a son and a daughter). Ziba lost her mother when she was only five years old and was raised by her father, his brother, and her aunt. She came from a very close-knit family who lived in a city distant from Tehran. "My aunt acted like a mother to me," Ziba recalled. "We all lived together. I had my father and my brother as fathers and then my aunt as my mother. Everybody took care of me." After Ziba's mother passed away, she remembers hearing her father crying time and again for her mother.

Ziba grew up believing that all men are kind and caring like her father and her brothers. She believed that the girls received more attention in her family than the boys. Coming from a lower-middle-class background and a religious family, she was nonetheless encouraged to pursue higher education and to move to Tehran, the capital. Although reluctant to leave her family, she was eventually persuaded by them to move to Tehran to work for her bachelor's degree in literature. The result was a teaching position in a northern city after college graduation. Again her family was encouraging and supported her decision to accept the position. The teaching position was particularly attractive because it was at an all-girls' school with a strong possibility of being transferred to Tehran after a few years of service. Ziba could not pass up this opportunity.

Ziba is a pioneer in terms of having had a long-distance relationship at the beginning of her marriage. Because her job was in a different city, she commuted for the first two years of their marriage. While Ziba believed that the dominant societal values severely restrict women's active participation in the larger society, she also theorized that women are controlled by their emotions rather than their logic. In her view, men could tower above their emotions; it is their logic that runs their actions. Women's excessive attention to minute details and mundane aspects of life and relationships, on the other hand, stifles their growth.

Ties That Bind

Mothers and Daughters

THIS CHAPTER EXPLORES RELATIONSHIPS between mothers and daughters. During the interviews, the women showed an eagerness to talk about their relationships with their mothers. This willingness inspired more attention to this intimate aspect of the family, starting in childhood and continuing on through life. The pictures that emerged from the interviews were of complex and emotionally charged relationships. While the mother-daughter relationship occurs in the private sphere, it is affected by a multitude of factors such as the impact of the father, siblings, relatives, and social forces. Ties with the mother, however, shape every aspect of the daughter's life in numerous ways. By examining this relationship, we can trace the conscious and unconscious repetition of those patterns that may harm the development of girls into mature and healthy adults, and, to a certain extent, attempt to undo the imports of patriarchy.

While the mother-daughter relationship varies from family to family, the fact remains that the mother functions as the primary caregiver in most families. This role is passed on from mothers to daughters and is carried from generation to generation. Mothers and daughters relate to each other in various ways; confusing feelings may be experienced by both of them, but these experiences are an inherent part of the mother-daughter dyad. There is a set of experiences, feelings, and thoughts embedded in every mother-daughter bond. There are also common themes that emerge from within the structure of family life. The interviews opened new windows for looking deep into this mother-daughter bond. Patterns and dimensions emerged that are long overdue for attention. These dimensions include the impact of the parental relationship on female children; the mother's position in the marital bond; and the role mothers play in shaping their daughters' thoughts and attitudes toward their fathers, family life, and men as future husbands. The result is a critical examination of the mother's role in the upbringing and socialization of children.

Examining the mother-daughter relationship also reveals the isolation and the powerlessness that some mothers experience within marriage. This powerlessness, at times, forces some mothers to turn to their daughters, most often eldest daughters, as companions, friends, or confidants. Having a mother confide in the female child brings the world of childhood to an abrupt end and puts the child in a contradictory position, forcing a too-immature entrance into the adult world and risking possible exposure to intimate but potentially disturbing aspects of the marital relationship. I explore ways in which mothers have internalized the dominant societal attitudes about the superior/male and inferior/female aspects of gender relations. The more-than-often powerless position of mothers in the marital relationship perpetuates a cycle of powerlessness in the female child and critically colors her attitudes toward the father and other men. Furthermore, this situation may retard the development of both parties in the future.

While the following chapter explores those relationships that are cherished by daughters, this chapter articulates the darker side of the mother-daughter bond and family interactions. Like all studies based on qualitative research, the sample in this study is small; therefore, caution must be taken not to generalize the findings to all mother-daughter relationships. It is important to emphasize the variability in mother-daughter relationships and avoid attributing universal and invariant features to them. Many women cherish close relationships with their mothers and have developed lifelong friendships. This chapter explores this multifaceted and nourishing relationship—a vital relationship without which the survival of the family institution as we know it today would be jeopardized. It also examines the ways in which patriarchy harms women and retards the development of happy and fulfilling relationships between men and women, husbands and wives, and mothers and daughters.

"Her Pain Is Mine"

When the interviewees talk about their mothers, they are speaking about a cohort of women who were born between the early 1920s and the late 1930s. For most Iranian women of this generation, marriage was not a personal choice based on romantic love. Rather, it was viewed as a family affair, decided by the parents of the young couple. All of the mothers with one exception had married men chosen by their parents. It must be noted that it was not only women who entered into blind marriages. The men whose mothers chose a wife for them and whose fathers approved of the choice also entered into marriage blindly. There were also occasions where the fathers gave their consent without consulting either the mother or their daughters. Therefore, an arranged marriage was a blind contract for both partners, often entered into with either minimal or no prior knowledge of the other person's appearance or personality.[1]

The mothers typically married at a young age, moved to a new house that they most often shared with the husband's relatives, were considerably younger than their husbands, and were expected to abide by cultural perceptions about appropriate gender roles. These factors led to unequal lifelong marital relationships. Thus, upon starting a new life, the couple played their roles according to societal expectations and dominant traditions that dictated an unequal relationship between the two partners. This created a situation in which most newly married women, young and inexperienced, felt lonely and isolated. Being responsible for the reproduction of family life, women conceived babies as soon as possible. Factors including the significance of childbearing, lack of adequate birth-control devices, and the social stigma against women with no children pushed young women into early motherhood. Many may have felt overwhelmed by these tremendous responsibilities of being a wife, mother, and daughter-in-law at such a young age. Required to respect the elders in the family, to value male supremacy (especially that of the husband and father), and to seek acceptance of the mother-in-law, the young woman/wife/mother may have experienced an acute sense of powerlessness. This may have led to an oppressive situation in which women/mothers, lacking a voice of their own or the ability to make personal decisions, sought solace in their children, especially the eldest daughter, who might have been the person closest to them and the person with whom they trusted and shared their lives.

Mothers are the primary agents of gender role socialization for girls.[2] In this process, social norms of the female role are passed on and reproduced. The mother represents the primary role with which the daughter identifies. During the formation of this primary mother-daughter dyad, the two partners develop a close sense of identification with each other. Mothers often see the daughters as extensions of themselves. "This generates between them a unique bond in which each feels the other to be a part of the self."[3] Seeing their daughters as extensions of themselves, some mothers tend to open up to their daughters and share with them their familial problems and marital unhappiness. However, this process not only hurts the child but also brings the carefree stage of childhood to an abrupt end because the child's eyes are opened to the adult world, in which relationships take on a different shape.[4] When mothers open up to their female children, the mother-daughter relationship is transformed: the mother, the all-provider and caring figure, is revealed as a vulnerable person. This change shatters the child's image and calls into question the degree to which the mother can protect her. The mother's world and her problems then also become those of the child. Not having adequate skills or experience to deal with these problems, children often create their own understanding of the situation. As Sima said, "From very early childhood, I was not my mother's child. I was her mother." She was the one who consoled her mother and listened to her stories.

Reaching adulthood, Sima even devised new strategies for her mother to use to handle the difficult husband/father. The young child became the caregiver and protector—a mother to her own mother and to the rest of the children in the family.[5] Recalling being disturbed at having her mother open up to her, Sima said, "It was only later on when I saw other mother-child relationships that I started to reflect on my relationship with my mother. I believe it is awful to open up to your fourteen-year-old daughter. That was the worst experience I have ever had in my life. Those talks disturbed me tremendously. They took away my youth from me. To this day, her pain is mine. Her problems overwhelmed me and I couldn't escape from them." Having to take care of her mother's emotional needs, Sima asserted,

I have concluded I was a sensitive child, that I didn't have the capacity for tolerating such pain so early in life. I compare myself with my brother and realize that he just turned off all his switches. No crisis or family argument affected his studies. I couldn't do that. Things affected me and there was no escape from them. Unfortunately, neither of my parents realized how sensitive I was. Or perhaps I was the weakest child because I stopped in life. I never progressed. I know I could achieve a lot more. But I didn't. The emotional burden was too heavy for me to bear.

Zahra recalled a similar situation from her own childhood. Feeling responsible toward the other children in the family and sensing the mother's emotional needs and dependence, Zahra said, "Sometimes when I look at the mother-child relationship I think it is the mother who is dependent on the child for her own life."

Having spent most of her time in childhood with her mother and older women, aware of her mother's unhappy marital relationship, Zahra asserted that she was never a child. "I don't know what it means to be a carefree child. I am glad my work deals with children. When I play with children I am playing my childhood games, which I never played." The women whose mothers had confided in them and shared their familial or marital problems did not like this openness. Zhaleh believed her parents should have kept their problems to themselves. "My mother opened up to all her daughters, but not to her sons," Zhaleh recalled. "I thought those problems were theirs and they themselves had to take care of them instead of dragging us children into their problems." Fischer suggests that, among various intergenerational relationships in the family (mothers-daughters, fathers-daughters, mothers-sons, and fathers-sons), mothers and daughters are likely to be most involved in each other's lives.[6] Confiding in one's daughter, especially the oldest daughter, is not a phenomenon unique to women in the Middle East. Fischer has shown a similar tendency among women in the West. It is interesting to note that, according to the daughters in Fischer's study, most of the mothers who confided in them confided quite a bit.[7]

Where mothers open up to their children and talk about the private aspects of their lives, the fathers and children become estranged and alienated from each other. The mother becomes an idol and protector as well as a victim of the father's unlimited power.[8] Reflecting on her childhood Zhaleh said, "When I was a child I thought my father ruled with an iron hand, that he repressed my mother. I believed my mother was a very unfortunate woman, or that all women lived such wretched lives after marriage." Forced to take sides, children often side with the mother because she is their primary caregiver. The family is divided into two fronts with the father residing in one, alone in his tyrannical rule, while the mother and the children, the powerless family members, occupy the other front. This situation poisons the atmosphere in the house. Most often, children assume the mother's attitude and beliefs toward the father before they ever get a chance to know him on their own.

Mothers also act as mediators in the family. They are the communication channel between fathers and children. That is how Zhaleh saw her mother. "I always thought if mothers had any problem or major disagreement with their husbands, they transferred it to their children and set him or her against the father," she said. "In this process, the father and child become estranged, alienated from each other. This distance affects all family members and it is impossible to overcome. Everybody is against the father."

Mothers have a certain degree of power in shaping the children's attitudes toward the father. Angry with the autocratic husband and powerless in their position, some mothers try to protect their children by creating a distance between children and the father. Opening up to the daughters (and sometimes to the sons) results in denigration of the fathers. In doing so, mothers have transferred their thoughts, feelings, and particular world view to their children.[9] Zhaleh believed that "children assume the mother's attitude toward the father before they themselves have ever had the opportunity to know their father." Acting as mediators in the family, mothers are in a position to define the father's personality and character. Fathers often are depicted as being too domineering. The father and the children are kept distant and aloof from each other. This serves different purposes. First of all, it further ties the child to the mother and guarantees the child's loyalty.[10] The child sympathizes with the mother and becomes her ally in the family. New familial/emotional alliances are formed between the mother and the children.[11]

Functioning as confidantes, daughters provide an emotional outlet by which the mother creates a new family of her own, separate from the father and the in-laws. In this scenario, any time the child trespasses the societal norms of propriety, the mother can discipline the child by resorting to the authoritarian father figure and threatening the child by going to him. Depicted as bogeymen, fathers become the all-too-powerful and oppressive male figures in the family. Mothers remain in the middle, friend of both sides; alliances are secured and children and fathers need the mother to communicate, to bridge the gap between them. Fathers too often are blamed for societal restrictions imposed on the children and for the lack of adequate economic means to establish a better standard of living. This will further inhibit the formation of a strong bond between the father and his children. As a power figure, the father is blamed for all the inadequacies and shortcomings in the family. According to Zhaleh, her mother "blamed everything on the father, anything that she could not do. My father was the primary reason that she or us, the children, could not do what we wished." The father becomes a complex figure; on the one hand, he is depicted as a tyrannical ruler. Everything has to have his stamp of approval. He is devoid of emotions and unable to establish close ties with his children. But on the other hand, the father is denigrated by the mother and is presented as the cause of all unfulfilled dreams for the mother and the children.

Knowing about the mother's marital problems, experiencing the father's oppressive rule at home, some daughters may turn against the father as the economic provider. Upon receiving her first paycheck at her first job, Zahra was advised by her employer to open a bank account. The then-nineteen-year-old woman refused to do so. "I wanted to spend money on the family to show to my father that what he was doing was not that difficult," she recalled. "That it was his responsibility to spend on us. I gave my salary to my mother, like men who give money to their wives for household expenses. I used to leave money for my mother, telling her this is the money for the house."

The parents' relationship—the father's utter rule and the mother's weak position in the family—leave a lifetime scar on some children. This may lead to a rejection of the idea of marriage. Zahra believed she could never marry. She built a dream world for herself, "a world without men." When her mother grew older, she regretted transferring her frustrations to the child. "Even my mother, who gave me all this feeling of hate and disgust toward sexual relationship and marriage, regrets it," Zahra said. Zahra befriended male relatives and colleagues at work, but she did not look at men as potential life partners. "When it came to more than friendship, when there was a talk of establishing a life together, I turned into a piece of rock because I thought people cannot be friends in marriage." Based on her observations, she asserted,

> In marriage men tend to ruin their wives. They want the wives to have no self-confidence. That's the way my father was with my mother. My father would not let my mother go to a hairdresser so that no one would know she was pretty. My brothers are the same. They destroy any sense of self-confidence in their wives so that they can completely own them, and the women won't even dare to divorce them. The man wants to prove his strength and I, as a woman, have to satisfy his needs, to show him that he is a man, to obey him, and to follow him.

Disturbed by the relationships she saw around herself—father-daughter, mother-father, brother-wife—she continued by saying that, "I see the same

relationship everywhere. At nights I wait for the eruption of noises and conflict among husbands and wives, among men and women. I listen sharply,
waiting and going to sleep only when I hear nothing."

Zahra's mother confided in her daughter, telling her about her unhappy
marriage and the difficulties she had to endure. When the mother attested
that she had lost in life, Zahra questioned the concept of loss on the part of
mothers. "I hear a lot of women saying they lost in marriage," Zahra said. "I
disagree with that because I believe when you have children losing is not the
issue anymore. When you bring children to this world you are responsible
for them and have to stake out for them." She reproached her mother by saying, "I am glad your other daughters don't have to hear you saying that you
lost, to learn that to be with men means to lose."

The father's tyrannical rule in the family and the mother's last resort,
confiding in her oldest daughter, had certainly shaped Zahra's attitude toward her father as well as other men and marriage as an institution. She,
however, refused to transfer her thoughts to her younger sister. She was careful not to repeat her mother's mistakes and not to influence her sister's
thoughts before she had a chance to develop her own relationship with men.
"Why poison her heart? Why tell her all the negative thoughts I have about
men," Zahra said. "I tell her you can find a good man, somebody who respects you, somebody who loves you. While I believe marriage destroys
women, I tell her you can make a good life together if both of you believe in
yourselves."

For Sima, marriage was not a viable option. "How could I dream of marriage given what I saw around me?" With no happy couples around her, she
said, "I am not brighter than other women. How could I be happy in my
marriage?" While her mother still dreamt about her daughter marrying and
having a family of her own, Sima was adamantly against marriage.[12]

Many women endure an unhappy marriage for the sake of children, believing that having a father present at home is better than his absence because
of the social pressure and stigma that a divorce may bring on the family. A divorce also tends to lead to a lack of economic security. To seek a divorce in a
traditional society, especially for women who are not economically inde-

pendent, is a tremendously difficult task. In many cases, going back to their families is not an option for women. Most families encourage their daughters to remain married, to hold the family together because of the shame that a divorce may bring on the family. Although granted in Islam, divorce is shunned socially. The more a woman suffers in marriage, the harder she tries to keep the family intact, the higher she is valued as a mother/wife. The family has remained intact because of her efforts, her sacrifices, and her understanding. The children have had a father in the house.

Although not all mothers open up to their daughters, children hear things and observe relationships. Hearing her mother talking to friends about a painful sexual relationship, Zahra said that as an eight-year-old girl she decided to sleep in her parents' bedroom. She believed her sleeping there would stop the father from approaching the mother and would protect her mother. She would stay up at night to make sure that there was no movement in the room. Her mother had been married off at a young age and experienced many marital problems. The unhappy marriage had its impact on the daughter, who as a young child decided to protect her mother against the father. Later, as a young woman, Zahra decided never to marry, seeing the husband-wife and father-children relationships as perpetually unequal relationships. Having to solicit permission from her father for continuing her education, for taking classes, for holding a job, and for visiting friends further affirmed her father's ownership of her:

> I have always thought that my father is a master and I am his slave. But even in this servitude I have my own position. If I were to marry, I wouldn't even have this position. The children would take that position away from me. I wouldn't be able to worry about my mother, sister, or brothers because I'd have my own immediate family to care for. When you have your own family, they are your priority in life. You have brought children to this world and you are therefore responsible for their welfare.

Although Zahra holds a job, is semi-independent economically (her salary was not adequate to enable her to be completely independent), and has gained more freedom as her parents have aged, she is still adamantly against marriage.[13] She was determined not to enter into another master-slave relationship.

> Once married, the majority of women tend to avoid divorce at any cost because they believe that the father's presence at home is crucial. I see a lot of women who put up with abusive husbands or even drug addicts. They continue living with them because they believe his presence is more important for the children. I ask them, "Why do you live with this drug addict?" They answer, "When he is around my house is safe, but when even this drug addict is not present, everybody, all the neighbors and relatives, say something. They harass us, me and the children."

This example questions the validity of the deep cultural belief that holding a family together at any cost is better than separation. It calls into question the significance of sacrifices mothers make and the eventual outcome for the children. Of course, the significance of strong social stigma against divorce and separation should not be underestimated.[14] Furthermore, in a society in which public services for divorced women with children are virtually nonexistent, where the larger society, friends, relatives, and neighborhood shun separated or unattached women, divorce becomes an almost impossible task if the women's families are reluctant or unable to help out or to take in the women and their children.

"I Call Her Every Day"

Not all mothers open up to their children from an early age and not all cases are as grave as Zahra's. Some parents, both mothers and fathers, open up to their children after a certain age, perhaps after they have reached maturity, are married, and have children of their own. Is that any easier on the adult children? There are also those mothers who develop complex expectations of their daughters even though they never established an intimate and close relationship with them. At times, forces of circumstance, such as the departure of all the adult children or the effects of previous decisions and lifestyles, put one adult child in a precarious position. Other unpredictable factors, such as instabilities associated with the eight-year war with Iraq or the increased dependence of aging parents on adult children, create a situation in which family members feel an acute need to stay in touch, to check on each other on a regular basis to ensure that everybody and all things are all right. Often several factors converge and create conditions that exacerbate an already-strained relationship. Pari and Tara's cases are two examples. Because of a variety of factors, they were the only adult children left in the country. This situation put them in an especially vulnerable position, in which they both needed to take care of their own families while having to tend to their own parents' emotional and physical needs and demands.

Pari's parents did not open up to her when she was growing up but waited until much later. In Pari's case, both parents started talking to her after she married. Perhaps the departure of all her brothers and sisters aggravated the situation. All adult children except Pari had traveled abroad to continue their higher education. Pari was the only child left behind.

> After I started college and married they both started talking to me more. Father complained about mother and mother criticized him. I couldn't take sides then. When mother said, "Your father has done this or that," I couldn't understand who is right or wrong. I didn't even know what to say. I couldn't tell the truth, to figure out who is right. Now I understand better. I was twenty-some years old when these talks started, when all my brothers and sister left the country. They felt lonely and needed to talk to somebody. Even now, when I go to places with them, they whine about each other whenever they get a chance.

While the degree of emotional harm in cases like Zahra and Pari cannot be measured or compared, Pari's statement is indicative of her feelings toward her parents opening up to her. "I get upset when they open up to me," she said. "To me, they were two separate individuals, each one after her or his life. There was a lot of distance between them. Of course, they traveled a lot, going to Europe and Japan when we were only thirteen or fourteen. But overall we did not share their happy moments." While Pari's parents kept their problems to themselves when she was growing up, she recalls hearing the discord:"We heard their arguments. All the conflicts and discussions were rooted in economic problems. Sometimes I felt sorry for my father because mother complained and criticized his every move. There were also times that I worried about mother. They had equal power in their relationship."

As the only adult child left in the country, Pari felt responsible for her parents' welfare. Pari talked on the phone with her mother every day. If she missed a phone call her mother got upset with her, worrying about her.

> We talk on the phone everyday. She gets upset if I don't call her. Sometimes, I feel like I need to pull away a little. There is no need for me to know all the details. But I try to either stop by or to call every day. Mother talks about her day and tells me where she goes so I won't worry about her and I must tell her about my plans so she won't worry about me. I prefer to reduce the contact a little bit. She asks too many questions and wants to know everything and I don't appreciate that.

Pari found the expectation to stay close, to have daily phone conversations, to pay regular visits, and to inform her mother about her every move burdensome. She preferred to have some privacy, to maintain some distance. But her mother's need to be in regular contact with her, the fact that her mother's feelings got hurt and she worried about Pari if she did not know where she was, stopped Pari from establishing a more independent relationship. Clinging to her daughter, Pari's mother probably saw any attempt on her daughter's side to establish a separate life as an insult.

Taking her side into account, Pari's mother had devoted her life to raising five children, four of whom had left the country and would never come back. Other than occasional short trips that the siblings might take, Pari was the only child left to tend to her parents' emotional and physical needs. Talking to Pari every day, seeing her every other day, sharing her day, and yearning to be part of her life was perhaps the most pleasant part of her mother's life and an affirming experience. This pleasure, however, denied Pari of her own independence and privacy. She was treated like a child and an adult simultaneously; as the mother of two children, Pari yearned for privacy and freedom of movement.

While Pari felt loved by her parents, Tara did not feel loved by her mother. Like Pari, forces of circumstances had again put Tara in a situation in which she was the only adult child left nearby and had to take care of her mother's emotional needs, functioning as her companion. Although Tara lost her father when she was fourteen years old and was mostly raised by her grandparents, she had vivid memories of her parents' relationship. She lived with her grandparents because her mother was working on her doctorate abroad and could not both study and take care of her first child. Furthermore, Tara had a unique upbringing.

> As a child I was put in a day-care center abroad when she was studying for her Ph.D. I was brought back to Tehran to live with my grandparents for several years when she was still working on her degree. Then in Tehran, I saw her a couple hours a week when my grandparents visited my parents. I moved in with my parents at the age of ten, living with her for another ten years, and then married early to get away. My understanding is that my mother does not see me as her child. When you go through trouble for something, whether it is a craft project or anything, you love that thing. She does not feel motherly toward me. I was not her child; she can't look at me as a sister either because I am not her sister.

What annoyed Tara was the way her mother differentiated between Tara and her two sisters. While her mother recognized the sisters' rights, she refused to see Tara as being entitled to any such privileges. "They [her sisters] spent considerable time with her," Tara said. "They even took their friends home and she catered to them, cooking lunch or dinner for them." But it was with Tara that her mother had a totally different relationship and unreasonable expectations.

Tara based the roots of her problematic relationship with her mother on several factors. She first blamed herself: "I have allowed this to happen." As a child who was not actually raised by her mother, she had observed her father and his relationship with his mother.

> My father highly valued his mother. He was so respectful toward her, trying to spend all Friday mornings with her or buying her different things. That is the kind of relationship I saw between my father and his mother. I thought I should behave in the same way. So I never reacted or challenged my mother when I was grounded. I thought I should keep quiet because the young kids in the family always learn from the older ones. I never challenged my mother, but my two younger sisters were not like that. They set their limits from the very beginning.

Tara's relationship with her mother was problematic. Her mother lived with her and her two children and showed a superior attitude and lack of respect for her lifestyle, which disturbed her. As Tara said, "I believed that our relationship could be much better—if each one of us had settled our limits. I actually thank God that our relationship is not worse. I believe that any relationship is shaped by the people's potentials and how much you let the other person get close to you."

Tara's mother had a multitude of expectations. While Tara tried to meet them, overall she found her mother's expectations unrealistic. Furthermore, meeting her demands did not allow Tara any freedom and independence of movement. Tara said, "When I go out with my friends, she asks me, 'Who are these friends?' She believes that because you [referring to herself] are not somebody important therefore your friends cannot be important either. 'Who are they? What significance do they have? Nothing.' So it is more important for me to run after her errands and take care of her needs." Tara's mother went as far as calling her daughter's friends to complain about how much Tara left her alone.

> I have two very good friends. We have been friends for fifteen and twenty years. Once she had called them, first making them promise not to tell me

that she had called, and then complaining about why I leave the house so often. Why do I take classes? I have a Monday morning class and a Thursday afternoon class when everybody is taking their afternoon nap. I prepare her lunch and then go to this sewing class. She has absurd expectations. She even complains about me to my husband and my children. She tells him that he doesn't know how to treat his wife properly, that he is not a man; that if she were in his place she would throw a fit about my outside activities. She asks him, "What kind of a man are you that allow your wife to behave like that?"

Tara's mother complained that when her daughter left home she felt lonely and scared. Confronting her, Tara asked her what she did when she was abroad visiting her sister who was studying to pass her doctorate exam. Apparently, her younger sister had told the mother that she could come for only one month and that during that time she needed to study long hours at the library. She therefore left the apartment at half past eight in the morning and came back at eight in the evening. Her mother's response was revealing: "Your sister was different. She had a job and needed to study for her test. She couldn't stay home like you can."

As an exceptional woman in her generation, Tara's mother had earned a Ph.D. abroad and had worked all her life. She had achieved an important position through education and hard work. Perhaps as a highly accomplished woman, she greatly respected those women who had advanced degrees and were career oriented. Tara had finished only her high school diploma; she was a housewife and a mother. In contrast, her two sisters had traveled abroad, pursuing higher degrees and establishing independent lives of their own. Perhaps it was Tara's lack of visible and measurable accomplishments that prompted her mother to believe that Tara was better off spending her time catering to her needs instead of cultivating her own interests. Although Tara lacked higher educational degrees, her voice throughout this research represents a complex image. Her voice is that of a woman who has passionately studied her society, who is sensitive and perceptive, and who genuinely believes in women's progress. What she lacks is only an official degree to decorate her voice.

"Do You Still Need More Time To Relax?"

Although some daughters must deal with the all-powerful father figure at home, they also have to defy the mother's internalized tendencies about the female/inferior and male/superior aspects of gender roles. Many daughters have taken advantage of the new employment opportunities and have embarked on new paths in their lives. It must be noted that they have had to overcome tremendous obstacles in order to be allowed to hold a job. These obstacles included parental and familial objections as well as societal taboos against women working outside the house, earning an income, and asserting a public presence. For most Iranian families, the first generation of young women who joined the paid labor force on a large scale occurred in the 1960s. Although living by themselves is an impossible dream because of societal restrictions imposed on single women, nevertheless holding a job brings forth a certain degree of confidence, economic independence, and social distance. As Sima said, "From a house [in which] there was no constructive atmosphere, I went to work and proved to be very successful. It was at work that I realized my potentials, my abilities." Furthermore, holding a job reduces the impact of traditions and enables women to initiate new friendships not rooted in familial relationships.[15]

Upon graduating from high school, Zhaleh decided to find a job because she was not accepted at the university. Her parents, however, intervened in her decision, asserting that the best jobs for women were in the Ministry of Education, i.e., teaching. "There were other jobs with more opportunities but I was not allowed to apply for them." She accepted her parents' choice and applied for a teaching job. Zhaleh continued, "That helped a lot. I was free to do a lot of things and they lost their absolute control over how I spent my time. I started to take some classes, . . .demanded more independence and with time they got used to it."

Daughters engage in a separation struggle with the mother in order to establish an independent identity of their own in the family and the larger society. Minoo took extreme measures for her time (in the early 1970s) to assert her independence. Her mother's temperament did not allow Minoo to bring friends home. "Every time I brought a friend home, she sat down with her and told her all the private family stories," Minoo recalled. "I was very young and didn't want her to talk about these things to my friends at work, especially because I never opened up to my colleagues." To stop this, she rented a separate apartment for herself and eventually stopped seeing her mother for a few years.

As daughters grow and mature into adults, mothers may experience a loss, sometimes referred to as the empty nest syndrome. Daughters, especially those holding a job, are no longer present at home at all times. Having the daughter enter into the adult world, meet colleagues, establish new friendships, and demand a degree of independence may threaten the mother-daughter bond. This is especially true about working daughters. "Maintaining a balance between attachment and detachment may require a considerable amount of effort."[16] A daughter tries to separate from the mother, desiring to establish her own identity by resisting the mother's hold. Isolated at home, mothers await the return of daughters from work. This isolation, especially if the mother sees her daughter as an extension of her life, intensifies the long daily wait. A mother looks forward to the return of the daughter from work, which breaks the monotony of the household and allows familial tasks to be shared and stories to be told. The gap can be filled by the mere presence of the daughter. Although some mothers wait to share with their daughters their daily problems, daughters tend to demand time and space, and at times may wish to fly away from the constricting family environment.

For many mothers, their daughters are the first generation of women to hold jobs. While fathers, husbands, and eventually sons who work is a fact of life, an expectation to be met, daughters who work comprise a new cultural phenomenon for the women born in the 1920s and 1930s. Work in the public sphere always has been the domain of men. Children grow up seeing their working fathers coming home tired. Fathers are often seen as "outsiders who come in with authority."[17] Given the traditional division of labor, home is seen as the women's work place and where every man can rule and have his needs attended to. Upon seeing the tired father, all interactions within the household change. Children start to hush up, disappearing into inner rooms so that they do not bother the father. Games come to an end. Silence reigns in the households, and mothers prepare to attend to the various needs of the father. Children are socialized to expect this kind of treatment toward the father; they have never seen the same kind of care and attention toward women, even working women. While daughters have full-time jobs and contribute to family expenses, most mothers have rarely had any experience working outside the home. They therefore show little understanding toward their daughters, their different lifestyles, and the challenges their jobs pose.

Seeing daughters as an extension of themselves and their familial lives, mothers might see their daughters' occupations as impertinent and inconsequential. This may lead to a lack of understanding on the part of mothers; they fail to see that their daughters may hold challenging jobs, that they need care, that both physical and emotional space is needed in order to resolve problems faced at work and to switch to a different mode of life, i.e., that of the family, once the daughters come home. While mothers respect that space for the men in the family, whether husbands or sons, daughters are denied the same treatment.

Zhaleh and her brother both worked. But she noticed the different kinds of treatment the two received. When Zhaleh and her brother got home from work, the mother left her brother alone to rest, believing he would join the family when he was rested and ready. "Then she would tell him the best news, only the good things and nothing that might preoccupy or upset him," Zhaleh recalled. "But she would never give me that break. She gave me the bad news or whatever that had upset her right when I sat to dinner. She never cared if anything bothered me or hurt me."

Although Zhaleh realized that perhaps her mother felt closer and more comfortable with her daughter and that perhaps she could not share those problems with her son, she concluded that her mother certainly loved him more because she was so respectful of his needs. Witnessing a lack of respect for her needs, especially when she returned from work, Zhaleh confronted her mother, telling her, "I am tired. Let me rest a little. I get tired at work. I need to rest after I get home." It may take a working daughter a few years to articulate her needs to the mother and it may take the mother several years to hear her daughter out and to respond to her demand. The mother submits eventually but reluctantly. She continues to see her daughter's work as trivial and her demand for space and time to rest after work as insignificant. Zhaleh's mother did not take seriously her need to have some quiet time after work. "She started badgering and mocking me, saying things like, 'Is it okay now to talk to you or do you still need more time to relax?' " Zhaleh believed that whatever rights she had gained in the family had been at the cost of confrontation, challenge, and struggle with her mother. Her older sisters received the same treatment:"My mother always showered them with her problems. She has started treating me differently because she thinks I am an unusual child, but she has not questioned the way she treats my sisters."

It is ultimately the gender of the adult offspring that determines whether or not she or he is entitled to some physical and emotional space to recover from the daily challenges of a job. Other mothers may act in the same way; while they await their daughter's return from work, their lunch talks are mostly about the daily family problems. Zhaleh and Sima posed the following question, "Do I get a break? Do I deserve some space?"

"Who Could My Father Blame?"

Some daughters saw the all-encompassing responsibility of mothers toward their family as a form of oppression. Spending most of their time with their mothers, Sima and Zhaleh saw their mothers as being oppressed in their marriages. Zhaleh said, "As a young child, I believed my mother was oppressed in her marriage. It was not fair. She took care of all our needs from school to shopping to going to parties and to the doctor."

Some mothers may blame all the personal, familial, and economic problems on the father. Fathers are held responsible for the social restrictions placed on the female children and the mother. However, the irony is that not all daughters in this research tended to side with the mother and accept her overall world view. Although as children they had accepted those ideas, as adults they may question the validity of the father's image as an authoritarian figure.[18] While Sima believed that her mother was oppressed in her marriage, she also believed that the tyranny she experienced could be reduced had her mother been more diplomatic.

"It was a kind of oppression that could be reduced if my mother was a more tactful person with him. I always thought my father is a heavy-handed and stern person. But he had valuable qualities and positive points, too. When I compare him with today's young men, I realize that he was a traditional man who did whatever he could for his family. He was a faithful man, dedicated to his family and devoted to the welfare of his children, but Mom underestimated these qualities and instead focused on his shortcomings."

Like Sima, Zhaleh believed that her mother portrayed her father as a tyrannical and insensitive person. For example, when Zhaleh's father did not grant permission to the children to participate in activities outside the family, such as going to movies or visiting friends, the mother explained the rejection by stating, "That is how your father is." Years later Zhaleh reflected on her mother's explanation. "She does not explain that he himself has never had or experienced entertainment in his childhood or adult life. My father had a hard life, a life of working from childhood. He was raised to work, to marry, to raise a family. That is all. It is not that he does not care for fun or entertainment for his family. He just does not know how. His life meant work. To be a man meant working and providing for his family."

While Zhaleh believed that her mother deserved better in life, she also took her father's side into account, saying, "Who could my father blame if his work was difficult, if he saw life as oppressing, if he was not enjoying his life?"

Zhaleh saw both parents as victims of their social conditions. As she matured and started working, she saw her father in a different light. Instead of looking at the father as a symbol of tyrannical rule in the family, she looked at other socialization factors such as his upbringing, childhood, schooling, class background, city of origin, and the impact of the larger society. "He wasn't taught anything else," she said. "He was not a happy man either. He was not a mean man. They were both victims of their society and the conditions under which they lived. I don't believe my mother was not oppressed, but I believe it was not my father's fault that she was oppressed."

Growing up and getting a job enables a daughter to look at her parents' relationship and the position of the men in the family and the larger society in a different light. Maturity and years of employment bring young women closer to the world their fathers inhabit. As an adult, Zhaleh said, "When I got older I decided that no matter what my father did, he did not do it on purpose. It was the society, his upbringing, his childhood, his schooling." She held neither parent responsible for their shortcomings. Although she acknowledged the distance between fathers and children, she also saw the loneliness the fathers may experience in their socially constructed tyrannical towers, as they are acting out their socially prescribed role. Taking both sides into account, Zhaleh raised multifaceted issues.

> I am sure he had problems of his own which he needed to share and to talk about. But what if my father sat down and opened up? What if fathers could open up to their daughters, if they could overcome the gap between them and their daughters? He could do the same and talk about his stories of hardship, his likes and dislikes, what he lost in life, my mother and the problems he had with her. He could tell us about his unfulfilled dreams or my mother's shortcomings. But he never did.

Minoo, whose father had divorced her mother when she was one year old and subsequently had never inquired about his daughter, said, "My mother opened up to me when I was a child. But when I got older I wasn't interested in talks like that. So I never asked her anything. I was curious what happened that there was no man in our house. But I never asked why my father divorced her or why she divorced her second husband." Although she had no recollection of her parents together, Minoo was well aware of her mother's feelings. "My mother always felt that she was oppressed in her marriage, that she was ignored, overlooked," Minoo recalled. "I, however, never accepted what she said at face value. I wanted to find out for myself, to figure out what had happened that their relationship had not worked out." Feeling distant from her mother, she continued, "I can't pinpoint any particular moment in which my mother and I felt a distance between us. We just grew apart from each other." Thinking back about her mother's life and the bitter memories her mother had shared with her, she said,

> She had a very difficult life with her husband and with her own family. Her mother died during childbirth. She had a stepmother who badly mistreated her. Her father passed away when she was only five or six years old. After her father's death, her stepmother managed to marry a young cousin, who actually wanted to marry my mother. He died too within a short time period and eventually her stepmother kicked her out of the house. Forced to marry at the age of sixteen, she was divorced at eighteen.

Not having an immediate family of her own to go to, Minoo's mother moved to Tehran to start a new life. Now Minoo, herself the mother of two children, said,

> Sometimes when I get very tired with the children, I think of my mother and her life, getting thrown away from her house, having to move to a different city with a baby girl. She could have had a good husband. She was beautiful. She could have married. But she carried me with her everywhere she went, like a cat. She did everything she could. But I think she had no more energy to deal with life. She was exhausted, tired of the challenges of life. She had become very embittered. We couldn't get along anymore.

Over the years, Minoo's mother developed a harsh temperament. Not only was she impatient with her daughter, but she also opened up to her friends and talked about private family affairs and her problems. "Even when I took a nap or slept she would come in and scold me for taking a nap," Minoo said. "She nagged and complained so much when I came back from work."

Although Minoo continued to support her mother economically, she refused to live with her in the same house in spite of strong cultural norms against women living by themselves.[19] As a child she had no option except to listen to her mother and share her problems and difficulties. As an adult woman, however, she refused to do so. Having resolved her feelings toward her parents, Minoo stated, "I never found anybody guilty. Sometimes I think I should dislike my father because of the way he was. But when I saw him for the first time I felt, 'This is my father.' Even though my mother had said negative things about him, I never disliked him. I was never angry with him for not taking care of my mother and I, for abandoning us."

Upon becoming economically independent, she not only took care of her mother's expenses but also housed her father, his second wife, and their children. "My mother didn't agree with me taking care of my father's family. I always thought that my father was a miserable person. He never made a life for his second family either." Although she saw her father as being responsible for all the difficulties they experienced, for having to move to a different city and having to stake out lives for themselves, looking at her parents with all their shortcomings, Minoo has forgiven them both.

For some women like Zahra and Sima, protecting the mother and the younger children against the despotic father becomes their lifelong destiny. Refusing to marry because they do not wish to exchange one master for another, they devote their lives to their families, trying to create moments of joy and comfort. Women like Zahra find their fathers too resistant to change, too entrenched in exercising authority and exerting absolute control over their families. Not able to bring dramatic change, these women spend their lives fighting against the authoritarian father. Although crushed to a great extent, the desire to bring change still motivates them to create breathing spaces. In this process, they may create moments of freedom and protection for the younger children and the mother, while they themselves may experience suffocation.

Women like Zhaleh and Minoo, on the other hand, developed a different relationship with their mothers and fathers. Perhaps their fathers did not depict such absolute dictatorial tendencies. Perhaps these daughters did see moments of softness, tender caring, and love. Perhaps those moments of tenderness enabled these daughters to see through the authoritarian image, to get a glimpse of the man who wanted to care but did not know how to show love and affection. These women were aware of the fact that their fathers were often raised by strict standards during a time when showing love and affection to children was seen as a sign of weakness and ruinous to the development of children. Perhaps women like Minoo and Zhaleh saw their fathers as men who wanted to care but did not know how show affection. Perhaps they saw their fathers as mere cogs in the working of the giant machine called society. Aware of the oppression their mothers experienced, they were also able to take into account their fathers' side.

Confined to their houses, hindered in developing their potential as complete human beings, trapped in familial relationships, expected to follow traditional precepts, some women/mothers experience their husbands as the primary agents of control and absolute rule in the family. The power of tradition renders every man a patriarch in his household regardless of his class background. Each man's household, be it a mansion or a shack, is his castle in which he can rule and expect to be taken care of and paid respect—a place where his rule will often go unchallenged.

However, inasmuch as this is the world that some Iranian women born during the 1920s and 1930s experienced, their daughters bring to light an additional perspective. The daughters' responses to how their mothers treated them varies. Overall, two distinct kinds of responses surfaced. Instead of holding individual men responsible for the unhappy lives their mothers led, some women looked at the larger picture. Although they did not doubt the suffering their mothers endured, they were able to situate their fathers within the larger social context. While each individual is accountable for her or his own behavior, some daughters realize that it is patriarchy that empowers individual men to rule over women and legitimizes their control over family members regardless of their economic means. It is the marriage of patriarchy and cultural traditions—the invisible cohabitation of patriarchy and economic systems within socially constructed norms—that renders women and men as powerless and powerful members of the society. The confluence of these forces yields tremendous power to individual men to reign in their own households if in no other place. There were daughters who saw a lonely and isolated man behind this facade of power. Some daughters saw their fathers as men who may not have felt loved in their own homes, who always may wonder if their children loved them, who always may experience a barrier between themselves and their children. A few daughters and fathers were able to bridge this gap, to openly express love based in parental affection instead of expressing respect based in fear and traditional cultural expectations; these relationships were the exceptions.

Whereas some women in this study were able to dissect the imports of patriarchy, others were traumatized by it, unable to look at the larger picture. Obviously not all daughters are able to take into account the social factors that shape gender-role formations. Therefore, many of the stories in this section have been gloomy and perhaps at times overly one-sided, blindly blaming either the mother or the father or both. Facing difficulties and not being able to resolve them, some daughters reproach their mothers, overlooking the degree to which societal factors (including religion, centuries-old cultural traditions and taboos, economic structure, and gender-role expectations) have determined the nature of their interaction. Those daughters who do not blame the mother have turned against the omnipotent authoritarian father, overlooking the fact that he also has acted according to traditional gender-role precepts.

Whatever life directions the daughters take, most have had to resolve feelings of powerlessness, reevaluate their worth as women, and reexamine their relationships with men and with their mothers. Emotionally wounded daughters have had to overcome their anger and frustration at one or both parents. However, blaming the mother for transferring her own troubled world view to the daughter and for shaping how daughters see the world around them is a way of clinging to the past. It takes energy away from any attempt to construct a new relationship, a new bond in which both partners will be more fulfilled as adults. Brooding over the ever-present tyrannical father and his injustices, past or present, leaves little emotional and creative energy to transcend the past and to build familial bridges.

Some women have suffered tremendously from the expectation that they would be mothers and wives. Isolated in their own households, separated from their immediate families, subservient to husbands and in-laws, and lacking independent economic means, some mothers have experienced extreme isolation and loneliness. This situation, compounded with experiencing a daughter as an extension of herself, led to the formation of unique bonds between mothers and daughters. As long as good mothers are defined as being those who see their own lives as entirely secondary to those of their children, women continue to see and experience their lives through their children.[20] Those women who have their own careers and work for progress at work are seen as selfish; they are blamed for believing in their own progress rather than the welfare of their children and families. Being a good mother means a lifetime of sacrifice, of devotion, of labor for children. After a lifelong investment in one's own children, it is extremely difficult, if not impossible, to expect women to step back, to let the child grow away and establish a separate sense of identity.

Mothers, especially those born during the 1920s and 1930s, were not raised believing that their daughters would have careers of their own, perhaps lives of their own. When this occurs, these mothers need to learn to let go of their daughters as they do with their sons. Obviously, some mothers have had a difficult time doing so, especially if they had a problematic marital relationship. They have tried to hold on to one thing, to one promising, fulfilling relationship, to the bond with their daughters, which has proven nourishing for both. In order to remain nourishing, however, this same bond has to be severed. Those mothers who refuse to let their daughters grow up, who maintain an overlong symbiosis with their daughters, who refuse to see their daughters as independent individuals, may retard not only their own emotional detachment but also their daughters' attempts to establish separate and independent identities. Where mothers see their daughters as companions and confidantes, daughters have expressed the need to break away, to distance, and to establish an independent sense of self.

This chapter is not intended as a critique of mothers or mothering, nor is it meant to castigate fathers. Rather, it is an attempt to depict the significant relationship between mothers and daughters and to show the isolation, loneliness, and emotional intensity that women can experience both as wives in their marriage and as daughters in their families. By articulating the strengths and the difficulties of their relationships with their mothers, the daughters have brought to light the silent experiences of women/mothers in the patriarchal family unit. By talking about their problems, the daughters actually are revealing their mothers' lives—the difficulties they have endured and the means to which they resorted in order to gain a limited sense of strength and power within their own families. This tendency is because of the patriarchal structure of marriage, in which women's individuality and freedom of choice are taken away from them.

Instead of being looked at as individual human beings, women in a patriarchal society are viewed as reproductive machines to produce the next generation and to socialize it on the right path toward maintaining and preserving the traditional family institution. The irony of this situation lies in the fact that, while it is the patriarchal structure that determines women's status, it is often the mother who carries and passes on to her daughter a devalued view of the feminine and of women's role in society. Socialized according to dominant gender roles, mothers pass on a cycle of powerlessness that becomes instrumental in perpetuating the patriarchal structure, in which masculinity and its attributes are more valued.

Entrusting their concealed pains to their daughters, mothers enter into a secret contract with their daughters. Assured of the mother-daughter bond, they share their hidden pain, unaware of the negative impact that doing so may have on their daughters' future. Ironically, by breaking their silence and talking about the problems and difficulties they personally have experienced with their mothers, daughters actually are articulating the painful experiences of mothers. Regardless of who is doing the talking, the revelations are made; a door has been opened to understanding one of the most intimate aspects of family relationships and to placing the mother-daughter relationship, with all its complexities, into the much broader social context.

While this chapter is devoted to problematic relationships between mothers and daughters, the next chapter opens a window to fulfilling relationships between the two women. As might be expected, there were daughters who dearly loved their mothers and who had developed mutually gratifying relationships with them. As the next chapter shows, not all daughters minded their mother's tendency to open up to them; some daughters invited that closeness, craving it from a young age. For others, closeness with the mother and awareness of her problems did not rule out attachment to the father. Both parents, in their own ways, proved to be crucial figures in the upbringing of their children.

Cherished Bonds

Mothers and Daughters Revisited

IS THE MOTHER-DAUGHTER RELATIONSHIP inherently problematic? Are there mothers who encourage the development of an autonomous personality in their daughters? Mothers who let their daughters grow and flourish independently? Mothers who do not apply double standards to their sons and daughters? Are there daughters who do not feel the need to engage in the separation struggle and who welcome their mother's openness and closeness? Daughters who do not mind the everyday contacts and entangled lives?

The women in this chapter loved their mothers dearly and highly valued their closeness. Of course, their family environments and circumstances varied. Despite coming from different classes of society, Layla and Roya enjoyed a content and happy upbringing. They enjoyed a supportive family atmosphere. Looking back at their lives, they appreciated their parents' constant efforts to provide the best for them and to practice modern ideas regarding their children's upbringing. Sousan and Azar, on the other hand, came from families in which power and control were clearly monopolized by their fathers. Sousan was quite conscious of the fact that it took her mother years to be able to express her opinions and to be heard. That knowledge, however, did not adversely affect Sousan's relationship with her father. Sousan's father remained a constant source of reassurance and support. Azar did not share the same sentiments about her father. Never attached to her father, she remained distant and suspicious toward him. What she and Sousan witnessed was, however, a complete reversal of power positions within their families through time. This dramatic change signified a fact of relationships: just because women begin their marriages in subordinate positions does not necessarily imply that they will always be subjugated.

Many factors tend to tip the balance of power in the family. The closeness of adult children, both male and female, to their mothers can be especially valuable assets that enable some mothers to gain considerable autonomy and status in their households. Furthermore, the women's devotion to their families and to the idea that the family comes first may again help some women to prove themselves to their husbands time and again. Time, devotion, perseverance, wisdom, and the presence of adult children may help some women to change their oppressive situation to a position of respect and power. Perhaps it is accurate to suggest that in traditional societies the beginning of a marriage is not an indication of how the marriage will evolve through life. Time may bring admiration, respect, autonomy, and power for some women.

"My Childhood Dream Has Come True"

There were mothers in the study who never opened up to their children. Are they those who were happily married and had a fulfilling relationship with their husbands? Layla's case is an example. "My parents had an ideal relationship. I can say their relationship was very different from what I see now among Iranian men and women. They are my role models. I learned how to treat my children from them. My father is so open minded. My family does not regard women inferior to men; there were no restrictions when we were growing up. We still have a very good relationship, all the four sisters and my parents."

Looking back at her childhood, at her relationship with her parents, Layla recalled, "My father provided the best for us. There was constant encouragement. My mother bought the best school uniforms. I always went to good private schools. Mother tells me that she made a difference between my sisters and me because she always bought the best for me. I was the brightest in the family. My father loved me dearly because I was so talented."

Layla's parents had a loving relationship but that did not guarantee that they did not have their share of problems. Layla's mother was the daughter of an immigrant family. Layla explained,

> She was a minority and my father was always so protective of her and her family. He was a very generous and kind man. He did everything he could for the people he knew. As a child, I used to think my mother was too in-volved with her own family. But now that I have my own family I realize that the more you give the more your family expects. Now that I look back I realize that my mother worked very hard for us. She cooked the best dishes for us. She even ironed our underwear. But I was so possessive. I expected her to be home when I got home from school. My grandmother's house was next door and sometimes when I got home and she [my mother] wasn't there I felt terrible. I wanted her at home. But now I believe they had spoiled me. I was jealous of her relationship with her family. My grand-mother was sick with cancer for one year. My mother took care of her the whole time. She did everything. There were nights that she didn't even close her eyes. I was sorry for her and even tried to help, but I was jealous too be-cause I didn't want her to stay there.

Layla's childhood dream eventually came true. In her forties she was as close to her mother as she had wished to be as a child. Although she still showed possessive tendencies toward her mother, she also saw their relationship in a different light. As Layla explained, "I have a very good relationship with my mother now. I can say my childhood dream has come true. I became very close to my mother after marriage. I enjoy this closeness. Now as a mother I can appreciate how hard she worked for us trying to give us the best she could. This is under the conditions that I experience no difficulty from my family, but her family had such a difficult time."

The nature of Layla's relationship with her mother is perhaps not that different from that between Pari and her mother (discussed in the previous chapter). The distinguishing factor is, however, how the relationship is perceived by the daughters. While Pari desired to maintain some distance from her parents, especially her mother, and did not enjoy their obligatory everyday telephone conversations, Layla enjoyed her regular contacts with her mother. "I call her every day," Layla said. "If I don't call her, she calls me. Of all the daughters, I am the one who has the most contact with her. The others are very busy with their own lives. When she is sick I cook and take it to her. Anything she needs I'd take care of it myself. I accompany her to the doctor although she tells me she doesn't need me to go with her. But I'd go with her anyway."

Layla enjoyed her regular contacts with her mother; the fact that she was the closest daughter to her mother and the one who catered to her needs was gratifying to her. Perhaps she was able to enjoy her close relationship because she was successful in her career as a dentist, had studied abroad for a short time, and was able to establish an independent and autonomous identity early in life. Perhaps the reason for her satisfying relationship was that it was based on mutual respect, love, and devotion instead of obligation, need, and expectations.

As a young teenager, Layla saw her mother helping to raise her uncle's children. Layla was jealous of those children, and explained, "She was so kind to those children. It got to the point I was so jealous of them I didn't want to see them. I liked them because they were younger than me, but I couldn't stand them." As an adult woman, Layla was still possessive towards her mother and did not enjoy sharing her care and attention with others. She even refused to see the video that her uncle's children had sent from abroad. Her jealousy seemed to have remained as strong as ever, but as an adult she had been able to focus her energy on the more meaningful aspects of her relationship with her mother.

Layla grew up believing that her mother was highly involved with her own family. To some degree, her mother's world was closed to Layla. "My mother never opened up to me as a child." As a daughter of an extended immigrant family, Layla's mother had her own share of problems and difficulties. Born on the border during the family's immigration, she was raised by foreign-born parents. Her uncle had traveled to Iran first, sending home beautiful pictures of the country. "That encouraged the whole family to immigrate," Layla said. "My grandfather was sorry about this move all his life." Layla's mother had to deal with the early death of her father, an uncle leaving his family and children, and other problems associated with the first-generation immigrant status in an adopted country. All these difficulties, however, did not prompt Layla's mother to open up to her oldest and brightest daughter. She endured diverse adversities, married a loving man, and raised her own children while helping to take care of other children in her extended family. Layla's father probably endured similar difficulties, acting as a bridge between his wife's Christian family and the larger society. Together they provided a loving and supportive environment for their children.

While Layla dreamt of a close and open relationship with her mother, that situation was to come about only much later in life. Her mother started opening up to her, sharing her past travails and present experiences, initiating the closeness at an age when their sharing could be mutual. Both women talked and heard each other out. Layla looked forward to sharing their lives together. Furthermore, listening to her mother did not involve an explicit or an implicit denigration of her father. Layla's parents remained her role models, setting an ideal image, a standard that she would later emulate as a parent. As a child she desired more time and intimacy with her mother, but her needs, whether normal or excessive, were not met. Attaining her mother's attention eventually came with Layla's maturity and marriage. By the time her mother was ready to or chose to open up to her, Layla was more than ready to hear her stories. The ensuing intimacy and closeness, the desire to take care of her mother's physical and medical needs, and the daily routine telephone conversations did not annoy her. Perhaps having to compete for her mother's attention throughout her life had enabled Layla to appreciate her final victory; of the four sisters she was the closest to her mother.

"Mother Was There for Us"

Like Layla, Roya appreciated her mother and the peaceful relationship that her parents had. She explained, "My parents were very kind and tolerant people. They never had any quarrels or arguments. They were that kind of people. My brothers have gone after their father. They are quiet people, willing to compromise and to listen. They are all very thoughtful and that affects their family life." Roya admired her mother for what she was. "My mother was a typical housewife," she explained. "She was married very young and was not educated. But she decided to go to school in her sixties, starting from the elementary school for adults. She wanted to have an education."

For Roya, it was her mother's modern attitudes that were a source of inspiration. Although belonging to the previous generation, her mother always looked forward to the future and was ready for change, for accepting new ideas in her life. As Roya said of her mother,

> She maintains a positive outlook on life. I look back comparing myself with other girls my age and realize that I have never had some of the problems they had. My adolescent years passed with no major trouble because my mother was there for us. I could bring friends home with no problem while in those days girls were not allowed to bring friends home. Later when I got older I had the permission to befriend boys, going out with them especially for long walks to the mountains. Some of them could visit at the house, those whom mother knew. I had certain freedoms. Mother was very open. She saw new things, thought about them and either accepted or rejected them. She was not a closed-minded person.

Her mother's diplomacy and attitude toward modern ideas such as allowing her daughter to bring friends home or visiting them at their homes, and to engage in sports such as mountain climbing with friends her age, allowed Roya to have a smooth adolescence. Given these conditions, she never saw the need to rebel or to challenge her parents in order to gain freedom and autonomy. Roya believed that, had her mother not been so understanding and kind, their lives could have been very difficult. "Her character affected all of us very much," Roya recalled. "We lacked so much in life but her love, tenderness, and thoughtfulness did away with a lot of shortcomings we felt in our lives."

A happy marriage and a fulfilling marital relationship can enable women to endure life's challenges and difficulties without having to resort to their young daughters as friends and confidantes, as younger sisters and a captive audience of the family drama. But a happy and fulfilling marriage is not necessarily the key to a content and satisfying relationship between mothers and daughters. There were women who have lived lives of sacrifice and understanding, who have shown a great extent of altruism. There were women who believed the women's role to be one of selflessness and sacrifice, who believed in creating a harmonious and calm environment for their families at any cost. To do so, they silenced their own voices, subjecting their own desires to those of their husbands, children, and the extended family. The impact of such beliefs and demeanor on children varied. For some women, a lifetime of sacrifice became their duty, perhaps setting up a negative image for their daughters; for others, altruism and devotion had long-term and unpredictable rewards. In these cases, the adult children, both male and female—and at times even the husbands—eventually came to recognize the depth of the sacrifices the mother/wife had made. These women were able to reap the results of lifelong devotion to their families.

Sousan's mother was a content and quiescent person who never challenged her husband. Instead, she was always accepting and supportive. Even as a child, there were times that Sousan and the rest of the children in the family believed that their mother's thoughts and actions were more sensible than those of their father. But she and her siblings never saw their mother opposing their father. Sousan recalled, "My mother is a very calm and quiet person. Whatever my father said my mother agreed. She always compromised and accepted his opinion. They never fought or argued in front of us. Of course, I am sure they had their own problems and disagreements but we never saw them arguing in front of us."

Sousan believed that her mother's approach to marriage, the fact that she neither questioned her husband's authority nor argued or fought in front of the children, had dramatically shaped her attitude toward marriage. As a quiet and calm person, Sousan saw her mother as a role model to be emulated. "My mother has influenced me more than anybody else in life," Sousan said. "I often catch myself doing the exact same thing. In my marriage, I am the one who tries to understand, to compromise and to yield. Consciously or unconsciously, my mother has influenced me dramatically."

A year after her parents' marriage Sousan's grandfather passed away. There were small children in the family as young as two years old. With his father's death, Sousan's father, who was the oldest son, became the primary caretaker of the extended family. Along with him, Sousan's mother became a second mother to all the children. They all lived in the same household. There were eight children in the family, so that Sousan's mother raised not only her own children but also eight other children. The workload was heavy, the responsibility horrendous. While Sousan's mother took it upon herself to raise all the children, her husband also took his responsibility seriously. The young couple raised not only their own children but also those of the extended family. Sousan explained,

My parents became the primary caretakers of this big family. My father believed that these children needed more care and attention because they were orphans. He even hugged and kissed them before he kissed his own children. We all lived in the same house. What bothered my mother was that nobody ever appreciated her work; nobody ever paid her the right respect for raising all these children. They all assumed that it was her responsibility, her duty. She played a mother to all of them. She is still upset about it. Her feelings were hurt, but she never complained to my father about it.

However, lifelong devotion, compromise, and accommodation led to a dramatic shift of power. While Sousan's mother had always accepted her husband's absolute authority, with time came a fundamental change. Whereas in the past it was Sousan's father's voice—charged with the power of tradition and authority—that was heard, now it was Sousan's mother who had exchanged places with her husband. "Now, everything is different," Sousan said. "He ruled during their early years. Now what she says goes. What she wants gets done. I feel that at the age of seventy-four, my father has decided to compensate for what he has done in the past, for how he was in his early days."

Observing the development of the marital bond between her parents, conscious of the hardships her mother endured and the dramatic shift of power, Sousan had come up with her own conclusions.

"I have come to believe that if you honestly try to build a trusting relationship, if you try to negotiate and to compromise in your life, you will develop a good understanding of each other in the long run. Sometimes, my husband knows what he is doing or saying is wrong but he says, "I can't do anything about it." Perhaps one day he will also come to a new understanding, the same way my father has come to develop a new appreciation of my mother. I hope one day my husband will come around, too."

Sousan saw her mother as a symbol of giving and forgiveness, a woman who put her family and her in-laws first. She willingly subordinated her own needs and desires to what was best for others. Her husband eventually came to appreciate her lifelong devotion and started to put her desires ahead of his own. Sousan's mother was her role model. She did not mind her mother opening up to her; furthermore, in opening up to Sousan her mother did not slander or vilify her father. Her father remained a source of support and encouragement throughout her life while her mother became her role model in building a marriage based on respect and understanding. While her father saw it as his duty to provide a decent standard of living for his extended family, to be loving and caring toward all the children, to encourage them all—boys and girls alike—to pursue higher education, her mother was dedicated to providing a home atmosphere where harmony and contentment reigned. Successful at their mission to provide for and raise fourteen children, Sousan's parents came to appreciate each other. A horrendous task was accomplished. Although Sousan's mother felt that her sacrifices and efforts were never fully acknowledged, her husband's final appreciation of her efforts, his surrendering of his power and autonomy to her, changed the balance of power in this family. Seeing the result of a life of devotion and altruism, Sousan was encouraged to take the same path to motherhood and marriage, believing that role reversal was inevitable with the passage of time and after the husband and wife show their true colors.

Women's lifelong devotion to their families does not necessarily guarantee that all those who were at the receiving end of this devotion would eventually come around to recognize the women's endless sacrifices and the fact that they willingly abandoned their rights for the welfare of the larger family.

For some women, devotion and altruism are seen as a life sentence; they do not have the pleasure or the hope of ever being acknowledged or thanked for their efforts. While some women may accept their conditions as the women's faith, there are those who individually rise up against such a belief system. Perhaps some women envision an end to lifelong sacrifice. Perhaps for some, there exists no other route but sacrifice and quiescence until they gain some measure of power in the family. For some women, the coming of age of children, both sons and daughters, is a turning point in their lives. Having enjoyed a supportive and caring mother, having shared her lack of control and autonomy, and having experienced the father's absolute rule in the family, some children form strong alliances with the mother. Together they rebel against the father/husband and question his authority. This alliance is crucial for the mother because it confirms her position and efforts within the family and provides unconditional support. While some men, like Sousan's father, willingly relinquish their power, others reluctantly lose their absolute rule to the mother and her adult children. A lifetime of sacrifice eventually pays off for some women.

Like Sousan, Azar loved her mother. She explained, "I can say everything I have is because of my mother. My mother was a very wise person. She didn't have much education, but she was the smartest person in the family. Now that I am reading psychology books I realize my mother practiced a lot of things in her everyday life, without ever having read any of those books. She didn't have much education but she was extremely smart. Furthermore, she was an exceptionally tolerant and dedicated person."

Azar, however, was not happy with the relationship between her parents. "My father was okay. Their relationship was not great. But we were more influenced by my mother." Azar's mother had always opened up to her, but her father had remained distant. "Recently, my father has started talking, opening up to me," Azar said. "I have always been very skeptical toward him. Their relationship was open to all of us. When we were young my mother was completely under his control. His parents were living with us and that exacerbated the situation by increasing his control over her."

However, the coming of age of the children changed the parental relationship and her mother's position. With the children growing older, Azar's mother gained more power and authority in her household.

> When the children got older, when they were there to support her, she changed completely to the degree that now she was the one who had control over my father. And that wasn't fair, either. But that was due to the early relationship that they had developed and all the difficulties she had endured. She was like a spring that was pushed and forced to be kept in place and when it suddenly snapped there was no going back where it was. Lately, it had gotten to the point that I did not fully appreciate how she treated my father. But I couldn't change anything. I said it many times to my brothers, but she couldn't control herself anymore. Nothing could control her anymore. For years we, the children, supported her in any way we could. It got to the point that I decided it is no longer correct to support her. I stopped, but my brothers continued to support her. It was too late. Only one of my brothers and I were more balanced towards my father, but she had the full support of the rest of her children.

Although Azar was skeptical toward her father and his motivations in opening up, she did not like her mother's attitude toward her father. She did not condone the way her mother treated her father, but this did not stop her from acknowledging her mother's positive qualities and constructive impact on her life. Aware of the hardships her mother had endured, Azar admired her wisdom and devotion to her family. These qualities had enabled her to raise capable and successful children who believed in her and her rights. Looking at her mother as a primary source of inspiration, Azar also was able to see her parents' shortcomings and the negative impacts of their relationship on her life. Azar believed that, had her parents' relationship been better, she could have been a lot more successful in life.

The reasons women open up to their daughters from an early age are varied. While it can be argued that those women who experience unhappy marriages tend to open up to their children, the cases of Azar and Sousan do not invariably provide support for such a conclusion. Rather, these situations show that even some women who experienced unequal and unhappy marital relationships did not necessarily feel the dire need to share their problems with their children. Perhaps taken together, these two chapters depict, more than any other evidence, the complexity of the relationship between mothers and daughters. Although there were more daughters (in this study) who had problematic relationships with their mothers, there were also those who admired their mothers and saw them as their role models regardless of the kind of marital relationship they had with their fathers.

Generational conflicts seem to be an endemic source of problems between parents and children. These conflicts are especially pronounced in countries where the rapid pace of change leaves many behind. Although many mothers and fathers strictly adhere to traditional gender roles, others try to adapt to the changing times. Therefore, while it is tempting to come up with grand generalizations and conclusions, the variety of cases in these two chapters shows the futility of such a tendency. There are daughters who came from very strict and conservative family backgrounds and still managed to challenge their parents on many grounds and to varying degrees. An example is Zhaleh, who constantly challenged her mother's strict rules about gender roles and developed a new appreciation of the world her distant father inhabited. Zhaleh challenged her mother on many occasions and, in the process, gained a level of freedom and personal autonomy not available to her older sisters.

Zahra, who came from a strictly religious, poor, and conservative background, questioned her father's authority in silence, in action, and in words from a very early age. For a woman of her family background, she had gained a high degree of independence through standing up to her father and asserting her position as the oldest daughter in the family. Zahra had internalized the suffering her mother had endured; this situation encouraged her to challenge her father. She rebelled by deciding never to marry and to financially provide for her family, acting as a breadwinner and a voice of protection for the younger children and the mother.

For others like Sousan, the internalization of the oppression her mother had experienced led to an ingrained inability to defend her rights and to voice her opinion in marriage. Believing her husband would eventually realize her worth, like her father had that of her mother, Sousan chose the same path her mother had chosen, a path of compromise and acceptance. While some women expressed anger and frustration at the relationship between their parents, there were others who were raised by caring and supportive parents. This, however, did not guarantee a successful relationship in their marriage, as we shall see later.

While the cases discussed in these two chapters allude to possible conclusions, perhaps it is better not to hint at any general inference. Instead, by reading the two chapters together one can further complicate the relationship between mothers and daughters while shedding light on the hardships endured by women of both generations. Individual cases might be stronger than others, and some voices are more convincing than others. We may find similarity with some while we feel sorry for or appalled by others' accounts or stories. Whether drawn to some and appalled by others, whether believing in a couple of stories and not in others, the fact remains that these are stories the women themselves have chosen to share. In this sharing the daughters have revealed not only their own lives but also those of their mothers.

6

Fathers and Daughters

"I Have Yet to See a Man Like My Father"

CHILDREN ARE GREATLY AFFECTED by the relationship between their parents. How they are affected, however, depends on the quality of the relationship. Fathers are the first men with whom children come into contact. A father's mere presence and interaction with the wife/mother and the child are the first lessons the child receives in the realm of gender roles. The parents provide a mirror in which the children see their future. They either try to emulate what they see, expecting their future to replicate the same image, or they may attempt to achieve what they always thought was missing in their parents' relationship. The parental interaction, combined with the inherent personality of the young child, creates diverse responses on the part of daughters.

Fathers have played crucial roles in providing economic and emotional support.[1] They have been a major source guiding their daughters through life, advising them about what to study, how much to study, what kind of jobs to take, and whom to marry. They have performed all these tasks according to their familial backgrounds and cultural precepts while constantly adjusting to the rapidly changing society. For example, if completing an elementary education was perceived to be enough for the first daughter born in the early 1940s in a traditional family, the third daughter, born only a few years later, faced no problem pursuing her higher education. If the desire to hold a job was a challenging experience for the first daughter, it was an expectation for the younger daughters in the family.[2]

The relationship between a father and daughter seriously affects the young child and colors her future relationship with her husband and her own children. While some daughters in the study, albeit a very small number, were turned away from marriage, others sought personalities similar to or very different from their fathers. While some felt especially appreciated and loved as female children, others felt overburdened or neglected because of their gender.

How the fathers influenced their daughters' lives cannot be categorized neatly. Some fathers were warm and supportive; they loved their daughters dearly—at times even more than—their sons. They provided lifetime guidance and support. They pushed and encouraged their daughters to explore paths hardly tried by any woman before them. There were also absent or distant fathers who, although they loved their daughters and left a positive impact on them, saw their work and career as more important. Responsibilities and decision making were delegated to the mother because the children were her domain of influence and action, considered too unimportant for the fathers' precious time. But needless to say, all actions had to have the father's stamp of approval. Another category that emerged from the research was that of the extremely controlling father figure who abided by conservative gender roles and tried to quell any desire for change that the daughters may have exhibited.

Fathers, the omnipotent force in the family, have played diverse roles, ranging from the very positive and constructive to the extremely controlling and destructive. While some fathers played absolutely positive roles, there were also those who left lifetime scars. Let us hear from the daughters themselves. What stereotypes are shattered, and which ones are reinforced? Is there a single image that can be defined as the Iranian father?

"I Have Yet to See a Man Like My Father"

Some women have fond memories of their childhoods. They were their father's sweethearts, having enjoyed his constant attention and love. Contrary to the dominant idea that parents prefer sons to daughters, there were daughters who actually felt that their fathers loved them more than their brothers. In some families, daughters were loved more than the sons. As Sousan said, "My mother is closer to her daughters than her sons. But my father cares for his daughters a lot more. He loves us. Even my brothers admit that he would do anything for us. We were a lot more important to him than my brothers. My older sister was like an idol for my father. My father always calls her Miss Katy and not Katy." Calling her Miss Katy showed his love and respect for her. "He agrees with whatever she says," Sousan said. Even in his old age, Sousan's father keeps up with his daughters. Although married with children, Sousan and her sisters know they have their father in addition to their husbands to rely on. "I feel more relaxed in my life because I know my father will be there for me if I need him," she said.

Layla's father also loved his daughters dearly. As a father of four daughters, he was not upset about having no sons. "On the contrary, he was happy that he did have daughters and to this day he loves his nieces more than his nephews," Layla said. Looking back at her parents, Zhaleh said, "My mother valued her sons more than her daughters. But my father was different. He actually liked his daughters more than his sons."

Sara lost her father when she was eight years old. She, however, remembers one story that was retold time and again. "I was told that he was happier when my sister and I were born than when my brothers were born because he believed that a female child will bring good fortune and symbolizes good luck," Sara recalled. Mina remembered her mother's words about giving birth to four daughters. "My mother loves her son. She tells me that when I was born she was very happy because she didn't have a sister to talk to. When my sister was born, it was OK. When the third daughter was born, she cried. With the fourth daughter, she was seriously distraught. But father was just the opposite. Unlike most Iranian men, he loved his daughters more than his son. He was a loving person, always providing for us anything we ever wanted."

Apparently, there were fathers who loved their daughters better and did not hesitate to show their affections. Openly expressing their love of daughters, the fathers became positive sources of encouragement who were always available for their daughters. Having such fathers enabled the female children to grow up feeling loved and cared for; they had a source of support, encouragement, and guidance throughout their lives. This enabled them to set high goals for their futures.

Loving daughters dearly or more than sons, however, does not mean that the fathers were overly indulgent with their daughters or allowed them to trespass culturally appropriate genders roles more easily. Fathers' love was expressed in different ways. One form of expression was a clear emphasis on higher education. As Layla said, "My father emphasized that I should go to college. I wanted to go to college mostly because of him. He stressed our education and believed that all his daughters should receive higher education." Layla's parents urged her to become a doctor. Upon graduation from medical school, her father helped her financially to set up her own private practice. She recalled, "My father used to tell me, 'you don't need to marry.' He told me that he'll buy me a car and will pay for my office expenses and that I never need to marry. He said, 'You can marry if you want, but don't worry if you don't.' " Layla's comments about her father's emphasis on education reminded me of my father's comments when I was about fourteen years old. "Study hard. Pursue your higher education. That will enable you to be economically independent. If you study hard, you'd never have to depend on any man. No man can harm you." This comment more than anything else inspired in me a desire for economic independence.

Quite a few fathers knew divorced or deserted female relatives—sisters or aunts. Cognizant of such injustices committed against divorced, widowed, or unattached women who had lost their livelihood, some fathers saw the need to protect their own daughters against such social ills. The best protection was obviously higher education, economic independence, and perhaps no marriage. As active members of the society, they saw possibilities for growth and for change in women's status, and they tried to channel their daughters in those directions. For them, education was the primary channel for economic independence. While they could try to protect their daughters by educating them and instilling new values in them, they could not alter the laws of the country or change adverse social attitudes toward women. Seeing education as the primary channel for economic independence and social mobility, fathers encouraged their daughters to pursue higher degrees in order to have their own careers. By providing various kinds of economic and emotional support, they were trying to ensure their daughters' success in the realms of education and work. For them, marriage was a secondary goal, having lost its primordial significance. Perhaps they saw marriage as a trap that might stifle their daughters' growth and independence.

It is important to note that it seems that most fathers did not, however, question their role in the family and in relation to their wives. Rather, they dreamt of a different world for their daughters. Most of the daughters saw their fathers as supreme authority figures at home, never seeing their mothers daring to challenge them. The contradiction is that, while most of the men played a very traditional role in relation to their wives, demanding nothing short of complete compliance, they envisioned a better world for their daughters, a world free of patriarchal forces at work in the family. What remains puzzling is the men's double standard for their wives and their daughters. While they expected their wives to be accepting and accommodating, ever catering to their needs, they attempted to raise strongly independent daughters who had high aspirations for their lives. Such daughters would certainly have had an extremely difficult time in traditional society.

Seeing a constructive relationship between parents or feeling especially loved by the father are not situations that automatically lead to a positive future marital relationship for the daughters. Having been raised by parents who had minimal conflict or who believed in providing a supportive family environment for their children seemed to have left some daughters at a loss, not knowing how to deal with problems in their own marriage. If love, respect, and affection were the predominant sentiments to be exchanged in the family, where could the daughters learn how to get there, how to establish a mutually respectful relationship with their husbands, how to resolve conflict in the early years of marriage when the two partners were simply getting to know each other? Feeling a sense of loss, some daughters looked back to their fathers, comparing their husbands with them and wondering why their husbands—these young men of a new generation—were so archaic. Experiencing an unhappy marriage, Layla commented, "We [she and her sisters] thought all the men are like my father. But we were mistaken. Between my parents, everything is shared. They make all the decisions together. They have so much respect and love for each other. I have yet to see a man like my father."

Sara had fine memories of her father. Even as an eight year old, she remembered how seriously her father took her mother into account and respected her opinions. Sara was, however, quick to add, "Don't get me wrong. I am not saying my family was a matriarchal family, just that my father was very respectful toward women. He saw my mother as a strong and frugal person. He always talked about her qualities, giving her his paycheck, telling her she knew better how to spend the money. Even when he was dying he said his mind was at ease because he knew that my mother was a very strong person."

Having such memories of her father, Sara grew up believing that all men were like him. However, like Layla, her expectations were not met. Her own marriage shattered that image, bringing forth a different understanding of men. Growing up, she saw that her father always consulted her mother for both major and minor decisions; she expected the same kind of treatment from her husband. Seeing her husband making important decisions without consulting her, she felt not only insulted but also astonished because, "I thought that all our interests, emotional or financial, were the same. Why shouldn't I know what kinds of decisions he makes?" In Sara's case, time helped, and her husband eventually started to involve her in his decision making, realizing that her input was reasonable. But that occurred after more than a decade of marriage. "It was only with time that he realized that a woman can also be involved in decision making," Sara said. While Sara eventually was able to convince her husband that her opinion counted, Layla's attempts constantly failed. Her expectations to be respected, to be valued as a dentist, to remain independent in her marriage, all met with severe resistance. The image her father created never would be lived out.

Mina's father gave her and her four sisters a relative degree of freedom; he was a loving father. The combination of a passive mother and a loving father, however, did not prepare Mina and her sisters for future difficulties. "Marrying an authoritarian man was puzzling," Mina recalled. "Nobody in my family ever told me 'Don't wear this' or 'Don't go there.' My father didn't even tell my mother what to wear or who to befriend." Mina's marriage, however, brought her together with a man who, because of his upbringing, believed his word was the final word. "That was difficult for me," Mina said. "He wanted to control me." Having been raised by a caring father who never imposed his will on his daughters and a submissive mother who quietly suffered through years of marriage and never voiced any objection to her husband left Mina with no defense mechanism, no survival strategy to handle difficult situations.

In a patriarchal society, an all-caring father who encourages his daughter to grow wings, to fly over distant horizons, and to see the world through a nontraditional lens may actually train his daughter for failure. Looking back at their lives, these women saw their fathers as being representative of all men. They expected their husbands to be supportive and encouraging, willing to take women's sides into account and see them as equal partners. Those daughters raised by caring fathers may feel deprived and neglected in their own marriage. Ironically, living in a supportive family environment and enjoying companionship and advice from a caring father seemed to have set up daughters for a life of disappointment. Their husbands were obviously far from prepared to live up to the standards set by their fathers.

"I Could Be A Lot More Successful"

The nature of the relationship between fathers and mothers affects the daughters in various ways. Whether mothers play a passive and compromising or an active and involved role shapes the female child's perception of her rights and position in the family. While some daughters found themselves acting just like their mothers (accepting and compromising), others wished for a more involved and equal role, trying to create what they sensed was lacking in their parents' relationship.

Sousan talked about her mother as a very quiet and tolerant person. "My mother agreed with whatever my father said," Sousan said. "Even when we kids believed that he was wrong, she agreed with my father. She always compromised." The nature of this interaction and her mother's acquiescence in her marriage affected Sousan to the degree that she found herself acting just like her mother. "I catch myself time and again compromising when I believe what I am saying is right. I am the one who tends to compromise." Mina felt the same way. Her mother was a reticent and quiet person. Shaped by her mother's reserved and quiet attitude, Mina said, "Most of us [four sisters] became very subdued people. We cannot defend our rights. My father was a soft and calm man, but he never understood my mother. He didn't know how he should treat a woman." While she was growing up Mina saw her father making all the decisions by himself and never consulting her mother.

> My father is a rich man, but my mother owns nothing; she has nothing registered under her own name. My father has saved a lot of money, but none of it is in my mother's name. My situation is the same. I was raised by a mother who never objected to anything my father did; she never struggled. She never fathomed the idea that she has any rights in her marriage. When I married, my father gave me everything I needed, a complete dowry, from glasses to a complete set of furniture. We were both students. I wonder how come after fifteen years of marriage and working full-time I do not own anything. I own nothing. My mother was not in a position to give me any advice because to this day she herself does not own anything.

Seeing their mother never standing up for her rights and never challenging her father about any of the decisions he made for them, Mina and her sisters became introverted women who did not know how to stand up for their rights in marriage. Although Mina saw her father as a source of support and encouragement, a father who loved his daughters more than his son and who allowed them abundant freedom of movement, she nevertheless was influenced by the nature of the interaction between her parents. The passive role her mother acquired throughout the years never taught Mina to stand up for herself. Obviously, her father's love did not give her enough self-confidence or a better understanding of men. What mattered most was how her mother had succumbed to her husband's authority. Although Mina enjoyed her father's love and support, she did not learn how to ask for more respect and an acknowledgment of her rights and contributions within her marriage.

Many daughters expressed a yearning for a better relationship between their parents because they believed it would have helped them to build a more constructive relationship with their husbands. Pari, whose father was self-employed, did not see much of him while growing up. "By the time my father came home we were asleep," Pari recalled. "The leadership was in my mother's hand. Of course, he would tell a lot of things to my mother, but we usually heard the 'No' from her." Reflecting on her parents' relationship, however, Pari asserted that the relationship was not close or intimate. "I felt they were separate individuals," Pari said. "Each one had his or her life. There was a lot of distance between them." Sensing the lack of intimacy and closeness between her parents made Pari determined to look for companionship in her marriage. When she began thinking about marriage, she recalled, "I wanted a friend in marriage, a partner. I didn't care about money or other things in life. My parents didn't have that sense of intimacy and closeness that I wished [for] in marriage."

Azar wished for a more positive relationship between her parents. In Azar's family, the children were quite aware of the nature of the relationship between her parents. She said,

Their relationship was open to us all. When we were little, my mother was under my father's absolute control. The fact that my grandparents also were living with us doubled his control over my mother; that exacerbated the situation. I could be a lot more successful in my life if the relationship between my parents was good. I didn't grow up seeing a constructive relationship between them. It was because of their relationship that I concluded early in life that a woman should be economically independent, that she should try not to be under her husband's control. But overall, some things are etched in your mind when your parents' relationship is not constructive.

The interaction between parents, the coming together of individual personalities and characters, leave their impact on the children. While the ultimate outcome, the blooming characters of daughters, cannot be predicted in advance, when they look back at their parents' relationship the daughters are in a position to trace back certain personality traits and expectations to their parents. Reflecting on their relationships with their husbands and children, women can find traces of their mother's imprints in their own doings. Whether emulating their mothers (consciously or unconsciously) or attempting to act differently than did parents, the parents' behavioral patterns are re-created and resurface time and again in the wide range of choices daughters make throughout their lives. Watching the interaction among mothers and fathers, daughters pick up those mannerisms that suit their personality traits. While some have realized similar tendencies, others have deliberately chosen a different path, wishing for a relationship that would be different from that between their parents. But whether daughters emulated their parents consciously or subconsciously, the fact remains that the parents' relationship affected the ways in which the daughters saw themselves, the lessons they inferred about appropriate codes of conduct, and the dreams they harbored for a more fulfilling marital relationship.

Tara's father passed away when she was fourteen years old. Raised by her grandparents to the age of ten, she did not see much of her parents. Tara, however, has delicate memories of her father and the relationship between her parents. Her father paid visits when she was living with her grandparents. He used to take her and her younger sister for walks, carrying the two year old on his shoulder and holding Tara's hand. He played games with them; a game she enjoyed tremendously was called "Catching Cats." They would run in the neighborhood streets following cats. "And we took it so seriously, running after cats," Tara recalled. "Of course, there were no cats. The next night I couldn't wait to go and run after cats again." Reflecting on these memories and the games her father played with them she said, "Now that I have become older, I realize it is very important for parents to know how easily they can entertain their children. This game cost nothing. If only parents could realize there is no need to spend any money for a meaningful relationship and lasting memories. At the age of forty-four I still have sweet memories of those bygone days and the games my father played with us."

Tara's parents had their own problems.

> My mother was a perfectionist. My father believed in a system like socialism. He tried to run everything in the house on that basis. Mother, on the other hand, wanted the best of everything. She was right, but my father was not a good partner for that kind of lifestyle. He always thought that we are part of the masses of people and that if we know a little more or have more than others it is because of the conditions under which we were born. He saw no reason to believe that we have to have the best in our lives.
>
> I went to the best schools. So did my sisters. Mother thought that we should have the best opportunities in life. Father, on the other hand, believed that even a garbage man's son should have access to higher education to become a doctor or an engineer, that a domestic's son could become a doctor without going to the best schools. For him, there was no need to send your children to the most expensive schools in order to guarantee their success. They were both right in their thoughts but it was their differences that caused all the conflict.

Strong beliefs in different ideological systems created constant conflict between Tara's parents. Looking back at her parents' relationship, Tara recognized different dimensions.

> My mother came from a matriarchal family. Family matters were under her control because my father preferred to spend his time on his work. He was not much involved with everyday family affairs. We always had to have permission from mother in order to do anything. He in a way was not doing his share of fathering. He used to tell us to go to Mom to get permission for everything. That was his way of making a decision about our lives. When he

died, mother became both mother and father and that was under conditions that she was working full time. She had to work very hard in order to keep her job, to show her expertise; she had to be the best in many areas.

The belief that those conflicts were not serious and could be avoided compelled Tara to choose a different strategy in her own life. One of the indirect impacts on her of her parents' relationship was to cause her to avoid any conflict rooted in money. "When I married, I decided to avoid any condition that might lead to such problems," Tara said. "Now I realize that was not good because I made so many sacrifices in my life. I was lucky because my husband was a good man, though."

In emulating their parents or devising new lifestyles, the adult daughters' actions or inactions were tainted by how their parents related to each other and what kind of relationships they developed over time. Watching the family drama only too closely, children could not change the channel. They were provided with one scenario that furnished lifetime images either to be re-created or edited according to the young viewers' perception of what is correct and possibly ideal.

"He Was a Good Man But Not a Good Father"

Sousan, Mina, and Layla received plenty of love and attention from their fathers, but not all women grew up knowing their fathers. Minoo grew up without having a father present at home. This fact, nevertheless, had not critically affected her life chances. Minoo said, "I never missed not having a father. It was only when I started going to school that I felt I didn't have a father because the principal wanted me to take my father to the school."

Minoo grew up to be an economically independent woman. She started to work at the age of sixteen, and a few years later she managed to buy a house. "My father was in a bad economic situation and I took him to the house that I had bought for my mother and had him and his wife and children stay there." In the meantime, Minoo took in one of her stepbrothers and raised him in her own apartment. "I did that because my father never cared for children," Minoo said. "All those years when I was a child, he never bothered to see how I was doing. He didn't come to visit me even once, wondering if he had a daughter, asking whether I needed anything. I always wondered how he could be so careless about his life and his children."

But after she grew up, her economic independence allowed Minoo to see her father in a different light.

> Sometimes I think I should dislike my father because of the way he was. But when I saw him for the first time, I felt, this man is my father. I have never disliked him. I was never angry with him for not taking care of me for years. I housed him, his wife, and three children. I always thought my father was a miserable man. He never made a life for his second family. Everybody in his family suffered because of his neglect. I never felt he treated his other children better than he treated me. I thought that was his nature; that was the way he was born. He was a careless person. He was a good man but not a good father. I have seen him buy bread and by the time he got home, the bread was gone; he had given it away to the people on his way. That's how he was.[3]

Minoo's father's absence and lack of caring, along with her mother's difficult character, did not stop Minoo from advancing in life. She was perhaps the first woman among her family and relatives to seek a job, to accumulate enough money to buy a house, and to be able to house her father and his new family. She grew up to be an amazingly strong woman, managing her husband's business and later seeking an independent position.

"You Never Gave Me Anything"

While some women had fine memories of their fathers, upholding them as sources of guidance and lifetime support, there were also those women who experienced their fathers as an omnipotent force who attempted to control every aspect of their lives. Some fathers upheld specific traditional precepts, such as restrictive movement in the larger society, while challenging those norms that prevented the young women from pursuing higher education or seeking gainful employment. There were also those fathers who believed in fixed gender-role formulations and suppressed any desire in their daughters to express the smallest amount of independence and freedom. Extremely prejudiced in their attitudes toward women, this last group saw women as being totally inferior to men.

Sima's father was strict. The children had to obtain permission for any kind of outside activity. While some fathers held the mothers responsible for the children's needs, Sima's mother was reluctant to accept such a responsibility because she knew that, regardless of what she said, the final word was that of her husband. She therefore sent the children directly to him to ask for permission to see friends, go to the movies, or invite friends home. The father represented the voice of authority. As an independent woman Sima did not appreciate the fact of having to acquire permission from a very young age. "I didn't like to ask for permission for doing what I wanted from the time I was very young, about twelve or thirteen years old. I had to ask for permission even if I just wanted to go for a short walk in the neighborhood. I used to confront my father, telling him that 'You inquire about my whereabouts only because I am a girl.' He disagreed. But he continued to monitor my every move up to the time I was in my mid-twenties."

Seeing this condition as belittling, Sima tried to devise ways of maneuvering around her father's absolute authority by sneaking out, by inviting friends to her house without asking for permission, or by simply hiding what she did. However, the pressure was reduced only with the aging of her father and after she had proven herself time and again. "After he became old and grew dependent on me, he tried to adjust to my needs," Sima said. "I am not saying he accepted my demands for independence and privacy. He just adjusted. I was the oldest child, the person who took care of his needs." Looking back at her parents' relationship, Sima said, "I have always thought of my father as a domineering person. Of course, he had valuable qualities, too. He is a traditional man. He used to tell Mom not to spend so much money, but the fact was that we always had everything we needed in life. He was dedicated to his family, to his wife and his children. Mom wanted a more extravagant kind of life, but we always had whatever we needed."

Sima was able to distinguish between the domineering side of her father's personality and his caring attitude toward his family. Years of living with her parents allowed her to establish a truce, a state in which her father implicitly accepted her demand for freedom and independence. But that came after a life of sacrifice for her family; she did everything to meet her aging parents' growing needs, which happened at the cost of not having any of her own needs and desires met. Although Sima had a problematic relationship with her father from a very young age, she believed in her father's positive qualities. This knowledge enabled her to come to an eventual peace, although their personality conflicts continue.

Some, although not all, of the women who had tyrannical fathers managed to fight back and to assert a certain degree of autonomy. The fight, however, was very difficult because they were not only struggling against centuries-long traditions but also against their father, the most respected and valued member of the family. Standing against the father and challenging his absolute rule in the family is neither taught nor expected. The father in a traditional family context has the first and the final word. He is ever hardly challenged by his children. This lack of challenge, however, does not signify a passive acceptance of his command over the household and the various family members. Young and old, there have always been women who have risen to challenge their fathers' absolute rule in one way or another.

Raised within a particular class and family background, fathers have acted according to specific precepts they inherited. While many questioned those precepts, others blindly accepted dominant cultural norms. For example, while some fathers strongly encouraged their daughters to pursue higher education, there were those who saw an elementary education as being adequate for the daughters. While they did not feel comfortable allowing their adolescent daughters to walk the streets unprotected going from class to class, at times the fathers had a hard time fighting the constant demands of their daughters and the continuously changing society. Many fathers had to adjust to the rapidly changing society, allowing more freedom of action for their daughters. However, some did not feel comfortable with the flow of change and did their best to halt it; they only managed to postpone the change.

Coming from an impoverished family background, Mariam's father is extremely prejudiced against women. In return, Mariam does not harbor any positive feelings toward her father. She always saw him as a tyrannical force, dictating his rule over the family. She questioned everything her father stood for. "My father is a very strictly religious but an ungodly man," Miriam said. "He tried to force religion on me, which had the opposite effect. He made me hate everything religious. He forced us to fast, but I would sneak into the kitchen and eat. He would wake us up for the morning pray, yelling, 'Get up, I am feeding a bunch of heathens.' I would get up and put on my chador, and pretend to pray under my breath."

Raised as a religious zealot, Miriam's father tried to force religion on his children, but to no avail. His forceful approach had the opposite effect on at least one child, Mariam. He forced his daughters to wear chador even before the Revolution. "We were always fighting about the chador in my family," Miriam recalled. "He forced us to wear chador when we left home, but my sisters and I managed to sneak out. We would sneak out without a chador, or we would wear it and then take it off a couple blocks away from the house where we knew we were safe. We put the chador back on when we returned home."

Mariam's father did not allow any interaction with friends; she was not allowed to bring friends home or to visit friends at their houses. "The mother of this girl would plead with my father, 'Mr. Kohi, I have only daughters in my house. We live in the same street, very near your house. Please let your daughter come to our house and play with my children for just an hour.' So, he let me go to her house for a short time. My father didn't let me go anywhere. My co-workers invited me to their houses. How many times I have had to endure beatings in front of my brothers. I would endure the beatings and the curses and still go to my friends' houses. He could not stop me."

It was not only her father's interpretation of religion that was a source of conflict. Mariam had a suitor, a cousin on her father's side in another city, when she was sixteen. She did not have a chance to turn down the suitor's offer. Given her family background, it would be quite normal to marry off young women early. Furthermore, her mother wanted her to marry soon. However, after initial arrangements and a small engagement party, she and her mother found out that the groom-to-be was a drug addict. They tried to call off the engagement, but her father disagreed and exerted strong pressure to force her into the marriage because he had given his word. He believed that an honorable man does not change his mind. When Miriam tried to explain to her father why she did not want to marry her cousin, her father did not listen. Miriam recalled, "He beat me till I was black and blue. I still wouldn't give up. To spite us he took some money my mother and I had saved up. He thought we'd be sorry and would agree because of the money. Eventually, he kicked us all out, my mother and her eight children. We lived with my uncle for some time. But all the pressure did not work."

Mariam resisted her father and did not give in. Eventually the family came back together after her uncle and other family elders tried to mediate. Mariam, however, had to pay the price for her insolent behavior. She was taken out of school and was not allowed to finish her high school diploma. Her contact with the outside world was minimized under the assumption that the real reason she broke off the engagement was that she actually loved somebody else.

In contrast to women who saw their fathers as a source of support and encouragement throughout their lives, Mariam saw her father as a destructive force. "I had decided that under no circumstances was I going to return to my father's house," she recalled. "Once I had left that house, I was gone. No matter where it led me, I was not returning." It is customary for women to return to their parents' house in the case of divorce. Having to fight against her father from a very young age led Mariam to develop survival strategies that allowed her to succeed in life. Knowing she had no option but to make a living separate from her family, she struggled hard to find a job and to choose a husband who would be a partner for life. Successful and happy in her marriage, she was glad she never again had to depend on her father.

Zahra's story is similar to that of Mariam. She too had a domineering and controlling father who deeply believed in the inferiority of women and tried to raise his daughters according to extremely conservative gender roles; he did not allow his daughters any breathing space or freedom of movement. Zahra was accepted in the midwifery school in another city, but her father did not allow her to attend because he believed it was not appropriate for a young woman to live by herself. Of course, she was not going to leave her family behind, either. Having to take care of her family because of her mother's paralysis, Zahra was like a mother to her siblings, raising all of them from a very young age. She was a primary source of help and support in the family; that fact, however, did not bestow her with much power in relation to her father. She was still a daughter who had to conform to her father's tyrannical rule. But she was enraged at her father, who was a traditional man from an impoverished background. To discipline her and the other children, her father resorted to physical punishment.

But there came a time when Zahra stood up against him. "Before I got my high school diploma, my father hit me and I raised my hand to strike him back, even though he was so much bigger than me," Zahra said. "I did not do it for myself, but for the other children. He acted better after that, because he was afraid I'd do something to shame him in front of the family."

Reflecting on her past, Zahra saw her father as a detrimental force, a force she had to fight against. Furious at the extreme control her father exerted on the whole family, she felt smothered. When Zahra wanted to take a night computer class at the university, her father allowed her to go to the class only if he walked her to the class and stayed in the classroom with her. The teacher agreed with the arrangement. She sat in the front and her father in the back. One night, when they were returning from the class, a man said something to Zahra in the streets. Angry, her father got engaged in a fight with the man. Zahra, however, continued to walk and did not stop to see what happened. Upon his return, her father reprimanded Zahra: " 'Don't you even care to stop when your father is being beaten by someone on the street? Your work and your studying is more important to you than your father.' " Zahra knew her father was hurt, but other feelings were involved. "I was happy to have gotten some measure of revenge for all the times he'd tormented me, and, yes, money and work was more important to me."

As a single woman, Zahra had to live with her parents. Her family background, their meager economic situation, and her low salary did not allow her to live by herself. The culturally prescribed practice of living with her parents was not attractive to her. Aware of the deep-rooted conflicts between her parents, she asked her mother how she felt when her father went on his occasional trips to his hometown. "She has the same feeling I do," Zahra said. "When he is not around, she is more comfortable and can think better, more clearly. She is even more comfortable with the children when he is not around, because he has his selfish needs and wants to order the children around. He feels jealous about the children. They defend her against him."

At the age of forty, Zahra had managed to gain some freedom of movement. When she first started to work, as an eighteen year old, she was not allowed to go places with her co-workers or to bring friends home. "Slowly these things changed, but they still bother me sometimes," Zahra said. Once, during the early years of the Revolution when the country was in political turmoil, her father went to pick her up from work. She was not there. Confronting her at home, her father told her, "Don't you think your parents worry about you? Why do you even come home? You might as well have stayed wherever you were." Her response was the answer of a woman who was repulsed for being monitored at every step of her life. " 'I would come and go as I please. You have bought me only one pair of gold earrings in my whole life.' I threw them at him. He left me alone after that. He knew I wasn't going to drag down the family name. I wasn't chasing boys or running wild. So, he left me alone."

In her early forties, Zahra goes on work-related trips without even telling her parents. If she senses any opposition to such situations, Zahra packs and leaves, then calls them later to let them know that she has gone on a work-related trip. She eventually has managed to exact some measure of independence, although for many women from her class and family background freedom of movement, going on office-related trips alone or with co-workers, visiting friends, or bringing friends home are not feasible ideas. Given the worst of situations, Zahra has fought the hardest and has not yet reached the end of the line. The search for freedom from family ties and imperious expectations for single women proves to be an especially arduous road. Single women have to struggle especially hard until society comes to terms with their plight and begins to see them as competent, responsible, and reliable individuals. Unattached to men, single women have to struggle much harder against both society and their families in order to acquire a minimal level of freedom.

Over time Mariam grew stronger. She defied her father's absolute rule and managed to find the best husband among the many suitors who came to ask for her hand in marriage. Zahra, on the other hand, refused the idea of marriage. Deeply scarred by her father's abusive behavior, the relationship between her parents, and her mother's paralysis, Zahra was determined to stay single all her life. Zahra's life, her accomplishments, and her success at work—in spite of her restrictive family background—testify to the extremely resilient character she has developed throughout the years. While remaining single may be considered as a sign of failure among her family members and in the larger society, it shows Zahra's strength to stand against all the odds and to assert her own wishes.

Some fathers openly appreciated their daughters more than they did their sons. A female child was a symbol of good luck; for many it reinforced their ties to their mothers. Recognizing the limitations women experience in a traditional society, some fathers, especially the educated and those from middle- to higher-class backgrounds, encouraged their daughters to pursue higher education and to have their own careers. There were also fathers who, because of their class and family backgrounds, were personally untouched by the pace of change in gender roles and did not appreciate their daughters' move toward a more independent lifestyle. The daughters, however, constantly pushed to enlarge their scope, to change with time, and to assert a certain degree of freedom.

The irony is that it seems that no single mode of fatherhood is adequate to explain or to predict what kinds of future lives the daughters will develop. Some daughters who had open-minded fathers did not develop adequate strategies to fight adverse relationships in marriage. They were brought up believing that most, if not all, men would be like their fathers. Dismayed at finding the opposite, they have led unfulfilled lives. There were also those who recognized their mothers' faults and tried not to replicate her mistakes. Taking into account their fathers' side, some daughters were able to establish more fulfilling relationships with their husbands. On the other hand, some of those who came from very strict and rigid backgrounds developed strong survival strategies. The desire to lead independent lives had created forceful personalities who would fight to gain a measure of freedom. Their stories are a testimony to success of the spirit to surpass limitations imposed by both society and the family. For them, life is a never-ending struggle and they are strong players in it. There were daughters whose spirit of independence was never suppressed; they fought with some measure of success. In this fight, however, they lost their vivacity and their youth, feeling suffocated by the pressures they endured and never having the chance to reach their potential.

Experiencing understanding and supportive or rigid and strict fathers is only the beginning of a woman's encounter with the world. Having a supportive and caring father does not guarantee that a woman will marry a supportive husband. Coming from a problematic background does not negate the possibility of a constructive marriage. Many other elements, such as the mother, the family's socioeconomic background, the city of residence, and the changing cultural scenes are also at work. It is critical to remember that parents provide the first long-lasting image of the relationship between men and women, between mothers and fathers, and between husbands and wives. These etched images, consciously or unconsciously, lead us through life, providing either clear pathways to follow or unlit passages for stumbling. Neither route, for women in this transitional generation, is without hardship.

Marriage and Courtship

"I Wasn't Looking for a Husband"

Nobody thought I was the marrying type. All my friends had decided I would be the last person in the group to ever marry. And I was the first person who married.

—Azar

I wasn't looking for a husband. I was in my own world.

—Layla

He knew everything about me, my name, where I lived, what I wore, all sort of things. I was so surprised. . . . I got interested in finding out who this stranger was.

—Mina

WHY DO YOUNG WOMEN decide to marry? What are their reasons and motivations for marriage? Is it love, romantic love, love at first sight? Do they marry because marriage and forming a family is still the ultimate goal in most human societies? How did their parents respond to the decision to marry? What role did the parents play? Was their marriage arranged and decided upon by their parents? Who were the primary players, the key decision makers in this game of love and lifetime commitment? Would the women do it again (marry the same person again)?

As the following life stories depict, women in this study have married for a variety of diverse reasons; the reasons include parental pressure and familial obligations, the desire to start an independent life separate from their family of origin, and mere curiosity. Some women married because they met a suitor at college or through family and friends. Colleagues and friends played an important role in bringing together young single people.

Several important features emerge in the women's accounts. Regardless of how the couples met, no woman had an adequate opportunity to truly get to know her husband before marriage. It must be noted that the same was also true for the man; husbands did not really know their future wives before marriage. Of course, the men had perhaps more time to observe the woman of their interest because they were the ones who traditionally approached women to propose. Cultural taboos about intimate relationships between unrelated men and women severely limited the duration of friendship before marriage. While a limited number of women had the luxury of a relatively long engagement (i.e., two to three years), the majority of women married shortly after they met their prospective husbands, usually within a year. Most of these women had not been thinking seriously about marriage, but apparently marriage was awaiting them. Some had other aspirations in life, such as leaving the country and pursuing higher degrees. Marriage brought an end to some of these ambitions. Other women were able to continue their educations and seek gainful employment after marriage.

"I Met My Husband in College"

Some women met their husbands while attending college. For them, college provided an avenue to meet people from other classes of society and parts of the country. Even in the West, college can function as a marriage market. Many young people meet their future spouses during the college years. However, a distinguishing element of these relationships in Iran was that, although the family context was missing and it was the two young people who met on their own, they rarely trespassed the rules of social propriety. While colleges brought students together, it is interesting to note that most young men and women tended to act according to socially sanctioned codes of conduct. Furthermore, colleges and universities in Iran had their own reputations regarding their degrees of adherence to socially appropriate rules of conduct. While some colleges and universities, mostly those in the physical sciences, adhered to more strict and traditional precepts, others, such as those in the fine arts, were more lenient.

Azar met her husband in college. He was a year ahead of her. It was acceptable in her college for men and women to be friends, to engage in various social activities, and to attend college-sponsored field trips as a group. It was, however, not acceptable to embark on romantic relationships with other students. Therefore, he proposed to her. Apparently, he knew well that he wanted to marry her, but his interest came as a complete surprise to Azar. "I didn't have good eyesight, but I didn't wear glasses," Azar recalled. "I wanted to look pretty so I didn't wear glasses, but that made me unable to see clearly. Apparently, he was interested in me for a couple of years, but I hadn't even noticed him." The desire to look beautiful stopped her from wearing glasses and therefore reduced her ability to see clearly.

Azar's future husband approached her after two years with a marriage proposal. She was caught off guard. "Of course, I wasn't even thinking about marriage." In fact, in a game to predict who would marry first and who would be the last person to marry, her classmates had ranked Azar as the last candidate for marriage. "Nobody thought I was the marrying type," Azar said. "I didn't want to marry because I was happy and had fun in my life. That [college] was the best period of my life. My golden days were my college days. I had so much fun. I didn't have a thing to worry about. I thought of myself as successful. I was set economically. My wish is that I could repeat that period. I had no boyfriends, either."

When her future husband proposed to her, Azar was faced with a dilemma. What amazed her was that she had absolutely no feelings toward him. "When he proposed to me I thought, 'I am a little unusual,'" Azar recalled. "I went to a psychologist and I asked her, 'How could this be possible? There is this guy who has proposed to me and tells me he loves me, but I have absolutely no feelings toward him?' She asked me whether a boy's hand has ever touched my hands? Whether anybody has ever hugged me?" Her answers were negative. After a couple of sessions the psychologist decided that her lack of feelings were quite normal. Her recommendation was to do some research about the suitor and his family's background. She recommended marriage if he came from a respectable background. The reason for her counsel was that, because the man loved her, Azar would grow to love him with time.

Upon researching the suitor's family background, Azar's father found no faults; therefore, marriage was recommended. The proposal was accepted, and Azar was the first person in her class to marry. She presents an unusual case because referring to a psychologist or a counselor is not a common practice in Iran compared to the United States, where people may seek counseling over the death of a spouse or parent or upon getting a divorce. In Iran, going to a therapist or a psychologist is still looked down upon and is considered to signify a troubled mind. However, as an educated person, Azar sought a specialist's advice regarding what she perceived as an anomaly. Her potential husband came from a good family and had chosen her among so many women attending the same university. These were good enough reasons to persuade her to accept his proposal. Like her psychologist, she believed true love is something that develops with time and a sound knowledge of one another.

Other women in the study met their husbands in other ways. At times, friends at school or work brought the couple together; a friend at work or at the school, a friend who studied with a brother, or two colleagues taking the same bus introduced potential marriage partners. In a closed society, any possible encounter within socially acceptable parameters is a situation ripe with the potential of bringing together single people. A good number of women met their future spouses through friends, work, or college. Like Azar's case, the approach is most often direct. Sara worked at an office. Her co-worker introduced them.

His sister was my colleague, but he worked in a different office. We rode the same bus back home. One day my friend told me that her brother had graduated from university and had completed his military service. She said he is gainfully employed and is interested in marriage. She wanted to know if I am interested in marriage. She was very direct with me and recommended that if I was interested we should meet and decide on our own whether we wanted to marry. He had asked for my phone number, and my friend wanted to make sure that it was fine with me to give him my number.

Upon meeting each other, the couple started dating and eventually married after two years. Sara's mother and sister both approved her choice. "I wasn't in love with my husband when I married him," Sara said. "I was actually in love with somebody else, but my mother didn't agree with our marriage. He even came to our house to meet my mother and ask for my hand, but my mother turned down his offer. He was young and not established in his life yet."

Sara's mother did not allow her to marry the person she loved. In those cases in which men and women fall in love, parental approval is crucial. Without their consent, the woman would lose all the familial support in her marriage. Because marital laws do not work in the best interest of women, maintaining familial support is of critical value to women. Twenty years later, Sara still remembered the man she once loved and wondered about him and his life. He remained a dream. Perhaps even if Sara's mother had agreed with their marriage, it would not have been successful; but not being able to challenge her mother and having to accept her decision turned the man she actually loved into a dream. He became a ghost Sara carried with her throughout her life, so that she always wondered what might have happened if she had married him. What if Sara's marriage were based on love instead of a rational decision and recommendation made by her mother?

In the cases of other women, the potential marriage encounter is made more playful or mysterious. Mina was seventeen when she met her husband. "I wasn't even interested in marriage," Mina said. "Neither was I thinking about boyfriends or falling in love. It all started with some curiosity." She and her friend visited often. Once when Mina was at her friend's house, there was a telephone call for her. She answered. "There was a man on the other side," Mina said. "We talked. He knew everything about me, my name, where I lived, what I wore, all sort of things. I was so surprised, wondering how come he has called here." However, her absolute trust in her friend, or perhaps her naïveté, did not allow her to make any connection between her friend and the caller. "He even knew what I had on or where I was going that night," Mina said. "It was mere curiosity that I got interested in finding out who this stranger was because I truly wasn't interested in boyfriends in that stage of my life."

Mina's friend denied having any information about the man. It was only much later that she remembered her friend had mentioned a man who was going to college and wanted to marry. She had wondered if Mina was interested in marriage. Mina's answer was an absolute no. "Not only I am not interested in marriage, my father wouldn't allow me to marry a college student, either," Mina said. "But I didn't put the two together until much later."

Curious to find out who the secret caller was and urged on by her friend, Mina agreed to meet him. "I was very scared." She was only seventeen when she met him. After being engaged for three years, they married when she was in college. In the meantime, she also started working full-time. "I think any other father would have objected to our marriage. But my father was so caring. He told me he respects my feelings. He just told me that because I was interested in him he would ask around to make sure he came from a respectable background. If he was a good guy then I could marry him. My husband turned out to be a very trustworthy, competent, and moral person. But at that age it could be a wrong choice. I decided so blindly, not knowing anything about him. I was seventeen and he was twenty-one when we first met."

Although Mina's father did not object to his daughter's decision, he made one condition: Mina should continue her higher education with no obstacles. His condition was met. Her husband never objected to her education. She quit her gainful employment only after her one daughter became a teenager and required more direct supervision.

While Azar wondered about her lack of feelings or passion, Mina was intrigued by the mystery of the secret caller and found the experience exciting. There were also women in the study who eventually succumbed to a marriage proposal because the future husband-to-be was persistent. Layla married upon her return from abroad. While in the United States to study dentistry, she received a fellowship from an Iranian university. She found the opportunity attractive and returned to finish her studies at home. As a young woman returning from the United States, she acted freely, wearing fashionable clothes, coloring her hair blond, and smoking cigarettes at the school's cafeteria. "I was the only daughter in my family who never wanted to marry," Layla said. "I wasn't looking for a husband. I was in my own world. Those students who were looking for a husband were careful about how they acted, what they said or wore. They were careful not to laugh out loud."

As in Azar's case, a senior student showed interest in Layla, but she was not interested. He continued to call her, inviting her to various places while receiving no positive feedback from Layla or her family. However, for some reason two years of perseverance eventfully paid off and convinced Layla that it was time to marry. Layla acquiesced. Reflecting on her age and her choice of husband, Layla stated, "I was very inexperienced. My life was limited to home, school, and books. I am not saying this is good. I used to beg my mother to go out with the children so I could have the house to myself to study. I had no understanding of men, of social relationships, of interactions among men and women. I was so ignorant about my own country and different ethnic groups in the country. When my husband said what region he was coming from I didn't have a clue where this region was. I was so naïve."

For many middle-class and upper-class women born in the 1950s in Tehran, marriage was a personal choice supported and sanctioned by their parents. While parents offered recommendations and suggestions, they mostly let their daughters decide on their own. School, work, and friends brought potential marriage partners together. For most women, the men who approached them to propose were the first men who had shown any serious interest in them and were persistent enough in their pursuit. Inexperienced, young, eager to start their own independent lives, and perhaps not taking marriage seriously, some women accepted the proposal only to recognize too late that they did not have a sound knowledge of their husband and his family and of the fact that different family backgrounds, value systems, and beliefs might lead to serious marital problems and lifelong unhappy marriages.

"Tell Him Yourself; Keep Us Out of It"

While some parents allowed their daughters to choose for themselves, others exerted a great degree of pressure. Believing they knew best, they tried to channel their daughters into a certain direction. Parental control happened in many ways, from implicit advice to explicit and forced intervention. Some parents, albeit a minority, play a minimal role. Like Mina's parents, some take their daughter's opinion and feelings into account, respect her wishes, and agree with her decision. They do minimal research on the husband's family background and his life chances, report the findings to their daughter, and let her decide on her own. Some parents—the more modern ones—may not even engage in such background inquiry, finding it old fashioned. They agree to whatever their daughter wills. There are also those parents who are actively involved in the process to the point of making a decision for their daughters. This direct involvement again has varied degrees, ranging from dictating the choice to screening the available supply of eligible men. Some suitors are turned down immediately, some are given more consideration, and others receive the full support of the parents. In this case, the parents and the suitor become one force in encouraging the young woman to accept their choice. They want the best for their daughters. In this process, what the young woman aspires for her life seems to be of secondary importance. Marriage to the most promising man is the ultimate goal of any parent. Parents believe that they know what is best better than do their daughters, whose world views and ranges of life experiences have been relatively limited.

Young and inexperienced, most women relied on their families for extensive advice. Pari had been preparing to leave the country for quite some time. Knowing that her parents would not allow her to leave the country alone, she planned to leave with her younger brother. "My brother and I were thinking about leaving the country together," Pari recalled. "We even took the language test [TOEFL] together. I used to study with him, thinking if my parents let him go, I could go, too. He is four years younger than me. I had not told anybody about my plans. My parents didn't know I was planning to leave the country. I had many suitors, but I didn't like any of them." Her secret plan, however, was interrupted by a particular suitor. "My family liked these people and they agreed to their visit," Pari said. "They believed that meeting the family wouldn't hurt and that after the initial introduction they could decide better instead of turning people down offhandedly. The family paid a visit and we met. I didn't like him [the suitor] at all."

Pari's mother, however, intervened. "My mother argued that, 'You can't make a decision like that. You should go out with him and try to get to know each other.' I did that and even then I didn't like him."

Apparently, her parents had approved the suitor. Her mother insisted that they continue to go out together in order to get to know each other better; she disagreed with a too-hasty decision. A couple of Pari's suitors were studying in Europe. Her older brother was living abroad and her parents were concerned she might leave the country, too. "They did not encourage those relationships," Pari said. "But this guy was living here so they insisted that I get to know him better." Adamant about her first impression, she remained uninterested. After seeing him for a month, her father entered the scene. He told her:" 'It is not appropriate to see him any longer. You have to answer him. You can't keep going out with him and saying, no, you are not interested. You need to make up your mind.' I exactly remember the last time we went out. My father gave me a ride. We talked very comfortably. It was easier to talk to him than to my mother. My mother was forcing me to make a choice, telling me what I must do. But father always gave advice, making recommendations instead of ordering me what to do."

The father's advice was to make a decision that day and notify the suitor immediately. "Tell him yourself," her father said. "Keep us out of it. This going out and him spending money on you is not correct. It is not proper to see him if you are not interested." Seeing each other for lunch, Pari could not bring herself to say no. "I don't know why, but I couldn't say a word," Pari recalled. "He took my silence as yes, believing my answer was positive. We had an engagement ceremony soon afterward. Even then I thought I could break up the engagement if I didn't like it. I thought an engagement is not a permanent arrangement." But Pari could not bring herself to upset everybody involved. "Maybe I was not courageous enough. He was thirty and I was twenty-three."

Perhaps Pari was not courageous enough to express her wishes. Perhaps she did not feel strong enough about leaving the country and pursuing her education. Perhaps she was too young and inexperienced. Perhaps her suitor was not courteous and romantic. Whatever the reason, Pari could not say no to the man her parents, especially her mother, had approved for her. She could not upset her mother by rejecting her choice. After the engagement, Pari could no longer say no to all the people involved. She just went with the flow of events, assuming the passage of time would take care of everything. A happy moment for her parents became the beginning of her surrender. Twenty years later she still remembered that she could not say no, that her lack of experience and audacity made her live with a man who was not her choice, to lead a life that she had not designed. The young brother left for the United States, where he still lives. Both her brothers and her one sister live abroad and she is the only daughter who has remained behind. Reflecting on the other men who wanted to marry her, she said, "I got to know a few of them, but my parents were not interested in them."

While Pari reluctantly accepted her parents' choice, there were women who willingly did anything their parents wished for without ever questioning the decision. Some women expressed strong faith in their parents, believing they would never make a mistake in such a choice. Such daughters always consulted their parents regarding crucial life decisions such as the choice of a major to study, where to go to school, what careers to choose, and whom to marry.

Believing her father knew best and because her mother had passed away when she was five years old, Ziba followed his advice. Although their distant families knew each other, she had only met her husband while visiting her brothers. "I liked him but I was not going to show any sign of interest because I didn't want to risk my father's reputation," Ziba said. "It could be a big embarrassment for all the family, so I didn't take any steps." But the feelings were mutual, and the man expressed his feelings. "Even when he showed his affections for me, I told him, 'I love you, too, but I will do whatever my family says. I will not take any step against their wish.' " While Ziba reciprocated, she showed him that her family came first. "I was that attached to my family," Ziba said. "If they had objected to our marriage, I would have never married him in spite of my deep love for him. I had faith in my family and knew they wouldn't make a wrong decision for me." When the man eventually proposed to her and formally visited her family to acquire their permission, it became clear that she had another suitor. Her family was interested in both men. Although her family asked her which one she would like to marry, Ziba did not reveal her interest, responding, "I'll marry whoever you choose. I have the same trust today. If my brother tells me today that you should separate from your husband [after twenty-two years of marriage], I'd leave him. I would shut the door and leave."

Fortunately, Ziba's father chose the right person, believing he knew her better than the other suitor. "My father told me, 'You have known each other for so long. He has seen how we have treated you in this family.' " The man she loved was chosen over the other suitor. "Relatives and friends recommended the other person because he was wealthy and more established in his life; he was a better groom," Ziba recalled. "But my father wanted somebody who knew me. Although he was a young, poor student, my father thought that he was young and could start a new life."

Ziba eagerly sought out her family's opinion and was not even willing to reveal her interest in the man she loved. Similarly, Pari reluctantly accepted her parents' choice, leaving behind her dream of higher education and travel abroad. Did anyone in the study stand up to her parents, defying their choice? Mariam was such a person, resisting her parents' decision with all her might. Coming from a small city and economically impoverished background, Mariam was under a great deal of pressure to marry young. "My mother was constantly harping at me." Her mother wanted Mariam to marry early, preferably to a relative from her hometown. She told Mariam, "The men in Tehran are all worthless. They all turn into drug addicts." Mariam was in her third year of high school, in the middle of her final exams. Telling her mother she had to study, Mariam tried to keep the suitors away. But the pressure was so overwhelming that she eventually submitted. "I finally decided I had to marry to get them [her parents] off my back, marry with just anyone," Mariam said. "Anyone my mother suggested. I thought they probably don't want me around anymore. I was tired of all the kids and wanted to get out of the house. So I agreed." The proposal came from a cousin who lived in their hometown. Since the groom was absent at his own engagement ceremony, his mother put the engagement ring on her hand. "He was illiterate and worked for a year or two in Tehran," Mariam said. "He had joined the army and was located to another city. Every now and then my aunt and her son would come to visit. I would try to escape these visits. Finally, I felt so bad about the whole thing that I revolted and said I can't stand it. I told my parents I wouldn't marry this man."

On a visit to the hometown, Mariam's mother found out that her daughter's fiancé was a drug addict. The townspeople told her, "What are you doing? You are giving your daughter to a drug addict." She and Mariam decided to call off the wedding, but what followed was a family scandal. Mariam, her mother, and the seven children were ousted from their house. She recalled,

My father kicked us all out of the house. We went to my uncle's house on my mother's side. My grandmother lived there, too. One day I thought I would go and talk to my father, who was all alone at home. I explained everything to him, why I didn't want to marry my cousin. He just said, "Even if I have to kill you, you're going to marry him." He had a thick whip and beat me with that until I was black and blue. I still wouldn't give up. I went there again to talk to him. My aunt was claiming damages. She wanted to frighten us with the threat of money and shut us up. My father blamed everything on my mother. He said she'd set this up and now she'd ruined everything.

Mariam's father wanted her to marry her cousin. She refused by saying, "You can marry my dead body to him, but I will not do it willingly." He stopped her from finishing high school, accusing her of having met another man; her father claimed that this was the real reason she did not want to marry her cousin. Mariam was bombarded with accusations for causing so much embarrassment to the family and in the neighborhood. Many people told her that nobody would ever approach her again to ask for her hand in marriage. Although Mariam had submitted to her mother's will to marry early, even her mother was angry with her for bringing shame on the family. However, the marriage proposal was eventually called off; the relationship with the cousin was severed. Mariam's uncle mediated and the family reunited.

Not allowed to get her diploma, Mariam took evening classes in order to be able to find a job. Although she preferred to finish school and go on to college, that possibility did not exist for her any longer. Finding a job and getting a steady salary proved to be more attractive. She decided it was more important to work and help out her family than to go to school. A couple years passed by and new suitors started to show up; Mariam was still young.

One day, upon coming back from work, she realized there were suitors at her home. She met them and felt that this family was better off than the others who had come earlier. She managed to exchange a few words with the suitor's mother and his sister but not with him. Apparently, they had seen her picture in the classroom photo that schools take every year. "It was not our custom to speak to the man before marriage, but his parents were very eager for us to speak together beforehand," Mariam said. "When they insisted, my father said that I could go to another room with my aunt and talk to him. I had never spoken to a man before and didn't know what to say."

Apparently, the man and her aunt did the talking. He said that he did not want his wife to work because it would ruin the marriage, and in general he was against the idea of women working. The aunt immediately agreed with his wish, declaring, "You are absolutely right. Why should a woman work? Who will raise her children? She will not work after you are married." As Mariam recalled, "She did all the speaking and I sat there mute. That was our talk." Although Mariam did not agree with the man, she decided to accept his offer. "I thought that if I didn't accept him, Lord knows who else might come for me," Mariam said. "If I remained in the house I would continue to be a burden and a shame for my parents. I agreed to marriage, thinking that if it didn't work, I would leave him. So, I accepted his offer."

But Mariam's major concern was keeping her job. Knowing that she might leave him one day, it was crucial for her to keep her job. "I thought if one day I divorce him and I don't have a job, what would I do? I just have these parents, which is as good as not having parents." After the engagement ceremony, she managed to leave work early one day to visit her fiancé and his mother at their house. Her words were,

> I can't marry you. I can't tell my family that I don't want to marry. My family won't accept it. But I need to keep my job. Not working will ruin me. It will leave me no security. I don't know you. Your son doesn't know me. If one day your son decides to divorce me, I will have to live on the streets and die of hunger. I have to continue working until I know my husband well. Perhaps I'll have to work all my life. Please go to my family and tell them that you don't want me. You can call off the engagement and tell them you don't want me as your bride.

After some negotiations, an agreement was reached; Mariam continued her employment. Upon marriage the couple moved in with the in-laws in the same housing complex—Mariam's mother-in-law on the first floor, the older brother and his family on the second, and Mariam and her husband on the third floor. After three years they bought their own apartment in a distant and poor suburb. Quitting her work also happened after three years of marriage and with the coming of their child. She decided to quit, although her friends at work and her parents were against her decision. Mariam's reason for quitting was to be with her children. Although her mother took care of her first son, she did not trust the kind of care that her mother provided. "I felt that these two children would be left motherless just because I wanted a pittance of a salary," Mariam said. "This salary wouldn't even buy me a pair of shoes or a uniform. In addition, we women have to put up with so much torture at the work place. It's not logical to do this." She worked as long as they were living with her in-laws. Working provided some distance from them. "I didn't want to get up in the morning and have to look anyone in the face," Miriam said. "When I returned from work I kept my head down and entered as quietly as possible so I wouldn't have to say hello to anyone."

Work was an emotional outlet, a precious time to be away from her in-laws. Mariam struggled against her family's impositions. Convinced that the husband they had chosen for her was the wrong person, she stood against her father, an act that her father, even as a man, could not have done (standing against his own family and telling his sister that her son was not the right choice for his daughter). He had given his word and, were it not because of Mariam's extraordinary perseverance, he would not take back his word.

However, Mariam stood against her father and his family and paid dearly for it. Pulled out of school, she was never allowed to finish her high school diploma. Seeing her mother and seven children having to move to an uncle's house, witnessing days of anger, tension, harsh words, accusations, and threats, she had nobody to blame but herself. But she persevered. Believing that her decision was correct enabled Mariam to defy her family, especially her father. Mariam has been remarkably successful in her marriage and is still married with three children. As an incredibly strong woman, she asserted, "Once I had considered everything, the whole world couldn't have stopped me."

Perhaps Mariam was strong enough to resist her family and to face all the relatives and neighbors. Perhaps she felt strong because she knew she was right; in contrast, Pari had no solid reason to believe that the man her mother had chosen for her was wrong. In a culture that does not consider love as a basis for marriage, merely not liking a person is not an adequate ground for turning down a marriage proposal from a respectable and promising individual. Women in traditional societies have always had to overcome cultural barriers that denied them their freedom of action. While some women are remarkably strong and take extraordinary steps, others abide by the rules and function within the parameters that the society has assigned for the female gender. Women like Mariam never proclaim, "I was too young or too inexperienced." Somehow she knew what was right or wrong for her. She knew she had to marry and marry soon, but she made her best choice by trying to wait for the right person to come along. For one of her background, she did not have any opportunity to meet men on her own. She therefore had to choose from the range of suitors who happened to pay visits to her family.

Mariam took active steps to try to shape her life within the culturally defined sphere. There were other women in the study who quietly took extremely courageous steps. Minoo married her cousin, an act viewed favorably by Iranians. The two were childhood playmates from a big family in which there were many stepmothers, in-laws, and others always present—a family in which there "was never peace." Her cousin wrote stories and brought them to Minoo. Loving to read, she always made suggestions and comments. "I didn't have any particular feelings for him," Minoo recalled. "But when he started to bring his stories to me things started to change. I always loved to read books. As a lonely child I didn't have any other outlet for fun except reading books. I got interested in reading his short stories."

Their mutual interest in writing and reading changed their relationship. The two families had many conflicts and did not approve of such a union. He secretly paid visits; none of the family members were aware of their developing closeness. "I took his stories to a publisher and invested in the publication of his first collection of stories," Minoo said. "I was willing to do anything for his writing. I had a full-time job then and was economically independent. I invested in his stories and had his first book published. I paid for all the expenses."

After having known each other for years, her cousin proposed to Minoo, telling her that he had loved her since childhood. "I wasn't thinking about marriage at all because our relatives were so hostile, so antagonistic," she said.

"I didn't even think marriage was possible between us. I told him that I was not interested in marriage, but since he was telling me that he had loved me since childhood and was still interested in me, then that was all right. Nobody else was in my life at that point."

Minoo's words, however, did not imply that she had agreed to marriage. Rather, her cousin had expressed his affections and she had accepted his feelings. The onset of the Revolution, however, created unpredictable changes. While she was living on her own—a rare act for young independent women in Iran—she lost her apartment. Looking for another apartment, she realized it was extremely difficult for a single woman to rent an apartment. Politically active groups rented apartments and engaged in antigovernment activities. Landlords therefore had become extremely cautious about renting their property, especially to single unattached men and women. Minoo explained her situation. "I looked very decent, no makeup or anything, and that made me look even more suspicious, but I wasn't involved in any political group. I couldn't find an apartment. One of his friends suggested marriage, arguing that I could get a house as a married woman. We accepted his suggestion, and because I couldn't get a house on my own, we married. We married in a legal office. His friend was our only witness, and because we needed two witnesses, we found a construction worker from the street. Nobody knew about our marriage."

After marriage, her husband was drafted and had to serve in a distant city. "There was an emotional tie between us, though," Minoo said. "We had become very attached. He started to seriously think of me as his wife. He had a key to the house and sometimes when he came and I wasn't home, he left a note saying, 'I stopped by and you weren't home.' That was surprising to me because I thought, I am not his real wife. Why does he expect me to be at home?"

While serving in the military, he called her long distance and told her that he could not live without her and wanted their marriage to be like a real marriage. "He asked me to join him there in that city and to let everybody know that we were married," Minoo said. "It was extremely difficult for me to tell his parents (my uncle) that I was married to his son. I told him that if he wants his family to know he is the one who should tell them." Reflecting on her past, Minoo said, "I always played games with two families. I always made sure my mother never saw my uncle. I didn't let my mother see his mother. I lived in such chaos, trying to protect everybody. They all believed that with my marriage all the troubles and family fights would start again. But that did not happen. I did manage to maintain peace between the two families."

As two adults, Minoo and her husband took extraordinary steps, maneuvering around difficulties created by the Revolution and problems endemic to large extended families. They surmounted family conflict, marrying secretly and eventually revealing their secret to both sides of the family—without regard to all the problems that doing so could create. Going against their families' wish and deciding to marry on their own without having any family elder present were grave steps taken by two young people in Iranian society. On Minoo's part, it was the Revolution that had made living on her own difficult if not impossible. On her husband's part, they were childhood sweethearts who eventually joined in marriage.

"I Saw Marriage as a Key to Freedom"

While some women unknowingly walk on the marriage path, there are those who clearly know what they want and take active steps toward their goal. For some women, marriage is a door to freedom, to an independent life where the ever-present parents and their constant surveillance is reduced. Upon marriage, the parents' strong sense of responsibility is modified; their daughter is married now. She is a woman and has to embark on an adult life of her own. Now she is expected to run an independent household with her husband.

Zhaleh has married twice. Her first marriage was quite "accidental." Zhaleh's parents were very strict. "My parents did not allow me to visit friends or to go on trips before marriage," Zhaleh said. "I had a very limited freedom. I was told I could do things only after I get married. Even going to foreign language classes was not allowed because they met in the evenings after work." Like many other women she said, "I was not thinking about marriage, but since I saw it as a key to freedom I decided to marry. Unfortunately, it was a bad marriage, but the result was that I was free to do what I wanted. They could no longer tell me what to do or where to go. They trusted me more after marriage." Her husband was living abroad and promised to take her there. "He was living abroad for years and we saw each other every couple of years or so and for a very limited time," Zhaleh said. "He kept telling me that he would take me there, false promises. But that never happened. He even eventually stopped paying visits."

Although Zhaleh's husband did not even live in the country, her parents believed she should not file for divorce because of the shame it would cause the family. Both of Zhaleh's older sisters were divorced and her parents could not handle another divorce in the family. Her family was particularly happy about her marriage because they thought that her husband would take their daughter abroad and settle her there, which would be a dream come true. That opportunity was too perfect to forgo. "My father was against divorce and believed that I should follow my husband wherever he went," Zhaleh said. "The problem was that he was not willing to take me. Although I was ready to file for divorce much earlier, I didn't do anything about it until my husband suggested divorce. Our divorce was finalized after a few years."

Her second marriage occurred eight years later with a distant cousin. This was his second marriage too; his first wife had left him. Zhaleh and her second husband saw each other for a year, but her family intervened and demanded that they make a decision soon. "My family pressured me to shorten this dating period," Zhaleh said. "They wanted me to marry him quickly because it was not proper for unattached men and women to see each other for an extended period of time." Zhaleh's family was there as a force to protect her purity and their reputation among relatives, neighbors, and friends.

Her first marriage was a door to freedom, which enabled her to take night classes, to go on trips with co-workers, to visit friends, and to bring friends home without having to acquire permission from her parents. She had become a married woman and the status in itself enabled her to make many decisions on her own. Going against her family's wish, she eventually agreed to divorce and gave up any hope of living abroad. Acknowledging that she and her family were deceived was painful, but necessary. In contrast, she chose her second husband, a man she had a crush on from a long time ago. Although her parents had lost their total control over her, they still made sure that she and the man she was seeing did not trespass appropriate social conduct. Allowing a certain amount of time for visiting, they demanded conformity to the rule that a couple should marry after a short period. Each marriage brought her a higher degree of freedom from parental control, freedom from constant surveillance, and the possibility to engage in personal activities such as visiting friends and taking classes in her free time.

The desire to establish an autonomous life and to defy parental control without openly challenging the family led some women to seek marriage as a key to freedom. Like Zhaleh, Tara's goal was to marry early in order to bring an end to her mother's incessant surveillance. Tara met her husband when she was going to get the results of her university entrance test. She remembered what she had been wearing twenty years ago on the day she met her husband. "I wore jeans when I went to school, jeans and tennis shoes," Tara said. "I really enjoy walking. Actually, that was the only kind of fun or leisure that my mother allowed." She went to her aunt's house to pick up something. "There was a guy who was leaving, saying goodbye. My entrance and his departure coincided. He stayed for a few minutes longer. We were introduced, but he didn't even shake hands. [After the Revolution, shaking hands with women came to be viewed as a corrupt practice of the past, an inappropriate act between unattached women and men.] He wore glasses and didn't have much hair. I always thought that those men who wear glasses and do not have much hair are married."

The next day, a woman called Tara's mother, introducing herself and asking for permission to come and visit the family. She wanted to come with her husband and son. Because he was going out of town soon, the man she had met the day before had asked his mother to call, making an appointment so when he came back they could meet. They met a week later. Tara recalls the meeting. "His mother was a very comfortable woman. She asked me to sit next to her. She took off her shoes immediately after she sat down and

said they were new shoes and hurt her feet. They talked about different topics, but nothing directly was said. They didn't even ask me how old I was and
what I was planning to do after graduation. The purpose of this gathering
was for their son to have permission to see me openly and for the two of us
to get to know each other. We didn't ask them any questions either."[1]

They married six months later and Tara moved in with her in-laws. Her
husband was serving in the military and was often out of town. They chose
an isolated room in the house, where they had more privacy. "I lived with
my in-laws at the beginning," Tara said. "We had the smallest room in the
house. It was like the maid's quarter, but we chose that room because it was
farther than other rooms and we had more privacy there. A year later we
moved to another apartment in the same complex."

Her father-in-law found her a job and she started working full-time. She
was nineteen at the time of her marriage. Unlike so many women who were
not thinking about marriage, Tara was determined to marry early. "I wanted
to marry early," she recalled. "Perhaps it was because of the family pressure,
constantly telling you what to do and what not to do." Her mother monitored her very closely and did not allow her much freedom. As Tara said,
walking was the only kind of activity outside the house that she was permit-
ted. Tara's father had passed away when she was fourteen. After twenty years
of marriage, she was still in love with her husband, but now truly appreciated
his qualities. "Now I realize what a compassionate and caring person he is,"
she said. "Knowing him to the extent I know him now, I believe I should
have been his suitor. I should have gone to his house asking for his hand. I
should have paid him mehr."[2]

Although young and inexperienced, Tara's choice turned out to be
right. Tara was happy to be out of her mother's house and, although she
moved in with her in-laws for a year, a situation in which supervision, control, and isolation can be potentially overwhelming, she preferred the new
arrangement. Ironically, living with the in-laws proved to be a constructive
experience. They cared for her and her children, found good job opportunities for her, and offered valuable advice, which enabled her to advance at
her work, to earn a good income, and to buy a house.

How often have parents intervened on the part of their young daughters and sons? Did that guarantee a happy and fulfilling marriage? It may have guaranteed the selection of a decent and respectable spouse who would be a lifelong companion, but it certainly did not guarantee for their daughters a union based on love and affection. That is not to say that in those cases where parents did not intervene the young women made the right choice. Perhaps such a possibility can never be guaranteed in any marriage.

Many women have lived with men their parents picked for them. The majority of these women will probably live with these men for the rest of their lives. However, a few will always remember the one man they loved, the one man who was their choice but was turned down by their parents. Some chose their husbands themselves, benefitting from their family's support. Still there were those cases in which the woman's decision truly was accepted and respected by her family. The parents were modern enough to bypass the cultural practice of any background search about the man whom their daughter had chosen. They believed in their daughter's sound judgment and her ability to choose for herself. It is actually the women from the more traditional and working-class backgrounds who have faced the strongest opposition regarding their choice, who had often fought their own families against being forced into an early or unwanted marriage.

Whatever the women's reasons for marriage, the fact remains that neither the men nor the women knew each other well. For some, the initial attraction and intrigue was the driving force, but a true understanding of the other person's habits, thoughts, and character was impossible. Although they were not contemplating the idea of marriage, some women blindly fell into it because they mistakenly took the suitor's interest in her, or his persistence, as a sign of love. Others willingly or reluctantly surrendered to their parents' wishes. While the women's reasons or motivations for marriage were varied, it seems that nothing guaranteed a happy and loving marriage. Parents may have done a good degree of background research to make sure that their future son-in-law was a decent man from a good family with great opportunities. But if the daughter was not seriously interested in the man, if the relationship between the young couple did not develop according to their expectations and dreams, the match would not necessarily work in the best interests of the young couple. The daughter would always remember that she was not given the option to choose for herself. On the other hand, some parents were modern enough to let their daughter choose. But that did not guarantee a contented marriage, either. Which route is the best remains a major question.

However, because of the fact that the Iranian Revolution further limited interaction among men and women, parents may have actually become bigger players in this game of life and marriage for their children. Economic inflation may have exacerbated the situation, forcing parents to be more involved, to do their best to choose a man with promising economic prospects. But to the same degree that parental supervision does not guarantee a happy marriage, neither does the future husband's financial status.

In a society that does not sanction a healthy relationship between unattached young men and women before a wedding, marriage becomes the only terrain to associate with the opposite sex within a culturally acceptable parameter.

"Would You Marry Again?"

"If you were to start all over, would you marry again? Would you marry the same man a second time if you could go back in time?" These are two interrelated questions, one dealing with the notion of marriage and the other involving the choice individuals have made or the decisions others—their closest relatives, i.e., mothers and fathers—have arrived at for them. All the married women in the study except Layla asserted that they would marry again. Their answers ranged from a firm belief in marriage as an institution that satisfies various individual needs to a belief in marriage as a form of resignation, a rite of passage one has to perform sooner or later, with one person or another.

Minoo believed in marriage because it meets men and women's needs for emotional closeness and physical intimacy. "Marriage, or actually being with a man, is crucial for a woman because it is only normal," Minoo said. "We need emotional attachment and closeness with the opposite sex, but this doesn't have to be in a marriage context."

In contrast to Minoo, who had believed in marriage as an ideal union between two equal partners, Azar seemed to have surrendered to the notion of marriage. She accepted the idea of marriage and did not believe that it could be any different from what she had experienced. Having an unhappy marriage had not turned Azar away from marriage, however. Her position on marriage was one of resignation. "I would have married again. All men are the same. It wouldn't make a difference." This fatalistic belief signified a loss of faith in men as persons who could be understanding and compassionate; in spite of these pessimistic thoughts, Azar did not reject the idea of marriage. Viewing marriage from different perspectives, Minoo and Azar nevertheless regarded marriage either as an ideal goal or simply as a goal to be achieved.

Layla, however, completely rejected even the idea of marriage. "I am totally against marriage," Layla said. "Although my father is such a nice man, I am still against marriage. But if more men were like him, perhaps I wouldn't be so adamantly against marriage." Although Layla's father exemplified a caring, loving, and supportive father and husband, it seems that it was Layla's husband who had left an impressionable mark on her attitudes about men and marriage. "I have transferred my thoughts to my daughter and, unfortunately, she accepts my position. She asks me, 'Do you think if I study and marry I'd have a life like yours?' " Trying to teach the best to her daughter, Layla repeated the same line her father had told her. "I have told my daughter you don't need to marry. Or don't ever marry an Iranian man. Or if you ever decide to marry, do it after you are forty." This is Layla's advice to her only daughter. The degree to which she will listen to Layla will be disclosed in the future. Obviously, Layla herself did not listen to her father's advice. Is there any evidence that her daughter will listen to her?

The daughter of a mixed marriage, Layla found Iranian men at fault—although her own father was Iranian and it was her mother who belonged to a minority group. "The best Iranian man entitles himself to more rights than women," Layla said. "Even if you hold a hundred Ph.D.s he still thinks he is superior to you because he is a man. I have told my husband that any right you see yourself entitled to, your wife has the same right."

Many married women experienced unfulfilled marriages, but it was only Layla who was adamantly against the idea of marriage. Other women had their own qualms about marriage as an institution. Pari had her own second thoughts. She sought a friend in marriage and believed that a husband should be a caring person, "somebody you could talk to and share your thoughts and interests, a person to enjoy his company. I don't know if I would have married again. To begin with, I think I must be older to marry, older and more mature and experienced. I believe if your husband is a good man, a marriage with no children doesn't do any harm because you can leave any time you want. But with children it is very difficult." Reluctant to leave their children, afraid the law might not grant them custody of their children upon divorce, many women stay in unfulfilled marriages year after year.[3] A divorced mother may limit the life opportunities for her children, especially for girls.

In relation to the second part of the question, whether the women would marry their present husband a second time, all the women except Tara and Mariam were adamantly against marrying their present spouse. Incompatibility was probably the major source of friction. Many women explicitly said that their husbands were good men. The problem was that they were very different from the women. Pari would not have married her present husband. "If I were to marry again I wouldn't have married my husband. He is a very nice man, but our families are very different. We come from very different backgrounds."

While differences in family backgrounds may not amount to much at the beginning of a relationship, they may loom enormous with the passage of time. Whether minor or immense, disparity in family backgrounds frequently led to emerging conflicts in the long term, coloring everyone's life and expectations. Differences in beliefs, attitudes, religiosity, or modernity affected the ways in which individuals related to one another. These disparities were felt more strongly in marriages in which relationships were not defined as equal, in which men adhered to traditional gender-role precepts, tried to control their wife, and saw themselves as superior to women. Incompatibility may simply lead to a lifelong feeling of loss and unfulfilled dreams. Although Pari expressed that her husband had never imposed his values on her, she felt an immense pressure because of the differences in their family backgrounds and upbringing. Solidified into insurmountable differences, the disparities only led to further estrangement. "I always tell my husband that my idea of marriage was to have a friend, a confidant, a companion, but I don't have that person in my life."

Having dissimilar family backgrounds and upholding divergent goals in life seemed to be major sources of conflict, perhaps the main causes of friction. Mina approved of the idea of marriage, but, like many other women, she would not have married her present husband. "My husband grew up in a family with a very despotic father," Minoo said. "His father was a very strict and authoritarian figure in his life. [My husband] is just like his father." She was, however, quick to add that, "Of course, he has changed a lot with time, but at the beginning of our marriage he was very strict. He has become much better, though. Nobody in my family ever told me, 'Don't wear this outfit or that color.' When I started my marriage, he wanted to impose his will on how I even dressed or what colors I wore. He wanted to control my every move."

Mina's style and color of clothing, along with her makeup, all became her husband's concern. "Although I loved him when I married him, it was very difficult. I believe dressing is one of the most insignificant issues and that a woman herself should decide about what she wants to wear. She should be free to make that choice. Furthermore, I myself was very careful, very modest in my attire. I never wore short skirts, revealing clothing, or even colorful lipsticks."

It was not only Mina's appearance in the public realm that concerned her husband. He also wanted her to cook in a certain way and to socialize with the friends he approved. "Even cooking was an issue," Minoo said. "I was the one who was cooking, but he was the person who said how he liked it. He wanted me to mingle only with those he condoned. After twenty years of marriage and my incessant struggles he is not like that anymore. He was a very strict and authoritarian person, but he didn't have any other problem."

For a generation earlier, a good man was one who provided for his family; being authoritarian and strict were expected. These were considered cherished masculine qualities. A generation later, those same qualities were not perceived as ruinous faults, but were considered by these women as reasons not to marry someone.

Layla and her husband had similar problems. He did not appreciate the level of freedom she expressed in her attitude and actions. Before marriage he asked her to stop smoking and coloring her hair. Upon returning from the United States, she had colored her hair blond and wore very fashionable clothes to the university. "If he found a pack of cigarettes in my purse, he would throw a big fit. He told me I had betrayed him, cheated him because I smoked behind him. He didn't realize that I had drastically reduced my smoking, but I couldn't call it quits. I needed more time. I used to smoke two packs a day. Now I smoke again. I have gone back to a pack a day and he is responsible for it because he was always after me, accusing me of cheating."

Coloring her hair was another source of conflict. Layla's husband wanted her to have her natural hair color for the marriage ceremony. She agreed and did not color her hair for a few years until her two children were born. "Then I got tired of my hair color," Layla said. "I needed some change. One day I had my hair frosted. He threw a fit when he saw me. Everybody was complimenting me, but he was not even talking to me. It is ten years now. Now he tells me, 'Don't you want to get your hair colored?' "

Another source of friction in Layla's marriage was child-rearing practices. Admiring her parents' upbringing, Layla was an involved mother.

My husband came from a very different family. In his family, it was the nanny who raised the children; they were not close to their mother. My parents provided everything for us, but his mother never did anything for him. He was against my child-rearing practices. He used to tell me, "Life is not all about children." And I responded by saying, "No, but children are part of our lives and we must do our best for them." I suffered a lot but I was able to enforce my ways of raising children. Anytime he threw a fit and became quarrelsome, I gathered the children and took them to the park or somewhere where they could play and have fun. I gave them a sleeping pill when I came back home. I didn't go to my father's house. I didn't want the children to see [my husband's] angry, violent side. I never fought back when the children were around. I never let the children know how contemptible he was.

Men's personal qualities, such as domineering attitudes, authoritarianism, and conventional expectations, are a primary source of discord in marriage.

Sara would not marry her present husband if she could start all over again. "Given what I know of him, I wouldn't have married him. He has certain qualities that force you into resignation. I have always tolerated his attitudes. I have had to put up with him for so long. He is too proud. He gives many credits to his family, but his family never returns his good deeds. They don't deserve all that he does for them. I have always had problems with his family. Now we have a good relationship; everything is peaceful, but I still can't stand them. And he still regards them highly."

Like many other women who viewed their married lives as a lifelong struggle, Sara was quick to report improvement in her marital relationship. "Of course, he has gotten much better because I have worked on him for so long. I have worked on him for more than twenty years."

While families of origin do function as sources of support and reassurance, they may also cause tension. In traditional cultures, marriage is not a union between a man and a woman. Rather, it is a union between two families with the young couple as easy pawns in the hands of the two families. The older family members believe they have more experience and freely shower the young couple with their advice, expecting nothing short of obedience because they know the best and they wish the best for their children. Married relatively young, the couple seek their family's approval. However, lacking adequate social experience, preoccupied with making a living, aspiring high without knowing how to achieve their dreams, many couples struggle to establish a new sense of self while having to espouse new relationships with their spouse, the in-laws, and friends they have in common.

Overwhelmed with the familial and societal expectations and demands and eager to prove themselves, it is only natural for the couples to turn against each other. Many couples never find the opportunity to thoroughly know each other. While many young men tend to dominate, young women either submit or begin their own process of quiet guerrilla warfare. Minoo commented, "In marriage, I see each person trying to dominate the other. Women think if they control their husbands they have been successful. Men assume if they dominate their wives and compel them to do as they please they have proven their masculinity. Many believe this is the right mode of interaction among husbands and wives. I yet have to see a relationship where the husband and wife complement each other and share mutual understanding."

Although the majority of the women would not have married the same man, they had only entertained the notion of divorce, never moving beyond mere thought to involve real action. None but Layla had seriously taken a step toward divorce. As Pari said, "I have thought about him not being there, but not about divorce. When his work takes him out of town for some time, I enjoy his absence. But he is a good father for his children. They need him. My son loves his father." While Pari enjoyed her husband's absence, Layla seriously entertained the idea of divorce. "I am going to divorce him when my children grow up," Layla said. "I wouldn't have lived with him if I didn't have children. Sometimes when he goes on a business trip and is gone for some time it is like we grow wings. The children and I have a ball. My workload also is reduced when he is not around. I don't have to cook, clean, or be on my toes all the time."

In the end, from the women's stories about their lives, their marriages, and their families, it is the sense of loss that emerges most powerfully—losses inherent in marriage and missed opportunities—unfulfilled dreams, unattainable love, and frustrations and failures associated with marriage. Espousing the idea of marriage, however, did not mean the women were happy with the choices that they or their parents had made. While Tara and Mariam decidedly said that they would have married the same man again, the rest of the women knew deep in their hearts that they would not marry the same men a second time if they were to start all over again.

Perhaps Minoo's words can shed some light on why the majority of the women were against marrying their present husband a second time. While Minoo believed in marriage as an ideal union between men and women, she questioned the kind of marriages she saw around her. For her, an ideal marriage was a relationship between equal partners; obviously not all marriages met such standards. Discussing the notion of hierarchy and dominance in all human relationships, Minoo called into question the dominant mode of interaction between men and women, between husbands and wives.

Marriage is necessary for a woman because it is only natural. We need emotional attachment and closeness to the other sex. People's needs and desires have to be met. But I don't see that happening in the actual relationships around me. I have not seen a couple that makes me think they truly complement each other. What I see in all these relationships is control and dominance. In marriage, one person tries to dominate the other. This is what many call complementing each other. Women think the right relationship is one in which they control their husbands. Men believe a good marital relationship is one in which they dominate their wives or have all their needs met.

I see many young couples around me. On the surface, it looks like they have a good relationship, but deep inside it is clear that they are having a lot of problems. People are facing a crisis. Or, perhaps, it is better to say that the family is going through a crisis in Iran. Family represents a micro institution. When this institution is not based on the right principles, it falls apart. When the family suffers, then the larger society is harmed. That, in turn, affects social laws, relationships between people, family members, and friends. When men negate the existence of women as human beings in the family, when women are not treated properly as equal partners, then the same thing happens in the larger society. We learn to negate each other in the family and that affects our everyday lives.

We are cruel to each other in the larger society; we can't see each other's success. People do not work together; there is a lack of trust. I don't see unity among people, among couples. A society like this is sick; it lacks human bonding, and the primary reason lies in the family. When relationships in the family are not based on principles of respect and equality, you can't expect the same principles to be practiced in the larger society.

When all the laws put women down and negate their equality, it becomes extremely difficult for men to accept women as equal. We can't blame the crisis in the family on the government. All families are in trouble. Men and women live in very stressful situations; they may lose it at any point, but they can't even afford to lose their control. They tolerate this situation because they can't do anything different. Women live miserable lives because they don't have any other model, any other way of living a more fulfilling life. They can't even fathom how to live a better life. Although their lives are filled with failure, they can't even choose a different path because they don't have any positive role models in front of them. I think this form of marriage is wrong. People are not happy. They are pressured by tradition, by religion, by their family. They are under tremendous pressure. This is a serious crisis. They attach themselves to their children, and it is the children that enable them to endure their everyday lives.

Marriage is a goal for women. When they think about marriage, they think about giving pleasure to their husband. A successful woman is one who keeps her husband satisfied. Her own feelings and thoughts don't count. She is there to serve her husband, to be at his beck and call. If you provide all the sexual services, if you keep your husband satisfied and happy at home, then you are a successful wife. When a man marries a second wife, everybody thinks that the first wife couldn't keep her husband sexually satisfied. When a woman gets sick, nobody finds any problem if the husband marries another woman.

Couples are in crisis because they can't satisfy each other. They have never learned how to satisfy one another, how to be humane toward each other. It doesn't matter who the oppressor is, male or female. They harm each other and this hurts the rest of the society. I look at people who have been married for years, who have been together for decades. They are living together only because they have to; it is not because they love each other. People marry, buy a house, and have children. Then one day they wake up and realize there is a major gap in their lives. They haven't learned to love each other, to respect one another. All of a sudden you realize it is not the material comfort, the size of your house, or having children that strengthen a family. If you have a strong and meaningful relationship within your family, toward each other, then that feeling can be extended to others. If you love your spouse and respect him or her, then you love your child, your friend, your neighbor, and your colleague.

Women's Lives, Women's Words

"In Those Days All the Girls Worked"

THE WOMEN IN THIS STUDY came from different walks of life. They represented the class diversity present in Tehran; while some came from very well-to-do families, others were from impoverished economic backgrounds in which everyday life proved to be a challenge for their parents. There was also the in-between class, the various strata of the middle class in which economic threat was not an ever-present harsh reality to be confronted on a daily basis. Regardless of their families' economic backgrounds, all the women in this research have, at some point in their lives, engaged in paid employment. Some women were still working full-time during the time of the interview. Others worked before marriage or had acquired jobs after marriage. The majority, however, were the first generation of women in their families who ventured outside their homes/private spheres into the public domain to seek employment.[1] Why did they take jobs?

For some women, employment was a door to freedom, to liberation from the constant supervision of parents, both mothers and fathers. Work represented freedom to spend their income as they pleased and freedom to engage in a social life as far as work allowed. Employment provided a legitimate avenue to leave the home. Other women sought jobs because "it was fun." Friends had jobs and were making money and the women did not want to fall behind. There were also women who had studied for years and were looking forward to reaping results from these years of accumulating knowledge. What is the use of years of a good education and higher degrees, they asked themselves, if they were going to stay at home? Some women worked to provide a decent standard of living for their families. Most of their parents were a major source of encouragement, always advising their daughters to hold onto their jobs regardless of how difficult the conditions had become. This was especially true after the women had proven the benefits of employment by securing a steady income and a respectable occupation. Apparently, many parents believed in employment as an escape from dependency, a move toward a more independent life for their children.

What kinds of jobs did the women take? How did their parents respond to their holding jobs, making an income, and coming home late? How did the women spend their income? How did the husbands react to their wives' employment? For these young men, too, their wives were probably the first generation of wives who had embarked on a public role. How was housework and childcare negotiated and managed? Did their work imply a second shift for women? If they quit work, what were their reasons? These and related issues are the topics explored in this section.

"My Father Believed in Women Working"

Many women started to work immediately after graduation from high school. Only a small number of women and men naturally have access to higher education in Iran, given the limited number of colleges and universities and the horrendously difficult entrance exams. Many young women were accepted in universities in cities other than Tehran, but their parents did not allow them to move to a different city on their own. This is a common situation even today; many parents still do not allow their daughters to study in a city other than their place of residence. Seeing the college doors closed to them, many young women viewed work as a viable option that allowed them some measure of freedom. As Zhaleh said, "I had the option of going to the university in a city other than Tehran, but my father objected to my living by myself at the age of eighteen and going to school. So I stayed in Tehran and started working." Pari was accepted at a college in Mashhad, but her parents did not allow her to attend that college. "My parents did not agree with me going to college in another city," Pari said. "I was allowed to attend college only in Tehran."

Confined to the capital city and unable to attend college elsewhere, women found work an attractive option and a door to a measure of freedom. Work was not new to Zhaleh. "I wanted to be independent and to have my own income. We, as a family, could have more income. We had an average life that could always be improved." As the youngest girl in her family, Zhaleh had seen her two older sisters seeking employment years earlier. "There were many obstacles when my older sisters went to work," Zhaleh recalled. "My father didn't like my sisters to have a job, to leave the house every morning and go to work. But by the time I went to work, there was no problem. My father had no objection because he had seen the benefits of women working and having a job."

Although Zhaleh's father did not see any obstacle to his eighteen-year-old daughter seeking employment, there was pressure to take employment only in certain areas of the job market. From her parents' point of view, only certain jobs were appropriate for women. "They even intervened in my choice of job." Zhaleh's parents, among many others, believed that the most appropriate occupations for women were in the ministry of education, i.e., teaching positions. Zhaleh explained the situation. "There were other places with better opportunities, but I was not allowed to work in those places. The only job I was allowed to take was teaching. Any other job was closed to me. In order to avoid staying at home all the time I accepted their choice. And that helped a lot. I was free to do a lot of things and they lost their total control over how I spent my time. I did manage to have some fun in addition to my work."

Zhaleh also started taking various classes; these activities enabled her to broaden her horizon and create a much larger world for herself. Although she was not accepted in college in Tehran, she managed to continue her education as she saw fit.

Regarding teaching as the most suitable occupation for women, many parents persuaded their daughters to move in that direction. Teaching was perceived as an honest, honorable job; this was especially true in a country where education was segregated and the possibility of contact with men was minimal, except for the limited number of female teachers who occasionally came into contact with male teachers. Parents' tendency to encourage teaching among their daughters is also reflected in the sayings of other women. Sima's father encouraged teaching as an ideal occupation. "My father didn't care about whether I held a job," Sima said. "That was my choice. I could work or not work. But he wanted me to pursue higher education. He, of course, told me that if I was looking for a job, he preferred teaching for a woman instead of working in an office."

Some fathers only saw the benefits of paid employment for their daughters with time. Others always believed in women working and played crucial roles in their daughters' lives, encouraging them to dream and believing their dreams would come true with higher education and perseverance. From a very young age, Layla knew she would be a doctor.

> I loved to become a doctor from a very early age. I can say I studied for my father. He worked so hard for our comfort, trying to provide the best for us. I went to the best school in Tehran and we were not rich. I decided the only way I can return my father's love was by studying hard, by showing him the best GPA. He always said, "Women should work, they should have a job. They should know everything and live independent lives." He was an intellectual, an open-minded man who believed in women's education.[2]

Believing in economic independence for women, Layla's father bought her a car and helped her to set up her private practice.

Sima's father encouraged his daughter to seek employment because he did not want to see his daughter wasting her youth. "My father always encouraged me to work," Sima said. "He didn't like me staying at home all the time doing nothing. That made him sad. He hated the idea of just hanging around. He was happy if I was even doing housework, but he worried about me wasting my time." The desire to see his daughter using her time productively, however, did not mean that he would be satisfied with any job Sima took. When Sima took a taxing job with low pay, her father suggested that she did not have to go to work if it was not worth her time. He believed the job was exhaustive and depressing, and he therefore did not recommend it. She, however, remained in that job and managed to advance considerably. Mariam was the first woman in her family who took a job before high school graduation, doing so because her father interrupted her education. Although she came from a rigid background, her father did not express much opposition to her employment. "My father was a government worker," Mariam said. "He saw many women who worked there. Even though in general it was not common for women in our family to work, he didn't object to my work. It was also partly because of money; he always had a difficult time financially."

Obviously, not all parents encouraged their daughters to seek paid employment and to establish independent lives. Some daughters had to fight against not only their parents but also other relatives in order to be allowed to hold jobs. Most often these women came from poorer families who had never seen women holding paid employment, who still had relatives in cities and villages who were not exposed to the idea of women working outside their houses. When Zahra took her first job she was eighteen years old. "Someone just happened to find me a job," Zahra said. "My father didn't object, but my uncle came to our house and cursed my father. He said horrible things to my father, disapproving of my job. My mother took my side, though." In order to circumvent the opposition, Zahra came up with ingenious strategies. She knew her father was actually against women working. "I did a lot of work at home," she said.[3] "I also tried to get along with him. I never expressed my opinion on anything no matter what he said. I brought my whole salary to him. I knew that if I bought even one new blouse, one new purse, my father wouldn't let me keep going to work. He would think I was too full of myself."

Zahra is forty-three years old and is still working. Somehow she was able to overcome her father's and the relatives' opposition. As a single woman coming from an impoverished and extremely strict background, her work enabled her to travel both in the country and abroad. With time, she was able to do things that are still impossible for most women from her background. Her work enabled her to assert a certain degree of economic independence against her father's domineering tendencies. Never married, she managed to establish her own social circle separate from her restrictive family environment. Although Zahra is still bound by their rigid standards, her job nevertheless empowered her to stretch her wings, to see worlds other than the world her parents offered.

Opposition was not always either so strong or based on the belief that women should be confined to the private sphere. Some parents discouraged their daughters from holding employment because they saw them working too hard or late hours. Pari started working when she was eighteen; she taught at a school in her neighborhood. There was no objection to her work. But when she was accepted in college she continued her work while taking night classes, so that by the time she came home it was very late. "I used to call my brother to come to get me at the beginning of the street," Pari said. "There were stray dogs in the neighborhood and I was afraid of them. I was not afraid of people but of the dogs." Her parents did not like her schedule and wanted her to quit work; they did not want her to come home after dark. With time, however, they harnessed their worries and stopped complaining.

Sara picked up employment right after high school graduation. Her reason, however, differed from those of the other women. Having seen her mother beginning full-time employment after her father passed away, she felt the necessity of finding a job. "I wanted to be economically independent. Perhaps if my father were alive I wouldn't have felt the need to be economically independent. My mother was working so hard. All of us wanted to help as soon as we could. We didn't want to be an additional burden on her. Plus, there was nothing else to do. In those days all the girls worked. They either became teachers or found some kind of office job."

Sara's story, however, presented an exceptional case. First, Sara's father had passed away and her mother was providing for her family. Secondly, she was the only young woman who was allowed to move to a different city, getting four months of training and working outside Tehran for two or three years.

Not only the parents but also the in-laws sometimes played a role in encouraging or discouraging their daughters-in-law to seek employment. This was especially true in Tara's case. She had lost her father at the age of fourteen. Upon her marriage, she embarked on employment due to her father-in-law's urging. She married after graduation from high school at the age of nineteen. Young and inexperienced, she did not have a clear idea about her future. "I had no idea whether it was a good idea to work or not," Tara said. "My father-in-law thought it was a good idea for women to work and suggested several possibilities." Having a problematic relationship with her mother, Tara could not turn to her for advice. "My mother didn't have a clear position," Tara said. "Her main stance was to disagree with me on any point. When we first married, she said that I must work. Then she said, 'There is no need for you to work.' " Upset about the situation at the time, Tara did not appreciate others deciding about her future. "At first I was upset with them for making plans for me. But those years proved to be very successful. I enjoyed working and liked the job my father-in-law suggested. It brought me into direct contact with people. Now that I look back, I realize that the experience was very good for my family and I. We bought a lot of things in those days; I even bought a house with my salary, a house that belongs to me. All that was possible because of the job he suggested."

Many parents were supportive of their daughters' employment. They encouraged their daughters to pursue higher education, to seek paid and worthwhile employment, and to establish some measure of economic independence. Those who showed resistance and were against their daughters' employment changed their opinion with the passage of time. The daughters were able to convince their parents that, not only did their job not damage the family's reputation, but it also benefitted the whole family. Depending on what order in the family the women were born (i.e., the oldest daughter or the youngest daughter), they met different measures of either support or resistance. Typically the oldest daughters received the most extreme resistance because they often were the first women in the family who sought paid employment outside their home. However, by the time the second or the third daughter was ready to seek employment, parents had seen the benefits of paid employment and did not show any resistance, especially if their younger daughters followed in the older sister's footsteps.

Even when parents showed no signs of opposition, they certainly had opinions about the most suitable jobs and pressed their daughters to take only certain positions. Fathers have played crucial roles in encouraging or discouraging their daughters to pursue higher education and to seek paid employment. As far as education and employment are concerned, it is important to reiterate the fact that women mostly talked or referred to their fathers as having been major sources of support or opposition. The silence on how mothers responded or what kind of role they played in their daughters' education or future employment is astounding. Mothers no doubt played a role, most probably a supportive one, letting their daughters know they would be there for them. However, the virtual absence of the mother's voice in matters relating to higher education or employment shows that perhaps these were issues to be negotiated with the father. Needless to say, education and employment belong to the public domain, and fathers knew most about these issues.

Some fathers harbored great aspirations for their daughters. Providing the best for their daughters, fathers taught them to aspire high and to struggle for their goals. Functioning as pivotal sources for emotional and economic support, they helped this particular generation of Iranian women to make a tremendous leap into the future, to pursue higher education, and to seek gainful employment in areas previously closed to women. This was, nevertheless, the first generation of Iranian women who ventured out of the private domain on a massive scale and asserted a public presence in many areas. For many of these women, their fathers functioned as their primary sources of encouragement.

Not all women benefitted from such abundant support. They had to rise against their fathers and their relatives. The degree of opposition obviously varied; some parents expressed concern over their daughter's public role, others acted as inhibiting forces. Regardless of the degree of opposition they encountered, the young women's determination to move with time and to demand freedom of action and thought, was not crushed. Some paid high prices, suffering long-term psychological and emotional scars in order to gain a minimal degree of independence. They fought individual fights, each one at her own home front against her father, brother, or other male and female relatives. But they were all fighting. Not aware of each other's individual struggles, they saw other women going to the university or holding jobs. Not aware of the prices others had paid for their relative independence, these women were willing to pay their dues in order to join the changing times. Willing to fly, they compelled many others—male and female, relatives and neighbors—to watch their flight. For either long or short periods of time, they all took jobs and formed the first generation of Iranian women who joined the paid labor force on a much larger scale than before. None of the women in this group stayed home.

"He Never Said, 'You Shouldn't Work'"

While some women sought employment upon high school graduation, others began working a little later, either during college or after graduation from college. For them, employment was not a choice; they had married and two incomes were necessary to support their families. As the chapter on marriage shows, many women married young men who were not yet financially secure. Although the parents (especially the women's parents) contributed significantly, both partners needed to work in order to get established. How did the husbands respond to their wives' employment? How did the women themselves perceive their employment? Was the women's employment a source of tension in the family or a source of relief because of the extra income it engendered? While some women had enjoyed their father's support, they mostly perceived their husbands as major oppositional forces with whom to contend. As Layla put it, "We [she and her sisters] thought all men were like our fathers. We were wrong." Obviously, the fathers' supportive attitudes or their eventual coming to terms with the changing times were attitudes not always shared by the younger generation of men.

The majority of the husbands were either implicitly or explicitly against their wife's employment. This opposition became vividly clear upon the arrival of children. Did the men object because they were playing their socially ascribed roles, seeing themselves as the party solely responsible for providing for their families? Women often read something more into their opposition. Zhaleh's first husband was against her employment. The way in which he voiced his objection was multifaceted; her office was too far away, he did not like his wife working, or they did not need her salary. But after their marriage, he did not bring up the subject anymore. "Of course, I didn't agree with him when he opposed my work because somehow I felt he is not truly against it," Zhaleh said. "He just pretended that he didn't want me to work. He didn't have enough money to support us and we really needed my money. Furthermore, he wasn't even living in the country most of the time. He couldn't tell me what to do. I worked all the time we were married."

While some husbands did not actively object to their wives' employment, there were also those who seriously objected. This opposition was not necessarily spoken out loud; some husbands chose ingenious ways of expressing their dissatisfaction with their wife's work. Layla and her husband married when they were both students in dental school. Practicing was never a question. They were both looking forward to having their own private offices. Layla's father was an encouraging force, always supporting her and believing in his daughter's talents. For him, it was not his daughter's marriage but her successful career and economic independence that mattered. Marriage was of secondary importance. Her husband, however, objected to her work. Layla described the change.

> I was a student when we met and we never talked about my work. After marriage and my going to work everything changed. Sometimes he tells me, "I don't want a doctor wife." I tell him that is too bad because when you came to marry me you knew I would be a doctor. He still hasn't said you

shouldn't work. But he made things so difficult. He created all different kinds of obstacles. I found a good day care for the children and continued my work. But he started nagging and finding faults with everything. The food wasn't appetizing; the house wasn't orderly. If he used to buy groceries for the house he stopped doing that. He never verbally said you shouldn't work. But he said that by the things he did or didn't do.

Jasmin was self-employed at home in order to supplement her husband's income. Upon starting her business, she found him growing increasingly demanding. Although he was not making enough to support the family, he nevertheless objected to his wife's work in different ways. He found faults with the food, left too late for work or came back early, showed up in his pajamas in front of her customers, and invaded their privacy during visits.

Needless to say, not all husbands were supportive of their wife's employment. There were certainly those who opposed it and did not believe in women working or spending their salary on the household expenses. Sara's husband never said anything about her work. After twenty years of a rocky marriage, she expressed her opinion about men. "Men are the same no matter who they are," Sara said. "There are some inherent biological tendencies in them, but because of some education or their class in the society, they realize it is not correct to say or to express a lot of things. They learn not to convey much of their attitudes or thoughts."

Sara's husband is an educated man, but according to her he thinks like a traditional man.

He believes that when a woman works, when women have economic independence, they will not follow their husbands any longer; they do not obey their husbands. Instead they want to lead. When I decided to quit [work], I told him about my decision. He started saying, "You have so many years of experience. Why do you want to quit?" I told him, "You have been telling me to quit for years." He always wanted me to quit, telling me his salary was good enough." He told me, "The money you make doesn't have any impact on our lives. I pay you that salary myself." And he had the money to give me my salary.

Obviously, Sara was disturbed by her husband's attitude toward her work.[4]

While some women survived the implicit or explicit resistance and continued to work regardless of all the difficulties they had to endure, there were also women who were glad to forgo employment to become full-time housewives. Sousan is the only woman who worked for two years before her marriage and quit right after her wedding. "I enjoyed staying at home," she said. "I was so tired of working that I looked forward to staying at home and resting for a while." Sousan and her husband were lucky because, while Sousan did not draw any satisfaction from work, her husband also did not believe in women working and earning an income. She presented different reasons as to why he did not like his wife to work. "My husband believes that women's income shouldn't be spent on the house," Sousan said. "That as long as there is no need for an extra income, there is no need for me to have a job. He believes that my presence at home is more important. Therefore, I didn't look for a job, but I did things on the side."

Interested in baking, Sousan began helping a friend who had a bakery. Her husband did not object to that arrangement because he trusted she could stop whenever she wished. To keep herself active, she took a variety of classes. "He was very encouraging about these classes and didn't want me to stay at home all the time by myself," Sousan said. "It was only going to work and being busy from morning to late afternoon that he did not encourage. He was especially against that because he believed that women's work is not valued in our society, that what you gain is not worth your efforts and time."

Sousan agreed with her husband. To support his opinion, she mentioned the example of a few of her friends, four out of seven, who worked and were unhappy about their work experiences. They worked because of economic necessity. "Only one of them who is not married really likes her work. She believes that her job takes her attention away from what she doesn't have in life." Convinced that society did not value women's employment, aware that her family did not need her economic contribution, Sousan was satisfied to be a full-time wife and mother, entertaining herself by taking various classes. These classes kept her in touch with the larger society, secured a measure of social contact with others, and kept her intellectually stimulated.

Layla had to confront fierce opposition in order to continue her work. Sousan's husband did not believe in women seeking employment. Fortunately, his wife agreed with him. There was also the rare example of men who were supportive of employed wives. Zhaleh's second husband was completely supportive of her work. "He supports women having social and active roles." It is Zhaleh, however, who is tired of working full-time. "My work is not interesting anymore," Zhaleh said. "The distance is also another problem. It is too far. Now I work three days a week. It takes me an hour and a half to get to work. By the time I get back home, I am exhausted." Before her second marriage, Zhaleh believed that she should work in order to maintain her relative independence from her parents and to have her own income. With her second marriage came a new perspective. "Before marriage I believed that I am solely responsible for my life, that there is nobody else to support me. So employment was not a choice. Now I feel that my life is more secure. I feel there is time to think about other opportunities because it is important for me to have a job. But now I can be more selective. My husband is also supportive, encouraging me to look into other options."

If a small number of husbands encouraged a wife's employment, there were also those who played no particular role, accepting whatever decision their wives made. Ziba started her job after her marriage. She worked in another city for two years. "My life was in Tehran and my job in another city. We saw each other every other weekend. I came with the bus. I had a contract for five years, but it ended in two years. I got transferred. He never objected to this arrangement. My husband played a neutral role in my work. He was neither encouraging nor discouraging. He let me do whatever I wanted. It was my decision; I liked my work, being with people, with my students. I felt successful at work. I was good at it. My students appreciated me and that was gratifying."

The sheer satisfaction she received from her work encouraged her to continue her employment; Ziba is still teaching after more than twenty years. "The money side of it was not an issue for me," Ziba said. "I wasn't working for economic independence." While Ziba did not sense any opposition from her husband, she wondered whether his position changed after they had children. The first child came after five years of marriage when she felt more settled at work and her life. "Maybe after I started having children he wanted me to stay at home, but he didn't say anything." Of course, her husband, like most of the women's parents, preferred her teaching to doing any other job. "Maybe one of the reasons he never objected to my work was that I was a teacher. I teach at a girl's school." For those families who depended on women's economic contributions, direct opposition to women's employment was often hardly ever explicit; employment was a necessity. Realizing the need for a second income, Mina's husband never expressed any concern over her work. "I started to work when I was a student," Mina said. "I had to work. He certainly wasn't against my work."

The coming of children, however, signified the beginning of change and new responsibilities for both parents. Mothers act as the primary caregivers and are naturally expected to raise the children. If husbands did not object to their wives working, the arrival of children often changed that relationship. For women, factors such as childbirth, number of children, age of children, and health status of parents or in-laws tended to affect their perspective on work. As Mariam put it, "It is only in reference to children that my husband ever raised any concern about my work. When the conditions are difficult, when good day-care centers are not available, raising children and full-time employment become critical issues." [5]

The arrival of children is a turning point in marriage. While some husbands insisted that women should quit work, there were also those mothers who found it particularly taxing to leave their children. They saw themselves solely responsible for the welfare of their children and they experienced employment as an additional emotional burden. Pari's husband had no objection to her work. "I think I was more rigid and adamant about my child rearing," she recalled. "He never said, 'Don't go to work,' or 'Don't leave the children alone,' but I couldn't leave them alone myself. After twelve o'clock I missed my son and felt that I had to be with him. I couldn't do it."

However, most of the women believed that their husbands were against their employment. Even when they did not disagree with their wives' careers, the majority of the husbands were certainly not major sources of support. More often than not, women were left alone to fend for themselves, to provide child care, to take care of the household necessities, to be both a full-time paid employee and a wife. Azar experienced tremendous pressure in her life after she had a child. "I work full-time and I am solely responsible for my daughter," Azar said. "All her work is my responsibility. Furthermore, I do all the house-work. I am not saying what I do is ideal, but I try very hard, doing the best I can to make sure everything is running smoothly at home. That's a lot of work."

While some fathers supported their daughters' adventures into the pub-lic realm, the husbands—men of one generation later—opposed those same tendencies. Why were the fathers supportive of their daughters developing new lifestyles while the husbands were not? Perhaps the answer lies in the different perspectives that husbands and fathers hold. For a father, to have a daughter who is educated and gainfully employed is a source of pride. His labor of love has come to fruition. Ahead of his time, he inculcated modern thoughts in his daughter, preparing her for the future. Successful at his mis-sion, he questioned deeply held traditional beliefs and attitudes and deliv-ered a modern woman into society. He was a pioneer in bringing change, in exploring new frontiers, in encouraging his daughter to delve into domains that had been closed to women a generation earlier and perhaps are still not completely open to many. The father and his daughter paved the way for generations of women to come. Furthermore, the pace of change the coun-try was experiencing was too strong to be halted. Such fathers saw the com-ing of change and, instead of resisting it, they joined forces. Change was inevitable.

Of course, most fathers enjoyed having a full-time housewife at home. The fathers were the dominant figures at home, their authority never ques-tioned. They did not bother with issues such as childcare and household chores. They benefited from the help and services of a full-time housewife. No negotiation was necessary to draw new lines, to share responsibility, to conceive of a nontraditional division of labor at home. Receiving services from their wives seemed only normal; encouraging their daughters to pursue higher education and to seek gainful employment did not present any inconsistency in their thoughts. Having working and employed daughters was a sign of prestige and culture. It signified a father's modern attitude regarding the generation of young women that was coming of age.

While working daughters were a sign of modernity for their fathers, for husbands having a working wife represented multifaceted challenges. On the one hand, her work called into question the young man's ability to provide fully for his family. On the other hand, an employed wife meant that sooner or later the household duties had to be shared or expectations were to be developed. Furthermore, economic contribution enabled women to develop relatively independent tendencies in both their actions and thoughts; they would be willing to express their opinions on various issues and were no longer totally dependent on their husbands for their livelihood. Gaining economic independence meant growing wings (although for some it took as long as twenty years), denoting intellectual independence that enabled women to develop new perspectives. An employed wife meant work at home for the husband. The home was no longer a safe haven where men could find refuge and be protected against more work, i.e., household chores. An employed wife meant that the food was not always prepared on time, that children needed more care and attention, that upon returning home from work both husband and wife had to start working again. Young and old, husbands were against their wives' employment because they were defending the last vestiges of home as a haven, a place where their needs were catered to and a place where men unequivocally could rule.

Both male and female, husband and wife, need a haven where they can be protected from the harsh realities of the public domain, where they can feel safe and secure. By resisting their wives' employment, the husbands were protesting the inevitable encroachment of change, the silent takeover of the last haven and the loss of absolute rule in one's own house.

"I Kept My Wage for My Own Expenses"

How did the women spend their salaries? Did they feel any pressure to spend their income on their families, or were they able to keep their salaries for their own expenses? For the most part, the young unmarried women kept their money for their own expenses. Before marriage, Zhaleh spent her paycheck as she pleased. "I kept my wage for my own expenses," she said. "I knew I could spend some money at home, but there was no pressure. I started my job because I wanted to have an independent income for my expenses. Once in a while I did spend some money on the house. But we [she and her sisters] mostly kept the money for ourselves."

Only one woman, Zahra, handed her wages to her father; she did so to pacify his opposition to her employment. "I brought my whole salary to him," Zahra said. "My father liked me to spend the money on the house." Bringing her money home was an attempt to get even with her father, to show him that making money and supporting his family was not a big deal.

> I had been waiting to make money for so long. I wanted to be able to spend money on my family. When I got my first salary, my boss pulled me aside and told me to go and buy a nice dress for myself. She said it was time to open a bank account and save my money. That day I got so angry and upset with her because I thought, why does she say that? I wanted to make money for so long. I wanted to spend my money on my family to show my father that what he was doing wasn't that difficult. That it was his duty to work and provide for us. That if he was more careful he wouldn't have so many children in the family. I spent my money on my family. I bought all sort of things for them.

Zahra gave money to her mother, telling her the money was for household expenses. Hoping she would marry one day, Zahra's mother spent some of that money to prepare a dowry for her. Determined not to marry, Zahra managed to sell everything her mother had purchased during a trip her mother made to her hometown. "That was stupid, but I never wanted to marry," she said. She resented the indirect pressure and the expectation to marry one day. Mariam also spent her money on her family, but not because of any pressure she felt. Being the oldest child in a poor family with five other sisters and brothers, she believed her family needed her income. "I really wanted to go to college," Mariam said. "I loved physics. But after I got my first salary, I decided that it was more important to work and help my family out financially than to go to school."

Apart from Zahra and Mariam, the women in this study kept their salaries for their own expenses while single. However, marriage brought a dramatic change in the way women spent their money. Most women started to spend their money on the house in order to supplement the family income. Zhaleh, whose first husband had objected to her employment, brought her money into the marriage. "I never asked for anything. If I needed anything I bought it myself. He showed no objection to this." For Mina's family, her income was crucial. "We both knew that both of us had to work. We couldn't survive without both of us working." Many employed women were proud that they never had asked for anything from their husbands.

Relative economic independence created a sense of self-reliance and pride. The women felt competent and self-assured not having to depend totally on the men of their lives. Seeing themselves as existing miles away from their mothers, they depicted an unusual sense of pride for never having to ask for any money from their husbands. Sara spent her money on the home. "I also spent it on my needs. I never asked for any money from him. Even when I bought jewelry I bought it with my money."

Some women were able to keep their salaries, buying fancy items for themselves and for the house or traveling abroad. Most of these women came from well-to-do backgrounds so that the economic survival of their families did not depend on their contributions. For other women, it was essential to bring the money into the household; their families depended on their income. There were also women who regretted spending their money at home on household expenses. This was especially true among those women who had quit their work after years of employment. They were used to having an income, spending freely without ever asking for any money.

Having lost their income, they felt economically dependent, a state difficult to live with. Some felt that they had been taken advantage of. Proud never to have asked for anything from their husbands, their new dependence was disheartening. Mina was dismayed at how she had handled her salary for years. "I brought my money into my marriage and never asked for anything," Mina said. "If I needed anything I bought it myself. I didn't even think about keeping my salary for my needs or even some of it for my future expenses. My mother never gave me any advice. She didn't know any better."

Jasmin was too proud to keep her salary. "Some women are too proud to keep any of the money for themselves, but with time they realize they have nothing. They own nothing. Their pride only left them destitute." As a married woman who had worked throughout her marriage, Mina compared full-time housewives with employed women. "Those women who work are reluctant to spend money on their personal needs because we realize how hard it is to make money," Mina said. "We don't even freely spend it on our needs. But I see housewives who easily spend half a month's salary to get their hair colored or something else. The woman who contributes to her family expenses never spends that kind of money."

Employed women were self-reliant; they also recognized the hard labor that had gone into making money. While they felt free to spend their money on either essential or fancy items, they also valued money on the basis of the sacrifices they made in order to earn it. Most women who were contributing to their families were therefore reluctant to spend money on fancy items. Their hard-earned salary was used to benefit all family members and not the specific interests of themselves. Mina believed that a woman who works to support her family does not learn that she has certain rights in her marriage. Comparing working women with housewives, she argued that housewives often know their rights in marriage. "A woman who marries and stays a housewife has her needs that have to be met. She makes sure her husband understands her needs and that those needs are met one way or another. Since she doesn't have any economic support, she approaches her life more rationally. She makes sure she has some kind of security to fall back on. I look around and see that housewives are in a much better economic situation, and have a lot more economic support. They spend money more freely than the working women."

Mina quit her job after fourteen years of employment because her teenage daughter needed more attention at home. She was worried about her and the fact that she was left alone for hours on a daily basis before Mina got home from work. "When I quit my job, I expected my husband to understand that now I have lost my income, my economic support, that he should do something to replace that, to console me, to comfort me. But he had no such understanding." Looking back at more than fourteen years of employment, Mina said, "My work never made any difference. He [her husband] never gave me any credit for working all those years. I was under so much pressure; I took care of my daughter all on my own and did most of the housework."

Experiencing a sense of loss, loss of not only her youth but also the result of more than fourteen years of gainful employment, she believed her working years were actually detrimental to her. "Perhaps if I had stayed at home from the beginning my husband would have understood that a woman has her own expenses, her own needs." Mina was quick to add that, "I am not saying he is a bad person; he just doesn't have any understanding of my needs. My pride does not allow me to ask him to buy this or that for me. The thought does not occur to him, either, because for years I never asked for anything. He never understood that I have my needs, too."Entertaining the idea of going back to work, she however asserted that, "Sometimes I think I don't want to have a job anymore because that would only add to my work load. Why should I do that? Perhaps the passage of years would make things a little easier. Perhaps I'd try to be less proud."

While most women spent their paychecks on the home, there were also cases that differed dramatically. Layla's husband felt ashamed of spending her salary on the household expenses. "He is embarrassed if a woman spends her money on the family," Layla said. "He is a good father and provides the best for his children. But I do my best, too." Both husband and wife worked as dentists and drew equal incomes. Her husband's reluctance to spend Layla's income on the home, however, did not stop her from spending on the family. She spent her money as she pleased, paying for private classes for her children and other facilities and expensive items that one income in itself could not provide. There were also women who were making considerably less than their husbands, working part-time or teaching a class here and there. For them, their income functioned as their pocket money to spend as they pleased. Talking about her own experience, Pari said, "I could spend the money on anything I wanted. Sometimes I spent it on the home, but more often on what I wanted. My husband was the one who was providing for the house. But I liked to buy more expensive stuff for him, for the children, for the house, or for myself. He left me free to do what I wanted to do with my money. My salary wasn't much, but he always told me to spend it on myself, on things I liked."

If the woman's money was not spent on the house, it was for multifaceted reasons; either the husband felt ashamed of such conduct, he was making an adequate salary, the woman's income did not amount to much, or because of the Islamic law regarding women's property.[6] Other women, especially those from less well-to-do backgrounds, were expected to spend their salaries at home. Furthermore, some women may have felt to be equal partners in making a living. They were embarrassed to keep their salaries for themselves; it was like they were cheating on their husbands. Jasmin thought it was wrong to keep her salary for herself. "It was embarrassing, shameful to keep my salary for my needs because I felt that I haven't contributed equally to our life, that I was a weak person," Jasmin said. "I didn't want to cheat my husband. But it is only with the passage of time that one realizes that all the money she has worked for is gone."

The passage of time brought a different perspective on how women spent their salaries. While they saw themselves as equal partners in making a living, they also saw their own needs ignored and forgotten. As equal partners, they contributed financially to their families' economy, but they saw nothing in return. If they helped out with finances, it was only natural to expect their husbands to help out with household chores. On the one hand, some women found themselves reluctant to accept any help with housework from their husbands at the early stages of marriage; they believed that the home and the hearth were their sole responsibility, their domain to control. On the other hand, the women who expected their husbands to help out with the household chores and childcare faced absolute resistance. Many husbands believed that employment was the women's choice; they worked only because they wanted to do so. Performing household chores or taking care of the children were not, however, the men's choice.

"I Didn't Want Him to Work Around the House"

Housework is a source of friction. Who does it? How much and when does it get done?[7] How do women feel about performing household chores? This is an area open to constant negotiation and conflict throughout marriage. After years of either full-time or part-time employment, many women had started to question past conduct and beliefs regarding housework. The women who had quit their jobs saw housework as their job, their responsibility, but they too questioned the constant demands they felt on their time.[8]

Minoo, a full-time housewife who had quit her work after a few years of marriage, put it this way, "It is correct that working for women in this society is very difficult. It is like having two full-time jobs. It doesn't matter what kind of degree or job you have. You can't expect any help from your partner. Housework is your work. I see many women around me who have good, well-paying jobs. They make as much money as their husbands, but they don't receive any help from their husbands. If the husband comes home and says we'll have twenty guests tomorrow, she has to cook and clean for all twenty people."

The societal expectation to be perfect housewives, combined with the husband's demands, tends to create an arduous task for many employed women. Minoo continued by saying, "Men expect the same kind of service from their full-time employed wives that they expect from their full-time housewives. This puts a lot of pressure on women." Recognizing the double burden that working women experience, Minoo is, however, quick to add, "Even though it might take years for the society to change, I believe economic independence is crucial for women in a patriarchal society." Unlike some women who had rejected the idea of employment because of the double burden they faced, having quit her job when her children were born, Minoo believed in women's economic independence.

There were also women who themselves turned their husbands away from doing housework. Young and inexperienced, they believed that housework was their responsibility; they were not enthusiastic about seeing the man of the house performing household chores.[9] Mina, who started working full-time right after her marriage, was under a lot of pressure. In addition to a new job, she also had her first baby. "I went to work at seven in the morning until three in the afternoon, and from work to school until nine o'clock at night," Mina said. "By the time I got back home, there was both housework and homework. It was very difficult." Mina's husband, however, was inclined to help around the house at the beginning of their marriage. But with time he stopped helping. "It was my own naïveté and stupidity that he doesn't help around the house anymore. I used to tell him, don't do this or that. I didn't want him to work around the house. Now he doesn't do anything anymore."

For many women, their own attitudes regarding men and the role of women in the family had become a question. As Jasmin said,

> There were things that were within me. When I worked I always had this thought that perhaps because I am working I am not spending enough time on the house. Therefore, I worked very hard at home, trying to take care of everything. When I worked I made sure that the food was always ready and prepared, that all the clothes were laundered and ironed, that all the shopping was done, that the house was impeccable. As a woman I had learned that the house is my responsibility, that I must run the house and take care of everything. That was within me; it was how I thought.

Seeing their mothers totally responsible for the house, many women believed that home was their primary responsibility. While they also engaged in paid employment in order to support their family economy, they did not have a different perspective on housework at the beginning of their marriage. Such a belief led to an acute sense of guilt because they were not spending enough time on the home; they did not take into account the fact that their financial contributions were as important. As Ziba said, "Perhaps my husband didn't even have any idea about housework. But I thought that I am doing less at home because I am working, believing my work is hurting my home. That maybe I am doing less than a housewife. Everything was always ready when he got home. He didn't have a clue about how things worked around the house. I did it all. And the more I did, the less he did."

It took some women years to develop a different perspective on their roles. Quitting paid work brought a new perspective for Jasmin. "When I stopped working I realized that I had been taking care of everything in addition to holding a full-time job. Now I had only one job to do." Looking back at her working years, she said, "All that was wrong. If you are working and putting so much energy at work, then you are equally contributing to your family. In those days, I didn't have any comprehension of equality. None of us knew anything. We didn't even have any idea about what a good marriage is like."

The deeply held idea of housework being the woman's job is obviously shared by both men and women. If employed women believed their job was hampering their ability as housewives, some men perceived women's employment as supplemental at best, if not detrimental, to their families. Even when a woman's salary played a crucial role in the family economy, some men continued to view it as an auxiliary kind of work. Women felt guilty for working; they were contributing to their family economy in a nontraditional way. To compensate, they worked extra hard, acting like superwomen. Men, however, felt entitled to certain privileges. At times, Mina was overwhelmed with work. "When I was working, any time I complained about housework or asked my husband to do anything around the house or in relation to my daughter, he responded by saying, 'Don't work. You don't have to work.'" All the housework, in addition to raising children, was women's responsibility; whether women worked or not was not an issue. Mina attributed a great degree of selfishness to Iranian men. "Iranian men are so selfish," Mina said. "They believe the salary women make has no role in the family. The money is used on the house, but Iranian men are not going to accept that their wife is working and putting in extra hours. He still thinks I owe him because he has allowed me to work. My husband tells me, 'Don't work. Stay home and we'll be just fine without your salary.'" Similarly, when Layla complained about her workload, her husband's response was simple. "'Don't do any housework.' I ask him, 'Who would do it if I don't do it.' 'Nobody. There is no need for it at all.' He is so stubborn that, although he knows if I don't do it it won't get done, he is not even willing to help or to thank me so at least I feel appreciated."

Full-time employment, combined with the existence of such attitudes at home, only exacerbated how some women felt about their work and their husbands. Not expecting much from the public realm in terms of day care or other facilities, they at least expected to be understood by their husbands, to be valued for their special contributions and the fact that they were performing two full-time jobs. The predominant attitude at home, as Sara put it, "injects a chill throughout your body."

The employed women experienced the second shift only too well. Perhaps it was because of such attitudes that some women decide not to go back to work. Although Sara was interested in having a job, she was not looking for a job. "If I get a job, I would have to do both my work and the housework. Why?" Unlike Sara, who had decided against employment because of the double burden she would experience on a daily basis, Minoo was determined about the advantages of employment for women. To Minoo, the loss of economic independence was tantamount to a major loss in life. "I took a leave of absence when my first child was born and then he said, 'Don't go back to work. We don't need your salary. I am making enough for both of us.' I agreed and quit my job; that was the biggest mistake I have ever made. That is the only thing I regret in my life. My mother told me over and over not to quit my work. I didn't listen to her because we had other problems; I didn't trust her judgment and attributed other motivations to what she said. Now I believe economic independence is the most important thing in life for everybody."

Regretting her decision to quit at the beginning of her marriage, Minoo made the effort to talk to all her women friends and relatives, encouraging them to retain their jobs and endure hardships associated with their work because paid employment is the only activity that grants women independence of thought and action. When Minoo's sister-in-law was getting married she was thinking about quitting college. "I told her that is the biggest mistake she can make," Minoo said. "It is correct that working for women in this country is very difficult, but it is certainly worth it."

"My Husband Helps Around the House"

For a limited number of women, housework was not perceived as a second shift. This was due to the fact that household responsibilities were shared and women were not left alone to take care of it all. Mariam said, "My husband helps around the house. He is an easy person and that makes everything a lot easier. I don't feel a double burden. He helps with the children's school, takes them to school or private classes. Today, knowing that I was coming here, he stayed at home with the children so I could come and visit with you."

There are, however, different degrees of helping with the housework. Tara, who moved in with her in-laws and lived with them during the first year of her marriage, felt no housework burden. "There was no work the first years. My mother-in-law was in charge of cooking and everything. So there was no work. I was responsible for washing the dishes. After we moved to our house, my husband helped around the house. Even my father-in-law, who is a military man, never sits idle. He is always doing something around the house like doing the dishes or something else. My husband did have a good sense of working around the house. I wake up in the morning and see him having done all the dishes."

While Tara's and Mariam's husbands worked around the house, Pari, a full-time housewife, knew there were limits in terms of how much help she could expect from her husband. "My husband helps around the house to some degree. Sometimes I ask him to do something like washing the dinner dishes; sometimes he volunteers to do something. However, if I ask him to do the dishes twice in a row he turns to me and jokingly says, 'You do it.' It is a joke, but when I think about it seriously, I believe he means it. That is what he truly believes in. I must be careful not to overstep my boundaries because his response would be, 'You are developing expectations of me.' "

Layla quit her practice because of back injury. After twenty years of marriage, and especially because of her back operation, her husband started helping with the housework. "There was a time when I needed his help," Layla said. "I wanted both of us to do the housework because I was working full-time, too. I wanted him to help me and me helping him. He didn't do a thing in those days. I learned to do everything on my own."

For some men, helping around the house is perceived as a favor to their wives; they are helping her with her work. In other words, regardless of whether women work or not, housework is women's responsibility and if the men are doing anything, they are reducing their wives' workload. Made to feel indebted if he did something around the house, Layla said, "No, I don't want him to do anything for me. He used to tell me if he does something, he does it for me and not for the family. I tell him you don't need to do anything for me. I can handle it myself."

Housework is the kind of labor that, when done, every family member benefits; when undone, all suffer. All family members enjoy the food, a clean house, and laundered and ironed clothes, among many other invisible tasks. As long as housework is perceived to be women's responsibility, then the men are helping their wives, doing a special favor. But if viewed as a series of responsibilities for the welfare of the family, then if men do housework they are actually doing it for the family and not their wives.

"Fortunately, My Mother Was Always Very Close"

How did the women manage their work, raising their children, and performing household chores? What role did their families play? Were there adequate day-care facilities or available kindergartens? Most women relied on their own families for childcare. Working and rearing children are two conflicting demands. This is especially the case in a country where many facilities are not readily available. The coming of children is usually a turning point in women's lives. Many quit their work because of lack of adequate help with childcare. Others are lucky to have families who are willing to help and to take care of grandchildren and nieces and nephews. Women's mothers have played a crucial role in providing full-time care for their grandchildren.

Without their mothers' help, many women would not have been able to continue their work. Roya's mother was a great help with her children. "Fortunately, my mother was always very close to me," Roya said. "I didn't have many difficulties when my children were born. Of course, I sometimes did think about quitting my work because of my children. I wanted to be with them and it was very difficult to work full-time and come home and spend the rest of the day with the children. Fortunately, my husband was of great help."

Azar's mother took care of Azar's daughter, acting as a source of inspiration. "After my child was born, my mother took care of my daughter. Now she is twelve. I took her to my mother's and picked her up after my work. When I got there, she was always so happy and cheerful. This ten year old would have so much fun with my mother, her grandmother. My mother could be a child with a child and an adult with an adult. She would take her to all different places, buying her clothing, jewelry, anything she fancied."

For some women, being away from their children was painful. Pari could not be away from her children for more than a few hours.

I could not leave my children alone. No matter where I was or what I was doing, after twelve noon I wanted to be with my son. I missed him and felt that I had to be with him. I couldn't have a full-time job. Now my daughter is still very young and I would like to spend time with her. I'll get a full-time job when she starts going to school. It is very difficult with the children, especially when children are left at home from one or two in the afternoon. A full-time job means I'd have to get back home around five and that is too late for the children.

Pari stopped her part-time job in order to be with her children. She did not feel comfortable leaving the children with anybody else, including her mother. "I didn't even leave my son with my mother. Didn't want to leave him with anybody. I started to work only after they got older. Even when I took classes it was always night classes. I made sure the children were not by themselves all alone. It was very tiresome because I was always running, taking care of their needs, cooking lunch and dinner, cleaning, and going to my night classes."

While most women turn to their own families for childcare, they usually do not expect to receive any help from the in-laws. Sara, whose mother-in-law was living with them, did not receive any help. Sara worked full-time when her children were going to school. She and her mother-in-law had developed a routine. She periodically asked her mother-in-law if she would be at home when the school bus dropped off the children or when she needed to run some errands. The answer Sara received was invariably the same. " 'No, I won't. I don't know whether I'll be at home.' I eventually arranged for the school bus to drop off my daughter at my work and we came home together when I was done. My mother-in-law was not willing to accept any responsibility for my children."

While most in-laws were not willing to help with the children, there were also those, no matter how small their number, who actually helped more than the woman's family. Tara's in-laws were a major source of childcare. "They helped me tremendously with my work," Tara said. "When I had children they helped me a lot. They took care of them and provided all kinds of services. I didn't cook for years. I'd go to their house, eat my lunch or dinner and then went to my house to rest." They were living in the same apartment complex and this arrangement did not bother Tara. She saw it as being very helpful because she received everyday services, care, and attention.

Like housework, childcare seems to be solely the woman's responsibility. If arrangements are to be made, it is the woman's responsibility to make them.[10] In most cases, it is the woman's family who provides full-time or part-time care for their working daughters, taking care of their grandchildren or nieces and nephews. Fathers, if economically successful, provided for their families' maintenance, but in most cases they did not play an active and involved role in raising their children. Many mothers felt the need to compensate for the distant and aloof posture the fathers maintained in their families. Layla tried to get her husband more involved with child rearing. "With time I realized he is careless about the children. He didn't keep up with their schooling, homework, or their growth and individual needs. Step by step, I carried his burden, his share of responsibilities, what to say to the children, what decisions to make, how to solve their problems. I went to their schools to meet their teachers and to have conferences with their teachers. He wanted me to do all this on my own because he thought I was better than him in these areas."

With the absent or detached father comes a higher degree of mothering. Woman start acting as both mothers and fathers, trying to compensate for the lack of attention on the part of aloof fathers. In their attempts to meet their children's diverse needs at different stages of their lives, some women are fortunate to have help from their mothers or in-laws. This valuable assistance enables the women to juggle family and work. However, if these sources of support are absent, employed women have to face the full responsibility of parenting on their own. The situation is further exacerbated when fathers tend to be distant and aloof and to relegate the job of parenting to women, seeing mothers as primarily responsible for the welfare of children while disregarding their wives' employment and financial contribution to the family economy.

"I Have Never Regretted Leaving My Job"

Women quit their job for a variety of reasons; the primary reason, however, is their children. Other contributing factors include poor physical health, boredom with a job and agreement with the husband that they can do without the salary, familial demands, and men's lack of support. Layla's back injury and a combination of other factors eventually compelled her to quit working. "Five years ago I developed disk trouble. There was the bombardment; the war with Iraq was in full force. We had to leave Tehran. My parents were both sick. I had an operation and the doctor told me not to go back to work for one year. The children needed more attention at school. I had to take care of my parents and my children. I wanted to do it all. I used to tell my children, I am a cook, a baby sitter, a private teacher, a chauffeur, a nurse, a doctor, everything."

Layla has not gone back to work for the past five years. One person, however, constantly asks her why she does not go back to work. That person is her father, who was a major source of support and encouragement throughout her life. He is the same man who was always on her side, raising her as an independent woman and offering to finance her private practice. Enduring years of opposition from her husband regarding her work, Layla eventually quit because of her physical health and emerging family needs. It seemed that everybody needed her more than she needed her job.

Sara left her job because of her daughter. One of her nieces showed her a letter written by Sara's daughter, which spoke of the child's fears of being left alone at home. Any noise scared her. The letter read, "I am always waiting for something to happen, thinking that somebody is going to open the door and enter the house. But I don't want to tell my parents because they can't do anything about it." Sara quit the next day. Her husband and colleagues asked her to reconsider her choice. Her husband told her, "You love your work. You'll be upset staying at home all day. Don't rush with your decision." She had made up her mind; she did not go back to work anymore.

Mina quit her work after fifteen years of employment because her daughter had reached a tender age and needed more supervision at home.

I worked under very difficult conditions. When my child was born, I got a nurse for the first couple of years, but later when I put her in the day-care center, I woke her up at five in the morning, dressed her and took her to the day care. I remember she cried the whole time. When I picked her up at three-thirty, I could see her sitting down, her head in her hands waiting for me. The teachers told me that she didn't even take an afternoon nap like other children because she was worried she might be left behind. She wouldn't even go to bed. When she reached her puberty, I felt like I can't do it anymore. As long as she was a child, I thought she at most cries a little or doesn't eat properly and on time. But when she got older it became more difficult. She was the only child, all alone at home.

Making enormous sacrifices, Mina studied for her bachelor's degree, worked full-time, took care of her house, and raised her daughter. Enduring horrendous difficulties during fifteen years of early morning hours and late nights, she eventually surrendered when her daughter reached an age at which being left alone at home was no longer feasible.

Tara quit work because, after years of receiving help and support from her in-laws, she was faced with a dilemma. Both her in-laws suffered from increasing physical ailments. Not only could they not take care of her children anymore, they needed help themselves. She continued her work for a while, but she realized that she was making too many sacrifices with having her in-laws ill, her children alone, and her husband away two to three weeks each month. "Up to this point it was them who were always helping me out," Tara said. "Now they needed me more than any other time. I thought this is not what life is about. It wasn't worth keeping my job. I realized my children gave me more pleasure than my work."

She quit and never regretted her decision. Mariam left her job because she found it extremely difficult to work and raise her children. "Taking care of my son was very difficult," Mariam said. "My work was far away. I was exhausted all the time. I would leave him with my mother for two days, with someone else for a few days. I didn't like the way my mother treated my child. I worried constantly. I felt like they didn't give him adequate attention."

Mariam lived with her in-laws on different floors of the same building complex. Buying their own house and the coming of the second child encouraged Mariam to quit. "At that time I decided to make do with my husband's salary. When I was living with my in-laws I continued my work, in spite of the fact that my child bore the pain of this. I couldn't tolerate being in that house. I didn't want to wake up in the morning and have to look anyone in the face. They didn't treat me badly. They were never impolite. I treated them properly too, but I just didn't want to be in the same house with them."

Determined to quit, Mariam had to convince her colleagues that she was not forced to quit and that quitting was entirely her decision. Her colleagues tried to change her mind, reminding her that her economic independence was more important. They apparently did not support her decision and believed that she might need her income at any point. Her response to her friends was, "If needed, I'll go and work as a maid from time to time," Mariam recalled. "There is always work. I can always work as a babysitter or a maid, but I just can't put my children through the pain." It was not only her friends who were against her quitting her job; her family also did not support her decision. "My father and the rest of the family objected strongly, saying, 'Why are you doing this? In a few years you can retire officially. Now you have a salary which is a help for your family; if you quit work, you'll lose all this.' " Determined to quit, neither her parents nor her friends were able to influence her decision. "I had decided and that was that."

Although some women received help from their mothers and sisters regarding their children, they most often quit working because of lack of adequate childcare. In addition, facilities that might help the women with the care of sick and elderly parents were largely absent. The elderly, if ill and in need of help, had to rely on their adult children for most kinds of care. Daughters are the primary care givers for elderly parents. They are the ones who provide care for both their own parents and their in-laws, as well as their own families and children. Responsible for the welfare of various family members, many women experienced enormous pressure on a daily basis.

Pressed to care, expected to give care, the women, as mothers and daughters, have nobody to rely on except themselves. As Sima said, "I am not one of those people who believes in giving, always ready to serve without expecting anything in return. I don't believe in constant giving. But I was always put in a situation to give. There was no way out." Regardless of whether women give willingly or reluctantly, the family dynamics, social expectations, and lack of adequate facilities position women to be in a constant state of giving. Not only women's immediate families but also the in-laws and the larger society benefit from the unpaid labor of love that women render. Born into traditional roles and expected to serve, most women live their lives in a state of perpetual giving.

A Man or a Woman?
Which Is Better Off?

"Women See a Lot of Things"

AS A YOUNG GIRL of thirteen or fourteen I wanted to be a woman because I believed being a woman would give me a certain power that could not be contained. Somehow, men's lives seemed already written for them. They had one path to follow: the path to manhood, to unquestioned masculinity, and to the task of being breadwinners. Women's lives, however, seemed full of mystery and closed doors.

I wanted more from life, and I presumed that being a woman would enable me to achieve more. Had I seen many powerful or strong women in my life that led me to believe in the innate powers of women? Women in control, who had achieved their goals or some measure of independence? Women who had fulfilled some potential other than what was culturally expected, i.e., being good daughters, sacrificing mothers, and faithful wives? Had the history I studied provided me with strong female characters? The answer to these questions is an affirmative no, yet still I believed in women's power!

Perhaps my ideas and ideals came not from everyday women, my aunts, friends, or women relatives and neighbors. Perhaps they came from stories. Every time my aunt came over for a short visit, we children would hide her shoes in order to convince her to stay for the night and tell stories. We managed to hide her shoes for two to three days at a time. In the meantime, we absorbed her tales and fables at bedtime and in the afternoons when all the grown-ups took their midday nap. Her reruns were as exciting as any new stories, and we never minded a repeated tale. There were tales of love and victory, with bright women who could outsmart all the mean creatures, who could overcome all the obstacles and win. There were also tales of noble and generous men who believed in justice and fairness.

Hardly remembering any of those tales now, however, I still remember the exalted feelings I had upon hearing each story. Perhaps I believed in those joyful and heartwarming stories more than the real-life cases surrounding me because they were tales of empowerment, of glorious, promising, future days to come. Such stories came from a woman who was divorced, who had been deserted twice, and who never again married. She raised her daughters on her own and never dreamed that she deserved better in life, never uttering a word of complaint in my twenty-three years of knowing her.

I wanted to be a woman because it gave me some mysterious power, but what about other women? Given a choice, would they rather have been a man or a woman? I asked the hypothetical question, "If you were to be born again, would you choose to be male or female? Why?" The answers I got were far from speculative, connected to some mysterious power; rather, the responses were rooted in the realities of everyday life. There were women who wanted to be male because they would have more power. There were those who preferred to be female because of the strong belief in women's inherent sacred qualities. There were some who wished to be male because they would have more freedom and they would be highly valued by society. There were others who were ambivalent, not willing to choose between the sexes. When pressed, some chose male because of the liberties men enjoy. For others, life was seen an endeavor, a series of challenges to be met by both men and women. Acknowledging the difficult times both sexes experience, they claimed to see no escape from life's tribulations. They believed it is just the nature of these challenges that varies according to one's sex. There were those who did not prefer any particular gender; they just wished for a more independent lifestyle. Some women wanted to be born female again because being female had not stopped them from achieving their goals in life. They viewed themselves as having been successful in their endeavors, never having experienced gender as an obstacle. Interestingly, there were also a couple of women whose answers were conditional, i.e., if social conditions were to remain the same they wished to be born male, but if the conditions were to change so that women could have better life chances then they wished to be born female again. One woman, however, did not want to be born again, male or female. Her life had taken her through a path she did not wish to travel ever again.

The accounts that follow show the diversity of the women's voices. This hypothetical question led to responses rooted in real life experiences, depicting complexity in each case. While a few women chose to say only a few words, others had more to say.

The majority of the women who responded wanted to be born female again. Their reasons ranged from having a belief in women's innate sacred qualities to having the desire for a second chance in life. The choice to be born female was not indicative of blindness to the oppression women experience. Rather, it was because of that oppression that the women wished to be born female again. While they criticized the situation of women, they also acknowledged those societal constructs that shape men. Individual men were criticized for taking unlimited privileges, but the impact of social institutions that shape men was also acknowledged.

The women's criticisms went beyond addressing individual men and instead questioned the society at large. It was the Iranian society and its many institutions that had specifically socialized men and allowed them to develop a different logic, a different approach toward life and problem solving. Recognizing the harming forces at work in the larger society, most of these women were beyond turning feminist consciousness into a war against men. Consciousness of the hardships they experienced on a daily basis had not turned them against men because of who these men are. They are their brothers, fathers, and husbands. For some, the women's goal was to change the society, to fight against inequality between the sexes, and to critique themselves and their own role in perpetuating the status quo.

Other women chose to be male to avoid all the trouble. Some dreamed of leaving the country and never having to look behind. They preferred looking only to the future, leaving the past and its fetters behind. Given their actual living conditions, however, their dream was going to remain a dream, for there was no realistic possibility of such a radical change for them.

"I Like Being A Woman"

Sima pondered on not knowing what it means to be a man. But given the chance, she wanted to be born female again.

I don't know how a man's world is, but I definitely want to be born a woman, go abroad, and never return. I very much like certain things in me, things that never got a chance to flourish, to develop. Don't get me wrong. I like men. But I wanted to leave the country, live abroad, develop my skills, and to grow. I wanted to live an independent life. I could improve so much in my work. I always believed I could become somebody if I had the opportunity, the chance. I have achieved so much without much education. I have been very successful at work without much formal training.

It was at work that I realized my potential. There was a woman counselor who helped me tremendously at work. She gave me confidence, the courage to ask for more, to succeed. She made me realize I can be successful. That is why I want to be born a woman again, because I know I can achieve more in life.

Instead of simply answering male or female, Zhaleh raised several points. Like Sima, she started by stating the fact that she did not know how it feels to be a man.

I don't know. I haven't been a man to know what it means to be a man. I believe both men and women have to overcome tremendous difficulties in life. But when you add societal limitations and expectations, then things become more difficult for women. At least men have a certain degree of freedom. They have the right to choose.

In this country, women don't really have the right to choose in many areas. It is men who make most decisions, in spite of all the difficulties they harbor, like providing for their family. This is a huge responsibility for men. Of course, there are families that are run by women. But in general it is the men's role as the family providers, which has received most attention in the larger society, and since they have more freedom of choice and action they can do a better job at it. Women, on the other hand, are under more familial and societal pressures because they have to deal with many constraints.

Sometimes I wish there were stronger women in this country or countries like ours so they could improve women's situation in this part of the world. Women definitely experience more pressure and constraints than men. But I like being a woman. I am not unhappy about being a woman. I look at other countries and see what kind of rights women have gained in those countries. Sometimes I wish I wasn't in Iran; I wish I were in a country where I could have more rights as a woman. But I have never thought about being a man. Even if I had to live in Iran, I still would like to be a woman but a very strong and courageous woman, somebody who could change things and rock the society.

It is interesting to note that for Sima and Zhaleh the way to avoid oppression was to leave the country rather than to change their gender. They did not wish to be male in order to have a better life or to have a more fulfilling life. Rather, they only wanted to change their conditions because they truly believed in their own potentials.

"Women Are Superior to Men"

Mina believed in the inner purity of women.

I wanted to be born a woman again because women are sacred and pious. I believe God has given women the power to give birth. In spite of the all the oppression women experience in the society, I believe women are superior to men. Their status is higher than men. It doesn't matter if the society recognizes that or not. What is important is that I do believe in the purity and ethereal quality of women. If I were a man I would try to empathize with women. In our society, the kind of socialization men receive turns them into inflexible, self-righteous beings.

For Mina, women's ability to give birth endowed them with a sacred quality and an innate source of power. The power to give birth overshadowed all the oppression women experience on a daily basis. However, Mina believed that oppression and power are not mutually exclusive. Women both endure oppression and yet draw power from their gender.

"I Have Been a Successful Person"

Minoo was certain that she would prefer being a woman.

I want to be born a woman again. I haven't experienced anything negative about my womanhood. Of course, I have had a difficult time in my life, but I have been successful. My family was never supportive. They created only obstacles and distress for me. Each side tried to concoct more troubles. I have resisted them all, but I don't know what will happen in the future. I don't believe my gender would have made a difference. I can do a lot of things that don't have anything to do with being male or female. It all depends on your personality, your outlook, and what you expect from life.

Having enjoyed an economically successful life before her marriage, Minoo believed in women's independence and self-sufficiency.

It is right [true] that the society works against women and is not supportive of women's efforts, but I never wished to be a man in order to be able to achieve more in life. I have been a strong person in life. I have lived a turbulent life, dealing with numerous complications. I have witnessed appalling things in life, but I believe this is what life is about. I look at other people and realize they have had to overcome their own predicament, too. Perhaps less than my share of troubles, but their lives haven't been easy either.

I think each individual is a unique person with his or her own problems.

Sometimes life becomes too complicated. But it is these same complications that make a person strong and independent. I have never depended on anybody; I didn't have anybody to depend on, neither a father nor a mother or a brother. There was nobody for me and that was dreadful. Sometimes you need support in life, somebody to take care of you, somebody to be there for you when you need it, somebody to lean on, but I never had such help.

Comparing the lives of men and women, Minoo deemed that a woman's life was certainly more difficult than a man's life.

Women's life is more difficult than men's in this society. When I look at people I try to go beyond the appearances. I am not deceived by the pleasant façade they portray. People usually present an image of their life and relationships that is far from reality. I am a perceptive person and I watch people. I often examine people's interactions, paying attention to who is jealous of whom, who is talking to whom, who is talking more to whom. Women are really oppressed in this country and I know it is the same in other countries. I read this in books and novels.

Women experience a high degree of oppression in the family. What is ironic is that even women tend to oppress women. They do it because they have been subjects of the same suppression. It is perhaps a kind of unconscious reaction, a suppressed response on the part of women to oppress those they can. It doesn't really make a difference who is oppressing who. The mother-in-law is a woman. She therefore shouldn't oppress another woman. Your mother is a woman, but she plays a crucial role in exerting power over her children.

It is the society that is responsible. When you have a sick society, both men and women are infected. Women's rights are overlooked in this country. Survival for a single woman, taking care of a family on her own in such a male-dominated society, is horrendous. Most families live together and tolerate all kinds of oppression and domination. But because they think separation will only create more problems, they continue to live their lives together awaiting their death. They just drag on; they are not actually living. They are passing their lives or perhaps it is life that is passing over their heads.

"It All Depends"

Roya wanted to be born female, but her choice was conditional and contingent on changing conditions.

> I want to be born female if the conditions were going to change. But if the circumstances would remain the same I prefer to be a man because they are the dominant ones. They [daughters] are better able to understand one's feelings. They are closer to you. In these conditions, I think daughters are better. My two children are boys and they are very close to me but sometimes I wish I had a daughter because she would understand me better. My sons are very close to me emotionally, especially my oldest. But I feel having daughters is better.

Roya believed that women use a different logic in life, that their outlook provides a broader perspective that is more inclusive than a male point of view.

> Women see a lot of things that men don't. They feel so much that men can't even come close to comprehending. Men's upbringing is different. It seems like they have never been exposed to certain things, like they have never been taught to feel, to develop emotionally. They are too logical and tend to impose their thoughts. They don't look at things from different perspectives. But women hear things, see details, sense feelings, discern vibes, and then make a decision by taking all these elements into account. Men are not like that. They say and do what they believe in without considering other people's perspectives. Even their feelings are masculine. Men make decisions very comfortably; they have a detached attitude and that makes them different.

Roya wanted to be a man—that is, if the conditions remained the same—because men are the ones who rule. But she apparently saw women's approach to and their understanding of life as being more inclusive than that of men.

"How Much Crafts, Sewing, or Embroidery?"

For Sousan, the important issue was whether or not she could choose where she was going to be born.

It depends on where you are born. If I was going to be born in Iran I'd want to be a man because men are more valued in this country. Women can't even start to show their abilities in this society. Men, on the other hand, can explore different paths in their lives. Our society does not even adequately value motherhood. This society looks at motherhood as a responsibility, as a duty. It is the women's obligation to bring children to this world, to become mothers. Some people even ridicule those mothers who have a number of children and say that their one and only skill is to bring children into this world. In other parts of the world women can be women and do men's jobs. They can accomplish so much. Women's gender does not stop them from exploring new areas of work and developing their expertise. Here women are very limited.

I know that my daughters will not have anything more than I have had unless they are extraordinarily strong women and want a lot from their lives. I think it is almost impossible for women to become what they dream in this society. Even going to the university is not going to open too many doors to them. I know women dentists who after years of studying and practice decide to become housewives. That is because their work is much more difficult as women. My own dentist is a woman and she always tells me about the price she has had to pay in order to become a successful dentist. It has taken years of hard work and sacrifice. This society kills any desire in girls to develop, to improve, to do better in life.

Everybody tells you that the best job for women is teaching. You hear that over and over. The whole society sends that message. Teaching is a good job, but there are certainly other jobs that women can do and are good at. How much crafts, sewing, or embroidery? Why not teach our children computer skills like that they can use wherever they go? It is a pity if they never get a chance to develop their potential. If our children are promising, bright, and eager, then they should be given the opportunity to advance, to go abroad for higher education. They deserve the opportunity.

Sousan wanted to provide the best for her daughters. She believed in their talents and knew they could advance dramatically if they studied abroad.

Criticizing a lack of possibilities for girls and women did not mean that Sousan was oblivious to the difficulties men face in making a living. "My husband's life and work is very difficult. He sees himself totally responsible for our life and that makes him very vulnerable. He works as hard as he can, but there is not much security in hard work. Sometimes I think I couldn't survive if I were in his place. Those who are not self-employed have an easier time. They may have less money, but things are easier for them."

While Sousan recognized the difficulties men experience on a daily basis, nevertheless she preferred to be born a man if the conditions remained the same. Comparing men's difficulties with the limited options open to women, she preferred the world of men regardless of its difficulties.

"My Mind Is Not Free"

For Pari the choice between being male and female was irrelevant. What she valued in life was independence.

I don't care about being male or female. What I care about is independence. As a woman, I'd like to be independent. I tell my husband I envy him because, as a man, he is not concerned about a lot of things. When I leave the house, my mind is on the house. I am constantly thinking about when to go back, what to do when I get back, what has to get done first. I can go anywhere I want to, but my mind is not free. I am mentally and emotionally chained to the house. On the other hand, when he leaves the house I ask him, "When are you coming back?" He says, "It is open. Don't know." He is not worried at all about when to come back. When he is at work his mind is free, but my mind is always preoccupied with the house. I am not saying he goes out to have fun, but at least he is not worried about the home and how things get done or how the house is run.

I envy men for being so unfettered, so free about the daily life. Sometimes I think it is my problem that I am so preoccupied with time, when to be where, and what to do when. Sometimes I wish I had no watch so I didn't have to keep track of time every second. But it seems like I cannot simply enjoy myself and get off duty once in a while.

Pari's account is a criticism of her world, a world in which being the primary full-time parent has proven to be overwhelming. She is free to have independent sources of pleasure and entertainment, but as a primary parent she feels chained to the house, responsible for everybody's welfare. Is it her motherly duties that bind her emotionally and physically to the house to the point that she feels engulfed? Does criticizing her world imply that she would prefer to be male? She envies her husband for the freedom he has in running his life, for the liberties he can take in administering his work. Pari yearns to have that unfettered approach to life so that she could live a more fulfilling and independent life. But she refused to choose between the two sexes because perhaps even men's world did not offer the kind of freedom and independence she coveted.

"I Wanted To Be a Man"

Three women in the study wished to be born male without raising any conditions. For two of them, Miriam and Layla, their personalities and their ventures into nontraditional areas were adequate grounds to convince them that they should have been born male. While there were certainly some very strong women among the first group, their strength or personality type had not persuaded them to choose the male over the female sex. The reasons to choose female varied greatly among the first group, and the logic to choose male also implied diverse perspectives on life. The women's starting points differed drastically; their reasons were rooted in divergent ideals, but they shared the desire to be male.

Ziba wanted to be male because she saw men's world as a safer place. According to her, men have better access to public facilities, a higher measure of freedom, and are more highly valued in society. For Mariam, women's logic was superior to that of men, but her strong personality, courageous tendencies, and resolute disposition made her believe she should have been male instead of female. Like Mariam, Layla wished to be a man because she found herself to be a capable person. As the oldest child among four sisters, she saw herself as the missing son. Raised to be independent and catered to by a father who loved his children dearly, accepting a subordinate role in her marriage was extremely taxing for her. Problems emerged from the very beginning for Layla. Marriage to a traditional man caused only frustration and unhappiness. Her choice to be male seems to be rooted in her relationship with her husband and in the way that women are treated in the larger society.

Like Zhaleh, Ziba at first was not sure which sex she preferred. However, upon thinking more about the question, she decided that to be male was "safer." "Perhaps I would have preferred to be male because it is safer to be a man," Ziba said. Ziba discussed several examples in detail to show why she preferred to be born a man.

> Transportation is a simple example. Even in the buses where the men and women's sections are divided, the section that gets more air and is more spacious is designated for men. Or men can easily get into any private car and get themselves to work. It is faster and easier for them. As a woman that is not possible for me. Sometimes I am late only because I don't have the same access to transportation that men have. I have to use either a taxi or a bus. I don't feel comfortable to use anything else. Even when I drive my car, if something goes wrong with the car, the men curse you, calling you names, yelling, "If you don't know how to drive why are you driving?" Because I don't want to face such a situation in the streets, I try not to use the car. So

there is more pressure; everything takes longer and I get more tired. It is simply exhausting. Men believe they are the best drivers. They claim mastery over everything as if life and the social world is theirs.

Even when comparing the salaries men and women make you see that more money goes to men because it is argued that men are the breadwinners and women are the bread eaters. These differences are there. Safety and the possibility of better functioning in the public realm are more readily available to men.

It was not only safety and the possibility of moving around more freely that proved to be important to Ziba. Lack of social freedom to equally participate in the society seemed to be as significant.

Women don't have social freedom and the liberty to participate in the public sphere on an equal basis with men. Our society does not condone women's active participation in the public realm. If a woman wants to be socially active, the dominant social norms frustrate her attempts. There is much gossip, as a way of implicit control to regulate her actions; facing all this resistance wears you out. In order to avoid the spread of nasty rumors women tend to withdraw, to avoid any serious involvement in the public sphere. This includes not only simple activities such as visiting friends and relatives but also engaging in educational endeavors.

Freedom to engage in socially meaningful activities is not possible even for married women who wish to be more active or yearn to improve their education. The dominant society stifles women's interests to the degree that women tend to unconsciously forgo social activities. These dominant attitudes don't allow women to show their abilities, to fulfill their potential, and to delve into nontraditional domains. Even if a woman is educated, she is still denied the freedom to use her knowledge and expertise in order to turn it into something the society can use. She is not granted many opportunities; nor do different firms or businesses consult her. All forces operate to squelch her attempts, to prevent her from fulfilling her potential.

Ziba's relentless criticisms were not just directed at the misogynist tendencies that inhibited women's freedom and growth. "Women's emotions dominate and shape their actions. Their logic is secondary to their emotions. Men can overlook their feelings a lot easier than women. It is their [men's] logic that governs their actions. Overall, men have been more involved in the larger society, in life. Things are a lot easier for them. We pay so much attention to details that we get bogged down with trivia. Men are not like that. They can ignore things; they are capable of solving the problems by looking at the larger picture, and go on with their lives."

While Ziba criticized the lack of possibilities for women, she harshly also criticized women for their lot.

Women are narrow-minded. In our society, women suffer from a lack of spiritual knowledge. We have many more uneducated women than men. Women's illiteracy rate is much higher than men. This lack of knowledge, the built-in inability to read, and strong inhibitions to socialize and spend time with other people turn women into spiders, spiders that constantly spin webs around themselves. They spin a world of their own and that world in turn stifles their world view. They remain in this world without ever leaving it to see what is happening in the society. They live in a closed world and never develop a broader perspective about life. This is due to the lack of decent education, limited contact with the social world, and inadequate contact with diverse groups of people.

Ziba's position obviously did not preclude an unequivocal acceptance of women or a one-sided criticism of men as tyrannical forces in the society. She believed that, overall, life is more difficult for men. "Men are held accountable to provide for their families. This is an enormous responsibility. The burden that the society has put on men's shoulders makes things certainly more difficult for them. Of course, they have accepted this charge. This does not mean that women don't want to work to support their families. But when a society emphasizes men's obligations and values their contributions more, when more work is assigned to men, their job obviously becomes more difficult. This leads to pivotal differences in the kind of jobs we hold."

For Ziba, it is the society that grants highly valued positions to men, thus making their task more difficult than that of women.

Overall, Ziba seemed to absolve men of their responsibility toward the making of the society. While she tended to criticize women for spinning a thick web around themselves, she recognized the all-encompassing societal forces that shape men. "Men are the creations of their society," she said. "They act according to the dominant rules. They do this because they are expected to act like that. They do it to maintain the family honor, to protect the family."

Ziba believed that being a man is extremely challenging, but being a woman seemed to be an unpleasant experience because of unlimited social constraints and women's innate tendency to remain in a closed world of their own making. Ziba's solution was to choose to be a man.

While Ziba preferred to be male because of the safety and the range of implicit and explicit privileges they enjoyed, Mariam wanted to be a man because she had lived her life like a man. Having struggled against many forces, she believed she should have been born male. "I always say I should have been a man," Mariam said. "My husband always says it, too. He always says I'm just like a man." Like Ziba, Mariam wanted to be a man, but not just any man.

I often wish I could have been a man with this same mind, not the mind that most men have. A woman's life is much more difficult than men's. Men experience some social pressure that they have to tolerate, but women have both societal and personal burdens to carry. Men do not feel the pain as much as women. They are protected from pain, or they learn to avoid it as they grow up. If the parents have any problem, the daughters listen to them. But if they try to talk to their sons, they'd say, "Get out of here." From childhood on, they learn not to care.

If I were a man, I would marry a very smart woman; my life would be made. I would have been more successful. I would have liked to be involved in trade, but I can't as a woman. On the other hand, I have done a lot of things irrespective of my gender.

I have bought and sold houses. I have gone to the realtor's on my own. I found a house myself; I myself went to the courthouse. It's customary and expected to take an elder with you when you are buying or selling a house. Of course I didn't feel it was necessary to take anybody with me, but my husband felt it was. He preferred my father to come in these situations. He would ask me to invite my father to come with us to sell or buy an apartment. I would say that we didn't need him. But if I went to the realtor's and my father realized I had gone without him he would be really cross. I would say, "Hey, I myself went and saw the house, I talked to the owner." My father would say, "Why do you want to come? The realtor is not a place for a woman. It's all men there." I'd say if I don't come we don't sell or buy. Faced with my opposition, he'd say, "Then put on a *chador.*" I'd say, "What do you mean, a *chador?* I'll wear a tunic." We were always fighting about the *chador* and the tunic in my house.

Delving into nontraditional activities and marrying a man who willingly respected her rights exposed Mariam to those social practices that undermine women. While her husband did not object to her exploring nontraditional areas, her father had serious problems with his strong-willed daughter and tried to limit her range of activities even after her marriage. Mariam had to fight not only her father but also the dominant societal norms.

Upon buying their second house, Mariam and her husband decided to register the house only under her name. They decided it was better for her future and that of their two children. But the official at the courthouse refused to do so.

When we went to the court to buy the house, it was supposed to be solely in my name, but the official who registered it wouldn't allow it. He said, "He has never seen a man put the house in his wife's name." My husband said, he had already decided to do it. Then he [the official] drew him aside. He didn't want to say anything in front of me, but I could hear everything. The official told my husband, "I have seen men who do this, and they later regret it. Don't do this." My husband said that he had made up his mind and he was going to do it. But the official said he wouldn't register the house only under my name. He added my husband's name to the contract and that was that.

But you see even if he had put it only under my name, I wouldn't have been happy because, if at some point we'd gotten a divorce, my husband would have gotten the children by law. If I knew that whoever was taking care of my children was doing it as well or better than I could, then I could be happy. But I knew that no one could do this, not even my husband. I could never be content with having the house under my name because my main right as a mother would have been taken away from me anyway.

Like Mariam, Layla saw the lot of women as being an unhappy lot. "I wanted to be a man," Layla said. "I was never happy with being a woman. Iranian women have no place in this society. Be they a doctor or a domestic servant. Neither has any status and this is under conditions that women work so hard." Raised to believe in her abilities and interested in playing a more active role, Layla had serious problems with those women who saw their sexuality as an asset.

Iranian men are like totems to be worshiped. He [her husband] doesn't care if you provided good care for his children, if you are a good cook. He doesn't need food, clothing, or anything. The only thing he wants is a doll-like woman who opens the door to him when he comes home, who kisses him and praises him. Unfortunately, I don't like that kind of lifestyle. He tells me, "This is what I like in a woman." I tell him, "I cannot be like that. I hate those women who use their sexuality to achieve their goals. I hate those women who play the role of the lover. These things are embarrassing to me. Mind you, these women are very successful, too. But I don't want to play that role in order to be successful.

I like a man and a woman to be equal in marriage. Life is not about eating, sleeping, going to parties, and sex. I want a lot more from life. Perhaps I am too much of a perfectionist or an idealist. I must say everybody loves him. He is such a popular guy. But perhaps I am as good as he is.

Layla chose to be male because of her experiences in an unhappy marriage. Furthermore, she believed women were not granted the value and status they deserve in the society. Her strong personality and her upbringing led to serious clashes with her husband. Raised to be independent and successful, Layla had accomplished a great deal in life. Her achievements came at certain costs, the heaviest being a complete lack of recognition or appreciation from her husband and not benefitting from his support.

Overall, Layla and Mariam chose to be male because the society relegated women to second-class citizens, denying them their due rights and status. Ziba, on the other hand, wanted to be male because of the higher status and unlimited privileges society granted men.

"I'd Never Wish for Something Like That"

Looking young and vibrant, planning to pursue her Ph.D., never desiring to quit her job, still seeking diverse sources of happiness and fulfillment, Azar was one woman who did not choose between male and female. Before considering a second life as either male or female, she rejected the notion of life and questioned the hardships that everyone has to endure. "I don't want to be born again. I'd never wish for something like that. But to be male or female, I don't know. I really can't say which sex I would have preferred to be. I just didn't want to be born again. I have had a very difficult life; I have been through very difficult periods in my life. That's why I believe it's not worth it to be born again."

Women's Words

"I Want to Be Me"

"WHAT KIND OF SPECIFIC PROBLEMS do you face as a woman?"
"What does being a woman mean to you?" In response to these questions,
the women raised multifaceted issues. The problems were social, economic,
legal, familial, and religious, and were all rooted in both the recent and the
centuries-old history of the country. It is impossible to dissect the importance of diverse factors and their specific impacts on women's lives. While
some women are better off economically because they either work or come
from well-to-do backgrounds, they may suffer from family conflict. Those
women who live in difficult relationships do not find the law to be in their
support. Those who happen to have good relationships with their husbands
may suffer from a problematic relationship with their own families. Others,
who have been able to reach their personal goals and marry the men in
whom they were interested, may find societal constraints unbearable. Some
women distinguished between the kinds of problems women and men face
in life; others found the problems women face horrendous while at the same
time believing in women's inherent strength to surmount most, if not all,
obstacles.

This chapter deals with the range of problems women face on a daily
basis. Having to confront them, obliged to move only forward, the women
have had no choice but to face their problems head on. The pace of the
struggle varied and the nature of the dilemma differed, but the accounts

shared here testify to the struggles women endured. Not all won; some struggles were chosen undiplomatically, and a tremendous amount of creative and emotional energy was wasted because the two people who were supposed to make a living together found each other situated on opposing fronts, their interests and yearnings divergent. Economic survival and societal constraints kept the husband and wife together, however.

Throughout their lives, many married women were compelled to question their worth as women along with the merits—or lack of merits—attached to womanhood. By examining their own upbringing in contrast with that of their brothers, the praise granted to men by society, the law, and religion, women assessed dominant societal values. Some rebelled; some resorted to silence. Some only harbored the idea of rebellion, dreaming of change, hoping for better days and more understanding. Some questioned other women, such as their mothers and grandmothers, their friends and relatives, their colleagues and neighbors. Others took to trial the men of their society, pondering why they were endowed with so many rights and privileges. The result is a series of questions and new outlooks. Although they began in the pre-Revolutionary era, the changes only started to rock society in the post-Revolutionary era. As Tara put it, "Women's issues have become like a flood in our society. There is no stopping it." This is a chapter on women's issues, the different kinds of problems women have faced, and the ways in which women have endured and coped with difficulties.

"The Invisible Contract"

For some women, limited social rights pose a problem. The family reigns supreme so that all individual rights and needs must be curtailed in order to safeguard this primordial institution. Family is viewed as the primary focus for women. Anything that takes women's attention away from this primary responsibility must be minimal. Zhaleh put it in the following words.

> If we work, if we socialize and meet friends, anything we do, as married women, must be limited to ensure that the family remains our central focus.

Of course, none of these activities ever will hurt our family. But there is this social contract, a social and religious contract, in this country to make women fearful anytime they dream about something that does not directly involve their family. To allow women to have their own friendships [after marriage] is a foreign idea to men. To grant permission to women to have their own relationships, even to have this little contact, is viewed as an act of extreme generosity. A man who does that is deemed enlightened and liberal. That is a big accomplishment for Iranian men.

Careful not to blame individual men, Zhaleh held society accountable for the superfluous rights enjoyed by men throughout their lives. "This is a right given by the society to men," Zhaleh said. "They then come to believe it is literally their right to control their wife, and whether or not to bestow certain privileges upon her. Women have to be accompanied by their husbands even for entertainment. If the husband is not there, then the children are." Reflecting on the lack of facilities for entertainment, Zhaleh continued by saying, "Of course the range of entertainment is very limited. Still more limited is the kind of activities you can do by yourself without your husband or your children accompanying you."

The lack of freedom to engage in simple activities such as visiting with friends or going to the movies along with having to acquire permission from fathers, mothers, and later husbands severely hampers women's autonomy and keeps them in a state of perpetual subjugation. Almost everything seems to be a right to be gained and negotiated. No right is automatically granted to women; arrangements have to be made. Negotiations are constantly in the process because some women wish to enjoy certain activities outside the family boundaries.

Living in a society that considers notions of freedom, privacy, and individuality as foreign imports severely limits women's ability to secure some private time and to cultivate their individual interests. The family and family-related demands are of paramount significance, and it is women's responsibility to ensure that all is running smoothly. The tremendous significance of the family in women's lives reduces all other individual concerns and interests to a secondary level. Traditional ideology holds fathers responsible for the financial support of the family. There is the tendency to assume that providing financial security is equivalent to good fathering. Unless something goes wrong, all that happens at home is therefore the responsibility of the mother. For men, their fathering is accomplished by the fact that they are providing financially for their families. For women, their mothering is an ever-present aspect of life, the core reason for their existence. Any deviation from the norm is reproached; any tendency for cultivating individual interests separate from the family carries with it not only social stigma but also a strong sense of guilt. Zhaleh explained, "Everything else is more important than what I am interested in. Everything else has a higher priority than what I need. But for men it is different. If they are interested in sport or some other activity, they plan it and simply do it. Nothing stops them; nothing intervenes with their hobbies and interests." Zhaleh was quick to add that her husband has never stopped her from doing what she wanted. "He tells me you create the opportunity and take advantage of it," she said. "But that is all he does." Zhaleh's problem was that, although her husband encouraged her interests, he never went beyond words in order to make it possible for her to engage in some activities of her own.

Zhaleh's husband seemed to be exceptionally open-minded and constantly encouraged her to do as she pleased in terms of her personal interests. She, however, felt the pressure to do her best as a mother and wife while believing there was no actual support in helping her do what truly pleased her. Given the fact that Zhaleh's husband was at least verbally supportive of her activities outside the family, one wonders whether or not it was Zhaleh and her deep-rooted belief about women's proper role and place in the family that stops her from engaging in activities not related to the family. Of course, another point to remember is that Zhaleh hardly creates situations that do not directly involve her family. It is hard to know what her husband's reaction would be if she really took his word and did create opportunities that took her away from her family on a regular basis.

As a young woman, Zhaleh had to acquire permission from her parents to engage in extracurricular activities after she graduated from high school.

Her job provided some measure of freedom; it relieved her of the constant supervision she experienced at home. Her first marriage brought further freedom because her husband lived abroad and visited only for shorts periods of time. Its dissolution, however, put Zhaleh again under the supervision of her parents. Marriage with her second husband, the man she chose and loved, brought confidence, security, and satisfaction. In spite of these positive experiences, she still felt solely responsible for certain duties and complained about an acute sense of lack of control over her time. Zhaleh explained. "For women, marriage is expected to fulfill all their needs, leaving no space for individual and personal growth or needs outside marriage. Social conventions and expectations confine women to the role of the mother and wife. All else is sacrificed to guarantee the survival of the family. Women's nonfamily-related activities seem to threaten the family and the assumption that a family is all women need."

Rather than experiencing marriage as an institution that expands one's horizons and allows one to develop her potentials and interests, Zhaleh experienced her marriage as an iron framework with bars blocking her view and locks inhibiting her freedom of action. She lived a constrained and static life, saw her opportunities restricted, and dreamed of some private time during which she could step outside the molding the society had structured for her and the female sex.

"The House Needs a Housewife"

For Azar it was not the lack of social freedom that hampered her engagement in nonfamily-related activities. Rather, she found the multilayered range of responsibilities overwhelming. Working full-time, solely responsible for her daughter, and in charge of most, if not all, the housework, Azar felt particularly frustrated. The fact that she came from a different family background than that of her husband only exacerbated her problems.

My husband is raised in one culture and I am raised in another. Now, after twenty-some years of living together, we are much closer in our cultures.

But it took so long for us to get to this point. He was the kind of father who believed his daughter shouldn't go out alone or even with her friends, or that she shouldn't talk on the phone. He exerted a lot of pressure and I believed that I must listen to him. But that was wrong. I shouldn't have listened to him. I realized that only much too late. I have many experiences like that, realizing too late that I shouldn't have listened to him, to everything he says, that I shouldn't submit to his rules.

Seeking professional advice from a counselor, Azar realized her mistakes and the degree of pressure they were exerting on her daughter. Talking to a counselor enabled Azar to realize what it was that she wanted for her daughter. "That is why I accepted all my daughter's responsibilities," Azar said. "I took everything in my hand. Now things are much better and my daughter is in a better shape after a whole year of trying to bring some change."

Differences between mothers and fathers and incongruent aspirations for children can lead to a constant power struggle. The parents may not share their dreams about the future of their children. While some mothers may aim for nontraditional goals, some fathers may hold onto more static and conventional ideals for their daughters. The result may be a perpetual conflict, which surfaces every now and then at different crossroads and stages of the children's growth.

Azar's husband did not want his daughter to take English classes because he was afraid it might result in a desire to go back to Australia, where they had lived for a year and both had lucrative jobs. Azar explained the problem.

I could no longer agree with him. We had sold our car and had not bought a new one yet. I told him, "I'd register her in English class regardless of what you say." But the class was very far. I went to work in the morning, came back home at noon, took her to the class, went back to work and picked her up again when her class was finished. By the time I got home, I was so exhausted. But I believed that my daughter must study English. The workload was horrendous for a few months. I did all that against his wish. He didn't fight over it and eventually said, "If you want to take her to classes everyday, do it." But he didn't offer any help.

For Azar, paid employment also represented its own challenges. While work enables women to earn their own income, it also adds to the range of responsibilities they face. Moreover, women's gender—the fact that they are mothers and wives—hinders their advancement. Regardless of the kind of occupations women hold, the family is expected to take the primary place, always demanding their presence and unequivocal attention. Acknowledging her unusual success at work, Azar remarked that, "I was much hindered at work because I am a woman. For example, my male colleagues may stay at work until eight and do their work. But I have to arrange my work so that when my daughter gets back home from school at two I am at home by at least three. I therefore can't be as successful as a man. Or, my colleagues do consulting, but I can't do that either because somebody has to be at home." Although Azar did her best at home, she regretted the fact that she did not have adequate time to spend at home. For her, home was a place of nurturing—in a word, a haven. "Somebody has to take care of the home," Azar said. "The house has its own needs; the house needs a housewife, a woman who tends to the plants, who beautifies the surroundings, who plays music. The house has its own soul and somebody has to take care of it."

It was not institutional discrimination against women that hampered Azar's progress at work. Rather, it was the house, the family, her daughter and husband, who demanded her presence at home. "It is impossible," she said. "I could be much more successful, but as a woman it is impossible." But Azar enjoys being a woman. Although she believes that it is her gender that has inhibited her progress at work, she does not wish to be a man in order to have more success. "I like being a woman, but I can't be a woman, either," Azar said. "A woman is somebody who takes care of herself, who plays music, who dances. I like these things, but I can't be that person." Azar's dilemma is probably the same conflict many women experience. "I wanted to be a university professor and at the same time a woman who is happy taking care of herself, her house, and the family. But that is impossible. Everything seems to be halfhearted, half-done."

As an accomplished person, Azar could not take pleasure in her accomplishments because she could not combine satisfactorily the life of a career woman and that of a housewife and mother. At work her motherly and wifely duties called on her; at home she felt inadequate for not being able to spend the same number of hours at work as did her male colleagues. Pulled in two directions, she could not truly enjoy her success; it was rather her shortcoming, her unfulfilled dreams that haunted her. Acknowledging her success, she was well aware of her unfulfilled dreams and the price she has paid for success.

Marriage had compelled Azar to question the principal values of the society.

> In the past, we were told that men are men, that they know better. Now I realize that men are not men at all. I tell that to everybody, to my brothers, to my friends. I tell them that real power is in the hands of women. My husband is a nice and successful person, but he has always made important decisions on his own. I never thought that he is like that. I thought that we should make decisions together, that everything has to be a collective decision. Now I realize if I had made decisions on my own, I would have been in a much better situation now. I now make all the decisions myself and I don't tell him directly in his face what I am going to do. But I have got to the point that I make decisions behind his back and do what I believe is the best.

A major problem that seemed to have shocked and hurt women tremendously was finding a lack of respect for their opinions. Working full-time, believing in their potentials and abilities, the women expected to be taken into account, to be consulted not only about mundane, everyday life affairs but also on important decisions such as buying a car or a house, vacation trips, and long-term plans for the family.

Decisions must be made and power struggles are an inevitable part of the decision-making process. Higher education and earning power has enabled women to develop a different perspective, seeing themselves generations away from their mothers and grandmothers. While women have experienced tremendous changes during the past few decades, men seem to have hardly experienced any dramatic change in their perspectives. Women's changing roles have given them a new outlook; men have continued to play their role as usual, albeit with some help from their working wives. This lack of respect for women's opinions, in addition to a lack of legal rights to protect women's financial security, exacerbates an already-strained relationship. While those women whose mothers were respected and consulted by their fathers expected to be treated similarly, those whose mothers were entitled to minimal if any rights reckoned they would receive a different kind of treatment due to their more active role in the family and in the labor force.

Experiencing a high degree of control from their husbands, some women learned to rely on themselves and to make decisions without consulting or even informing their husbands. It is significant to note that it often took women a decade or two to convince themselves that it was okay to make a decision on their own without checking with their husbands. It took the women a long time to realize that their opinions were valuable and that they could have sound judgment about many issues. Even those women who were academic high achievers and were straight-A students throughout their college years took a long time to recognize their potential, to realize that it was okay to make decisions on their own and to have opinions that differed from those of their husbands.

While the women saw the need to consult, to respect, and to defer to their husbands, regardless of the value of their position, the feelings were not mutual. Expected to abide by their husbands' opinions, the women's opinions were barely sought out or respected. Their happiness and sense of self-worth were eroded severely when they found out, only too late, that their husbands already had made a decision without even consulting them. Feeling powerless, the women tended to feel anger and resentment over these situations. Power imbalance and the men's willingness to use their power led to continual disappointment for the women. Some women eventually resorted either to manipulation or to acting just like their husbands, i.e., making decisions without consulting the spouse. Decisions must be arrived at one way or another, and some women were not going to abandon all their power—however minimal—in making decisions.

Although none of the women embarked on making major decisions such as buying a house or a car on their own, they nevertheless managed to make some daily decisions on their own. Twenty-some years of work experience and marriage brought Azar to the point where she now makes decisions on her own and ensures that they are executed as she sees fit, regardless of the price she personally pays for their attainment.

> I have learned (only too late) that I shouldn't listen to him. At least when it came to my daughter, I learned things kind of faster. I noticed that my daughter was under a lot of pressure. I felt that was wrong, that something was wrong. I went to a psychologist a few times. I used to read psychology books on my own but I hadn't reached any conclusive idea about how to raise a child, a teenager. The counselor was a great help. He made me realize my mistakes and that's when I started to accept all my daughter's responsibilities. Things have gotten a lot better. Last year I was seriously stressed out. But this year my daughter is in much better shape. I have made so many changes in my family and how I raise my daughter.

Aging in-laws or other family members also can be a source of stress in women's lives. At times, with the passing away of one of the in-laws or one's own mother or father, the remaining parent becomes the responsibility of the adult children. As in most traditional societies, in Iran it is the family that is the sole source of support and care for the elderly. The adult children provide care for the elderly's various needs. They are the support group and social security for the elderly, family members to fall back on in time of need. While the sons may offer housing and financing, it is the daughters or daughters-in-law who provide other services.

Upon the death of her husband, Azar's mother-in-law moved to Tehran. She had her own house, but she was scared of staying alone at night. Azar suggested recruiting a student to stay with her, but the answer was negative;

her mother-in-law did not want a stranger in the house. Azar explained the situation.

What happened was that the children started taking turns and spending one night at her place. One night the daughter, one night the son, one night she would come to stay with us or with her daughter. They called this arrangement separate living, but the situation only worsened with her deteriorating health.

I suggested hiring a nurse. They all disagreed. She was actually the one who didn't want a nurse in the house and the children agreed. When she got sick everything got worse. In the beginning, she moved in with us. Imagine how much pressure that was. Both of us worked full-time and had to take care of her. After her health improved, they went back to the old routine, each staying at her place on a regular basis until their own lives started to suffer. Now they are doing all that I said a long time ago, but there was so much pressure on me until they accepted my suggestion. Time has taught them what a mistake they made. She is killing her daughter. Now her daughter is mostly taking care of her and she is paying dearly for it. She is falling into pieces. They have hired a nurse but it is too late to do anything, to bring any changes, to undo all the spoiling they have done for years. She is a serious burden on her daughter.

Azar persevered and managed to keep her job while tending to the needs of various family members. Not only the in-laws but also one's own family and their problems can be sources of pressure. According to Azar, "Women are the primary caregivers to their families. It is the daughters and daughters-in-law who are expected to help out more than the sons, to sacrifice their lives for their families."

After her mother's death, Azar found herself responsible for not only her father's livelihood but also for her sister, who was suffering from depression after a short-term marriage and divorce. "I have to take care of her constantly." Although her sister lives with her father, Azar feels responsible for her sister's welfare, too. She is a wife, mother, and a full-time employee. She also takes care of her sister, father, and mother-in-law. "I can say I have struggled tremendously in my life to create a balance. I have been successful, but I have endured enormous pressure."

The combination of considerable accomplishments at work and horrendous difficulties related to her in-laws, her own family, her husband, and their child have created an extremely independent woman who believes in her abilities and potential. Struggling with her difficulties has taught Azar, among other things, about her strengths and power. The woman who did not wear glasses because she wanted to look pretty has come a long way to assert her independence, to confront challenges head on, to make decisions on her own, and to wish for still more in life.

"I Know My Father Will Be There for Me"

Comparing the difficulties that men and women face on a daily basis, some women do not necessarily divide the sexes into two separate groups. Although they realize that society grants men more rights than women, they still believe that not all men are oppressive and not all women are necessarily oppressed. For Sima, difficulty was an inherent part of life. "I believe both sexes can have very difficult lives," she said. "They share so many problems together. I never believed being a good father was easier than being a good mother. I never thought being a good husband was easier than being a good wife. But because this society grants more legal rights to men, perhaps they have an easier life than women." Sima maintained that being a good father, mother, husband, or wife were not easy jobs and that both sexes had to work hard at their roles. One role was not easier or more natural than the other. But the extra rights and privileges that men were entitled to because of their gender were significant. Because of the fact of birth, men were endowed with more social rights, putting women in a disadvantaged position.

Sima, however, claimed that not all men are inclined to use their rights. "You see some men who never use—or I should say, who never misuse—the privileges the society has granted them," Sima said. "They have these rights and they can take advantage of them. But they don't. Why don't they?" In an attempt to answer her questions, Sima came up with two explanations. The first focused on women's hidden power or diplomacy to control their husbands. The second took into account some men's realization of the unfair treatment women endure in society, and therefore their individual efforts to do right when wrong has been committed.

> When you see men who do not take advantage of their rights, who are good fathers and husbands, you come to think that their wives must be very clever. Even without the support of the legal system, these women have managed to have so much control over their husbands, to get them to take them and their needs into account. Or perhaps it is not the wives who are clever. Rather, it is the men themselves who have realized that society has been unjust to women. They therefore are motivated to be fair to their wives out of their own volition.

Between the two explanations, Sima was inclined to accept the first. "Because of the large number of unhappy women I see, I conclude that it is not the men who themselves have decided to be fair to their wives on their own. Rather, it is those extraordinary diplomatic women who have been able to control their husbands, to teach them to be fair and just." Whether Sima's conclusion is correct or not, what is significant is that, in the end, she is reluctant to credit those men who have tried to be fair. They did it because of their wives' wit and diplomacy; they did it because they were pawns at the hands of the wives; they did it because they were steered into fairness. Although Sima acknowledged that some men, albeit a small number, were fair to the women in the family, the men's motivation to be fair remains a big question.

While some women did not separate the roles of men and women, others distinguished between various aspects of family life and the differing involvement in it of men and women. Sousan believed that men's lives are more difficult because they are responsible for providing for their families. "I feel more relaxed in my life because I know my father would be there for me if I needed him," Sousan said. "That sense of security and support is not there for my husband. He works very hard to provide for his family. He doesn't have anybody to rely on." Sousan, however, distinguished between the financial aspects of providing for a family and the emotional dimension of family life. From an emotional standpoint, she believed her life was more difficult than her husband's. "I am highly involved with the children and worry about them more," she said. "He is more detached and believes that they will do something with their lives eventually. I cannot accept that and believe in doing the best I can for the children."

From Sousan's point of view, to be a man, a father, and a provider was a difficult task. Having to face the world, to overcome work challenges, and to fight economic insecurity put tremendous pressure on men. As a woman, she was glad she did not have to endure such hardships. Furthermore, the fact that her father could be relied on enabled her to feel safe and secure. Her father's economic resources gave her a sense of control over and contentment with her life. However, that sense of comfort and control was absent when it came to emotional attachments and her children's futures. Emotionally involved with her children, ambitious about their future, she believed her personal efforts would not necessarily yield guaranteed outcomes. Her children's future worried her—a worry not shared by her husband.

"He Is a Rational Man"

The kind of relationship fathers develop with their children has serious implications for the mothers. Maintaining a detached attitude or being overly strict with the children has critical consequences for all the family members. A potential source of problem in marriage is the different values and attitudes parents hold in relation to raising children. Some fathers, especially those from traditional backgrounds, adhere to more conventional attitudes. Having suffered from societal constraints and lack of support to engage in a variety of activities, many mothers try to provide the best for their children. However, in order to do so, they may have to fight the father/husband, who may have other ideals for his children.

When a husband imposes strict rules or maintains a detached attitude, a wife may be put in the position either to protect her children against their

domineering father or to try to establish a more balanced relationship between the children and the father. Some mothers take an active step, attempting to do away with the distance in order to bridge the gap between
fathers and children. For others, the distance further attaches the child to the
mother, turning the father and the children into virtual strangers.

Mothers often act as emotional bridges between fathers and children.
Caught between the two, they empathize with both sides and try to act as
communication channels. Realizing the significance of a strong relationship
between fathers and children, many mothers see fathers as being incapable of
establishing close ties with their sons and daughters. At times, differing character traits of the parents tend to complement each other. When a mother
cannot say no to her child, the father often is able to oblige his children.
Some mothers are too close to their children to act as the voice of authority
when it comes to constructive advice.

Sara could not disagree with her daughter regarding her choice of a college and had to rely on her husband to keep her daughter from attending a
college in another city.

> I couldn't say no. She was crying the whole time and she wanted to go to
> that college. But he said she can't go and that was that. My husband is a good
> father. He makes good decisions regarding rational issues, but when it comes
> to emotional matters, for example, to relationships with his children, he is at
> a loss. As a father he has been able to provide a decent living standard for his
> children and has been able to advise them well regarding which majors to
> choose and what to study. He, however, hasn't been able to connect to his
> children on an emotional level.

Sara is the link, the bridge between her children and their father. "I ask him,
'How much has this child talked to you for the last two months?' He says,
"Very little. I don't want to talk to her till she comes to talk to me.' I have to
work on him for so long so that he eventually comes around and starts talking to his children."

A strong relationship between parents and between parents and their children leads to a more constructive family environment, in which the children feel comfortable going to their parents for their needs and problems. But when fathers are unable to establish a close relationship with their children, likely because of a lack of a strong relationship between the men and their own fathers, maintaining an emotional link in the family becomes the women's responsibility. They are the ones who at times remind the fathers that they need to talk to their own children, to listen to them, and to be kind to them. For many fathers, their fatherhood is fulfilled as long as they have provided economically for their families. Not having had a close and intimate relationship with their own fathers, many fathers do not know how to establish an intimate relationship with their children. Fortunately, Sara's husband listens to her. "He has a lot of problems with intimate relationships," she said. "We talk a lot about different issues. He listens, and because he is a rational person, he is capable of listening when he thinks something makes sense. He even tells me to remind him what kind of decisions he should make regarding certain issues."

"My Mother Always Calmed Me Down"

Sara was proud of being a woman. However, she believed that women are seriously discriminated against in society. Major sources of discrimination for her and many others are the family laws that grant men unlimited rights. Men's willingness to take advantage of those laws also exacerbated the situation. One such law, which seriously hurts women and forces them to stay in unhappy marriages, is the child-custody law that allows divorced women to keep their sons and daughters only up to the ages of two and seven respectively.

> I think one of the reasons that Iranian women don't file easily for divorce is that they lose everything in divorce. They won't get their children; they lose their house. No salary. The loss of children hurts even those women who happen to be economically independent. The impact of this law is traumatic

for women. Iranian men know the women's vulnerable point and they seriously take advantage of this right. The men are safe and secure in their position. The laws in this country collaborate with the social customs and enable men to act more freely, to be more self-indulgent and less understanding. This disempowers women to the point where they forgo their rights. The woman has no option but to submit, to surrender because she doesn't want to lose her children.

Jasmin believed that it was not only the child-custody rights that hurt women but also women's modesty. "Women can't pack up and leave," Jasmin said. "Where do they have to go, to their fathers? Women have to make so many sacrifices if they want to keep the family together. Women's tendency to keep all family problems hidden, their belief in holding the family together at whatever cost, enables men to do more harm, to cause more emotional and psychological injury." Jasmin believed that, if there was a problem, women tend at most to go to their own parents. But she knew also of cases in which women had actually gone to their in-laws, stayed with them instead of their own parents, and told them about their son's mischief. "By doing something like that she questioned their son's actions and their upbringing, exposed his wrongdoings, and laid everything open in front of his parents," Jasmin said.

For many women, such acts, which revealed their marital problems and disclosed them to their in-laws, represent extreme immodesty. For Jasmin, such acts reeked of indecency.

Such shameless acts enable women to succeed. But if you are a demure and bashful woman who tries to avoid any embarrassment for all those involved, who doesn't want to take her problems to either her or his family, then sooner or later the men grasp that. They find out that this woman is not going to challenge or even object to their acts. Women's unlimited prudence in these matters is detrimental to both husbands and wives. When absolute power is not checked or kept in control, it has the potential to be ruinous.

A lot of men are not even interested in keeping the child in case of divorce. They keep telling the women that they can have the children, but they know that no matter what they do or how much pressure they exert, the women will stay in the marriage and are not going to file for divorce. They know that whatever they do is going to remain in the family; their misconduct is not going to leak out anywhere. That is the price of decency and self-restraint on the part of women.

Women are not brought up to defend their rights; instead they were brought up believing that they should hold the family together at any cost, that if there was a divorce it is their fault. It is the women who hold the family unit together. A good woman can make it work. Such beliefs have held families together, but they certainly have not guaranteed contentment and happiness. They have not produced mutual understanding and respect. Such beliefs have allowed men to reign supreme without having to question their privileges. Born to believe they are entitled to more liberty and authority, many men have enjoyed a privileged position in their families regardless of their class backgrounds.

According to Mina, women were not innocent parties in this game of socializing and preparing their sons and daughters to be future men and women. Mina held women strongly accountable for granting their sons more rights and privileges than their daughters, for perpetuating a system that has hindered women's equality. Acknowledging the role of other socialization factors such as the educational system, the media, and religion, both Mina and Jasmin nonetheless believed that women are capable of bringing forth constructive change. There was certainly a sense of self-criticism and blame. "It is our fault," Mina said. "It is us who socialize our men, who treat them like that, who value them highly, more than what they deserve. It is both the family and the larger society that grant men too many unwarranted rights and carte blanche."

Jasmin and Mina questioned not only the role the mothers play as agents of socialization, they also examined women-to-women relationships, i.e., friendships and colleague relationships. They argued that, while men expect submission and conformity in marriage, women friends and mothers encourage compliance and deference. Mina explained. "After so many years of marriage and a world of experience, my mother should be in a position to give me some constructive advice. But I see that even my own mother or others with the same or more experience are pushing me toward a more submissive position, that you should bend more, that you should tolerate more. These acts embolden men. The women who themselves have suffered a lifetime, who have felt oppressed all their lives, push me to be more lenient, more submissive, more accepting."

Given the stigma attached to divorce, many mothers have encouraged their daughters to accept suffering and to abide further. Perhaps they did this because they knew there was no return for their daughters, because they had gone through the same path many times over—knowing only too well that there was no option for them but to persevere and that they would survive one way or another.

Enduring a life of oppression, mothers know that their daughters could survive it too; perhaps mothers do not consider that the movement for change has to start somewhere, that there is hope for change and for more happiness and mutual understanding in marriage. Perhaps much has to be undone before anything positive can be built. But uncertainties attached to divorce; the loss of respect and honor among family, friends, and neighbors; the fact that a daughter's divorce reflects to some degree her family's failure and that society is not prepared to reabsorb unattached divorced women, that the women have to go back to their parents and again lose their independent status; all these factors are too much to endure after a lifetime of survival against all the odds. For many mothers, their own marriage was a struggle and they endured it; in a way, their marriage was their success story. If they were successful at survival, they feel that their daughters could be, too.

Mina's mother always urged her to submit to her husband's wishes.

"At the beginning of my marriage, my mother always calmed me down. That was because of her personality and character. She couldn't act any other way. She was not a happy or a successful person in her marriage. She couldn't give me any advice but to submit, to accept things as they were. But she did that unconsciously. Now that I am talking about these things it is because I have read a few books. It has taken me twenty years eventually to understand how I should treat a man."

More often than not, the women's mothers had entered arranged marriages. For their generation, mutual understanding and shared interests were not the criteria for a successful marriage. Rather, marriage was viewed as an inevitable event, perhaps the most significant rite of passage to adulthood. Love was not a basis for marriage; it was the stuff of poetry and literature. Successful marriages were marked by economic prosperity, family unity, and the raising of healthy children. Husbands and wives acted according to traditional precepts, each playing their role judiciously.

In playing their roles, the parents also socialized their children into specific male and female roles. Teaching their children gender-specific attributes, the parents presumably guaranteed the eventual success of their children. However, with time came change and divergent expectations; those same values that at one point had secured the survival of a marriage seemed now to undermine it. If traditional values were guarantees against separation and divorce for those of a generation earlier, these values now guaranteed unhappiness and discontent for some women and, perhaps, for some men.

Mina believed that women willingly and blindly award men with certain privileges and rights. "It is us who encourage men to act this way. Why? Because we were raised in families where our mothers never struggled, never objected. My mother never fathomed that she had any rights in her marriage. When I married, I gave my husband the same rights and privileges. I gave him some rights myself. He was young like me, too. I gave him many rights because I didn't know any better."

Of course, Mina is quick to add that she was not completely submissive. "I sometimes objected, too, but not to much avail. I always tell my husband that you were not lucky in your marriage either, that you should have married a girl who could always say 'yes,' agreeing with you, willing to follow you."

Obviously, Mina did not always submit to her husband's rule. At the beginning of her marriage she saw her husband as being entitled to many privileges, and she therefore handed over to him many rights and liberties.

While she conferred many rights, she also objected; she granted privileges, but she expected some recognition in return. The relationship, however, was not mutual. After years of marriage, she found herself in a constant position of giving; giving was her perpetual duty and obligation, so that feeling deprived and neglected was the end result.

In addressing men's power, Jasmin and Mina brought up multifaceted issues. While the detrimental impacts of laws and social customs were recognized, factors such as the role other women played in relation to each other were also scrutinized. It was not only mothers who never advised their daughters to rebel or to stand up for their rights; women friends also played a similar if not a more detrimental role. In Iranian culture, as in many other traditional cultures, women comprise a support group for each other; they are there for each other in times of happiness and hardship. But there are certainly limitations to this system. Not empowered in their own personal relationships, the women do not have much power to give to each other. Thirsty for power, the women may ally themselves with the men, hoping the alliance would render them a minimal power. "Unfortunately, a lot of women do not support each other," Jasmin said. "If they don't have certain rights in their marriage, they do not want to see other women enjoying those rights either." Jasmin recounted the case of a couple among her friends.

There is this husband who helps his wife with housework and cooking. All the women friends ridicule the husband. They all bad-mouth her, their own friend, as the most tyrannical person, as a poor housewife. The men do their talk behind [our backs]. My husband tells me they all say if they were married to her, they wouldn't stay with her for even one day.

Why do we women tend to undermine other women like that? We all know she goes to work early in the morning. There is no law legislating that the women should do the ironing, cooking, and cleaning. When this couple is not present at our gatherings, everybody is ridiculing the husband. I believe this is a betrayal; we are betraying ourselves. As a woman I should think what a nice guy who helps his wife around the house.

Is he helping his wife or actually putting in equal hours for his own family?

"A Society That Believes Only the Body Should Be Taken Care of Has a Serious Problem"

Even if strict gender roles were functional at some point, adherence to these roles may in the long run carry the seeds of discontent and eventual change. Successful or not, some women have felt the necessity to push for change. Others may not have felt the need to press for change. Mina criticized gender-role socialization.

> Unfortunately, in our society, the culture teaches Iranian women that they are born to serve their husbands and their children, to clean, to cook, and to iron. She does not have much understanding about life. She doesn't have any other goal in life. She is not familiar with studying, with reading. Those who have studied more learn about their rights. A woman who is not a good cook, who does not meet the dominant standards, stands out among other women. Obviously, she is inadequate at her most important job; she has failed not only her husband but also her children. Even my daughter asks me how come I am not like other women.
>
> There are only a limited number of Iranian women who take themselves and their interests seriously, who pay attention to themselves as individuals, who try to educate themselves beyond the formal education they have received, who try to be open-minded.

An attempt to broaden one's horizons beyond the wifely/motherly duties seemed to be an important goal for Mina. This tendency not only was evident among women but also was voiced in some television programs that criticized women's conspicuous concern with wifely duties. One particular show criticized those programs that channel women into wifely duties and instead emphasized other aspects of life and overall advancement for women. Jasmin recounted one such program. "You turn the TV on and there are cooking classes: How to make your dinner table more colorful, what to cook, how to cook." According to Jasmin, the woman behind the TV camera was saying, " 'Ladies, Imam [referring to the Ayatollah Khomeini] hasn't said that all life is about eating.' What happened to your enlightenment? What happened to your spirituality? What are your talents? Is your talent only in cooking more colorful dishes?"

But Jasmin was careful not to downgrade the significant role women play as mothers and wives; her criticism was not directed at those who devoted their lives to full-time housewifery. Rather, her criticism was aimed at the system of thought that limited women's existence to only such activities.

> If a woman saw her only function and expertise in cooking, then that is fine. Good for her because that is how she sees her world. That is how she relates to her surrounding environment. But if somebody wanted to use her time and energy on spiritual aspects of life, on expanding her horizons, on the creative development of her children or that of her husband, then what do we do? We can't call a person who is more interested in educating herself, in uplifting her spirit, a failure. A society that believes only the body should be taken care of has a serious problem.

Jasmin was looking for other ways of being; she was looking for a space for those women whose existence was not solely defined by motherly or wifely duties. "Such women are not rejecting motherhood or the responsibilities that go with it," she explained. "Rather, they are searching other ways of personal fulfillment, where they can lead happier lives with their husbands and children."

Like Jasmin, Mina believed that women's fulfillment should be defined in broader terms that would allow women to explore their diverse dimensions. "You have a right to live for yourself to a certain degree, to make the effort to cultivate new skills," Mina said. "The same is true about my husband, who leaves the house in the morning to go to work, but manages to do the kind of things that interest him, too. He reads his evening newspaper. I should have the same right to read my books, too. Not all my time should be spent in the service of my family."

Needless to say, one of Mina's hobbies was reading. She found reading to be educational and personally fulfilling, but making time to read required a certain degree of struggle.

> I never hide my interests in reading books. My friends tell me that you do your housework in the morning and when your husband comes home in the evening you sit and read your own books. Most women do their own work in the morning and when their husbands come home they go to the kitchen. I don't like to conceal anything from my husband. Hiding my interests would make me a coward, as if I am scared of him, that I am a weak person. I had to struggle a lot to gain certain rights. At times, I felt very weak, beaten at the struggle, but I did not give up.

As a proud person who did not believe in manipulation in order to gain certain rights in her marriage, Mina tried different strategies to gain power. Resorting to silence and deference did not grant her the freedom to cultivate her own interests. Ten years of marriage eventually brought an end to silence and deference. She explained.

> When I think about my marriage, I divide it into three periods. There was a period of silence, absolute silence. This period took about ten years. I tried not to talk, not to object to anything. Then there was the period of struggle or rebellion. I remember there was a time I told my husband, "I want to be me." He said, "What do you mean? You mean you haven't been yourself till now?" "No. So far, I have been what you wanted me to be. I am tired of that now." That took about five to six years. It was a daily struggle. We had a lot of problems, many conflicts. I even considered divorce. But now things have changed. I think he has recognized certain things. I have gained certain things, only certain rights, though.

Another area that Mina touched on was the situation of women before and after the 1979 Revolution. Comparing the two periods, she summed up the differences.

> In the past, women were mainly concerned about their looks; they were interested in presenting themselves. The only option women had was to exhibit themselves as objects, to dress, to look beautiful. This Revolution definitely affected the society. People are reading a lot more. They are interested in studying and in discussions; they want to educate themselves. If you ask me which period I like better, I definitely choose the present situation. Although so much freedom has been taken away from us, like why should I wear this uniform in this heat? Why should I be completely covered in dark colors on summer days when the temperature is so high?

Tehran's heat in summer months can be oppressively hot. Having to be covered during hot summer days—particularly in dark colors—is quite uncomfortable for both employed women and housewives. The combination of the summer heat and mandatory laws regarding veiling exacerbates the situation for some women. However, comparing the two regimes, Mina continued by saying that,

> The previous regime didn't offer us anything, either. Women have entered the public realm much more. Their roles have changed. In the past, they entered the larger society because of their looks, appearance, or the connections they had. But now women do play an active role because of their expertise and knowledge. Of course, there were women in the old regime who were also very talented, skillful, and played major social roles. But that has become a lot more prevalent these days. I certainly prefer this government to the previous regime when it comes to women's representation and participation in the society.

Change is coming slowly but surely. Talking about her daughter, Mina believed that the young generation of women is going to have a different lifestyle and mode of interaction with men.

I am forty years old and I realize I know much less than my daughter, who is only seventeen. She is a leader, a forerunner. When I confront a problem I see she is more rational than I am. She looks at things from a more logical standpoint than I do. Today's children belong to the age of technology and change. We lived more with our feelings and that's why we failed. But this generation is no longer approaching life with their feelings. The marriages I see around me today are very different from my generation's marriages. Both boys and girls have changed dramatically. In twenty years, it will be the men who will be complaining about women. Our girls have changed so much. They are a lot more open-minded. They are aware of their rights. The women easily divorce now. They know more. They are different from my generation. They are not like us.

Acknowledging the loss of freedom and the limitations imposed on women, Mina nevertheless pointed out that the two-decades-old government has brought positive results for women. For her, the changes in women's presentation were indicative of progress, of a step forward. She credited the new government with creating a new generation of women who tend to be more rational and challenging, exhibit awareness of their rights, and are more willing to press for change in both the private and the public domains. This new generation carries with it new hopes and dreams; they are ready to challenge and to be challenged. "This is an explosion period," Mina said. "Maybe we have reached the stage where our daughters are saying, 'Enough is enough.' "

"Veiling Is a Problem for Those of Us Who Were Raised Unveiled"

Tara was not interested in talking about the problems and difficulties women experience. Rather, she preferred to address change and what women are capable of doing. She said that being a woman has never been an impediment in her life. "I always have done whatever I have wanted to do. I don't think a government can have a strong influence on people's lives. The impact of the government is more cosmetic at best."

Tara compared the pre- and post-Revolutionary periods.

During the previous government, many women could achieve higher positions, but now their advancement is limited. Many never are promoted. But the impact you have on your society is not only through your position. After I quit my work, I worked voluntarily for different organizations. It was very satisfying. If I ever believed in a cause I worked for it. I worked with people who had lost their livelihood due to earthquakes. My gender never has stopped me from working in these areas. I never have had a serious problem doing what I wanted. I have worked with the poor, with patients in hospitals, those who need emotional support, be they male or female. My gender never has hindered me in what I wanted to do.

Tara discussed in detail some of the changes she had observed during the past two decades. The ability to participate in street demonstrations, work with different educational and community art programs offered by the government, and the increasing number of women's magazines were some of the examples she discussed in detail. "Now women can do a lot of things that they couldn't do in the past," Tara said. For her, it was the mere experience of gathering and demonstrating their unity for a cause that mattered.

Maybe the reason women go to the streets and demonstrate is not good or valid, but what is important is that now they have the experience. In the past, the women's families never allowed them to do such things. Parents and husbands never allowed their womenfolk to participate in street demonstrations for any cause. Furthermore, the women themselves never fathomed the idea of playing such active social roles. After the Revolution, such barriers that were rooted in traditional values and familial expectations were removed. These obstacles were invisible but they had very strong effects on how we lived our lives as women. The societal and familial barriers were there without ever being acknowledged or recognized.

The Revolution had involved women of all classes; its impact, the enthusiasm it created, touched all those involved. Tara explained.

> If a taxi driver did not allow his wife to play a socially active role before the Revolution, that changed because he heard it on the radio time and again that women have had demonstrations. Therefore, going to demonstrations, playing an active role in the society, became normal—a part of everyday life. In the past, women were allowed to become taxi drivers or work in gas stations. That was reported like a big achievement, a sign of progress. But there was wife abuse when the women got back home.

Tara related the story of a friend she had met at a community school. The woman, who was married to a taxi driver, came from a strictly traditional background. Even after a period of friendship, her husband still did not allow her to visit Tara at her house. "She doesn't have permission to come to my place. But she is allowed to go to the community school because it belongs to the government. She is forty years old. The first semester, her husband dropped her off every time and then picked her up. The second semester she came herself. The third semester she could ask him whether it is okay to go and visit her friend at her house for an hour. This is a considerable achievement for a woman from her background."

Tara argued that it was the masses of people who started the Revolution and the women were very involved from the very beginning. This massive involvement paved the way for many changes, on a fundamental level.

> Many doors are open to women. For example, women artists exhibit their work as a group. That was unheard of during the previous regime. Maybe they could do it, but it was once for ever. But now they do it so often. In the past, we had women in high positions as a form of show-off, window dressing, to show other countries that we have women in positions of power, that we are comparable with advanced countries. Now you go to an art exhibition, even in poor neighborhoods, and you find women artists who have put up a show together. That means that this woman has had the permission to leave her husband's or her parents' house and do art work and to organize an

exhibition. That is a tremendous achievement. Governmental support and a belief in their own abilities and skills have encouraged women to play a much more active role on a social level.

As Tara saw the conditions,

Women have come together as a group to teach different skills to the un-skilled. For example, those women who know about carpet weaving go to the surrounding areas and villages and teach this art to rural and village women. Then those women are encouraged to go and teach their skills to women who live in villages farther away. These kinds of activities never happened in the past. Some art institutions or community schools do a fabulous job. Each institution is teaching so many art classes, the kind of crafts that women could use and benefit from. Many of these institutions are in poor areas and reach out only to those who don't have easy access to such facilities.

Not only different arts and crafts are encouraged, but different cities have also opened new sport clubs. Now you can say that many facilities are missing in these clubs, but what is significant is that these places bring women together. It is okay for women to go to these places, leave their houses, parents, husbands, and children and join these facilities.

Interested in women's issues, Tara had followed the development of different programs and facilities for women over the past two decades. Her focus was on the more underprivileged women, women from traditional and poor backgrounds who had lived strict lives. The Revolution allowed some of these women to find a voice, to participate in social and political activities, and to seek jobs.

The sex-segregated policy of the government created many jobs for women and pulled them into the labor force. The Revolutionary slogan to emphasize the plight of the poor and the underprivileged encouraged many to venture out to explore what the new government was offering them. When women's rights were advocated within an Islamic framework, women's issues were brought to the surface.

Before the Revolution we had only a couple of magazines that were for women and they were junk. How many magazines do we have after the Revolution? And all of them are for women and about women and family. When you talk about family, you are talking about women. Newspapers and magazines are all writing material that is related to women's rights. Women lawyers who work with these publications do take into account women's legal and social rights. When you mention the word women in your talk, women realize that they are taken into account one way or another. They understand that they exist as members of society. Even though the ruling government may not grant women their total freedom, the women will ask for what they can. The impact will be much stronger and longer lasting because you have had to fight and struggle for your rights instead of being handed certain privileges.

Like Mina, Tara believed that the last two decades have brought a high degree of social awareness, creating a new generation of women who are more aware of their rights. Women (and men) have endured twenty years of hardship due to Revolutionary turmoil, a prolonged war with Iraq, and unstable economic conditions. This has enhanced their sense of urgency and political awakening. Tara explained the situation.

Women have become a lot more socially aware in the last twenty years. They have advanced a broader perspective. For example, now there is a lot more divorce in Tehran. Women no longer look at men the way they used to. In the past, whatever a man said, it went. That has changed dramatically. There is no doubt that all the family laws are detrimental to women. They benefit men and harm women. Men have child custody; economic dependence is a serious problem for women; the women don't have a place to go.

In many cases, the parents are not willing to take their daughter and the children back because of economic problems and social stigma. Unlike more advanced countries, this country does not provide services for domestic violence. There are no social programs for widows and single mothers. But because there is a need, it has to be met one way or another. I am not talking as an optimistic person. It is rather a matter of supply and demand. When the women's community is in need of support and protection, not only women will arise to ask for change, there will also be a group of powerful people who will hear them and are willing to create some change. Sooner or later the laws of the country will change to benefit women.

Having been married to get away from her mother's constant surveillance, now a mother of two and in love with her husband, Tara embraces life and its challenges. She believed in women's strength, in their ability to push forward to bring forth improvement in women's lives. Tara criticized society for not having cultivated women's potential, for not allowing women to contribute to the making of their society according to their capabilities.

Women are a tremendous source of power, but their potential hardly is used in this country. A woman has so much power; she is like an atomic bomb; she is that powerful, a power that never has been used. The Revolution brought to the surface women's issues. Women and their concerns have gained tremendous significance. It is like a flood. The flood is roaring; its pace is horrendous. Nothing can stop this tide. Laws may be passed against women's rights, but they will have a short-term impact. The only direction is forward. There are and will be victims for sure. But women have started to demand their rights and they will get them. They will not be satisfied with limited gains here and there.

Like Mina, Tara believed that the seeds of change have been planted.

The younger generation is going to be the agent of change. From the very beginning when they opened their eyes they saw that women demonstrated on television. It is correct that all those demonstrators wore black chadors. What is more important is that they were all women, demanding something. This generation has seen women playing an active role and has accepted that. Women of this generation believe that if they want something they have to struggle for it. The real energy and power is in the hands of this generation. They will become tomorrow's women. Veiling is a problem for those of us who were raised unveiled. Veiling is not a problem for those children who were raised with it. It is not going to stop them. I believe a piece of material is not going to stop women's progress. Even if tomorrow a law is passed to enforce the chador on all women, nothing is going to stop the movement that is created among women. Television programs and other public media are addressing the needs of the younger generation. I see success in tomorrow's children and today's youth. My eighteen-year-old daughter feels she has nothing less than the species called male.

Let women speak, utter their words, and you hear thunder.

Notes

Bibliography

Notes

1. Introduction

1. While talking to my American friend who had recently traveled to Iran, I realized that this is not a tendency unique to Iranians. He reported that, when he traveled to China in the past, he always claimed to be Canadian instead of American. During his last trip to Iran, he decided to disclose his true national identity and reported that people showed no hostility when they found out that he was American. Many actually felt very comfortable sharing their thoughts with him. I have noticed the same tendency among many recent immigrants from Eastern Europe and the former Soviet Union. When asked about their country of origin, many answer Europe instead of naming the exact country where they come from. The war in Bosnia, Serbia, and other republics has made many people uncomfortable about their national identity. Therefore, Europe comes to displace their country of origin.

2. Judith E. Tucker, *Arab Women: Old Boundaries, New Frontiers* (Bloomington and Indianapolis: Indiana Univ. Press, 1983).

3. An exception is Elizabeth W. Fernea, *In Search of Islamic Feminism: One Woman's Global Journey* (London: Anchor Books Doubleday, 1998). See also Elizabeth W. Fernea and Robert A. Fernea, *The Arab World: Personal Encounters* (London: Anchor Books Doubleday, 1985).

4. Badr al-Moluk Bamdad, *From Darkness into Light: Women's Emancipation in Iran,* trans. F. R. C. Bagely (Hicksville, N.Y.: Exposition Press, 1977). See also Guity Nashat, "Women in Pre-Revolutionary Iran: A Historical Overview," in *Women and Revolution in Iran,* ed. Guity Nashat (Boulder, Colo.: Westview, 1983), 5–35.

5. Janet Afary, "On the Origins of Feminism in Early 20th Century Iran," *Journal of Women's History* 1, no. 2 (1984): 65–87. See also Janet Afary, "The Debate on Women's Liberation in the Iranian Constitutional Revolution, 1906–1911," in *Expanding the Boundaries of Women's History: Essays on Women in the Third World,* ed. Cheryl Johnson-Odim and Margaret Strobel (Bloomington: Indiana Univ. Press, 1993) 101–21; and Ervand Abrahamian, *Iran Between Two Revolutions* (Princeton, N.J.: Princeton Univ. Press,

1982); Mangol Bayat-Phillip, "Women and Revolution in Iran, 1905–1911," in *Women in the Muslim World,* ed. Lois Beck and Nikki Keddie (Cambridge, Mass.: Harvard Univ. Press, 1978), 295–308.

6. Jack Zipes, *Arabian Nights: The Marvels and Wonders of the Thousand and One Nights,* adapted by Jack Zipes (New York: Signet Classics, 1991).

7. For a select sample of research on family planning in Iran, see Akbar Aghajanian, "Family Planning and Contraceptive Use in Iran, 1967–1992," *International Family Planning Perspectives* 20, no. 2 (June 1994): 66–69; Homa Hoodfar, "Population Policy and Gender Equity in Post-Revolutionary Iran," in *Family, Gender, and Population in the Middle East: Policy in Context,* ed. Carla Makhlouf Obermeyer (Cairo: American Univ. in Cairo Press, 1995), 105–35; Homa Hoodfar, "Bargaining with Fundamentalism: Women and the Politics of Population Control in Iran," *Reproductive Health Matters* 8 (Nov. 1996): 30–39; Yasmin L. Mossavar-Rahmani, "Family Planning in Post-Revolutionary Iran," in Nashat, ed., *Women and Revolution in Iran,* 253–62; and Carla Makhlouf Obermeyer, "Reproductive Choice in Islam: Gender and State in Iran and Tunisia," *Studies in Family Planning* 25, no. 1 (Jan./Feb. 1994): 41–51. For studies on marriage, see Haleh Afshar, "Women, Marriage, and the State in Iran," in *Women, State, and Ideology,* ed. Haleh Afshar (Basingstoke: Macmillan, 1987), 70–86; Janet Bauer, "Demographic Change, Women, and the Family in a Migrant Neighborhood in Tehran," in *Women and the Family in Iran,* ed. Asghar Fathi (Leiden: E. J. Brill, 1985), 158–86; Jacquiline Rudolph Touba, "The Effects of the Iranian Revolution on Women and the Family in Iran: Some Preliminary Observations," in Fathi, ed., *Women and the Family in Iran,* 131–50. For an analysis of temporary marriage, see Allameh Tabataba'i and Seyyed Hossein Nasr, "Mut'ah or Temporary Marriage," in *Shi'ism: Doctorines, Thought, and Spirituality,* ed. Seyyed Hossein Nasr et al. (Albany, N.Y.: State Univ. of New York, 1988), 213–16; and Shahla Haeri, *Law of Desire: Temporary Marriage in Shi'i Iran* (Syracuse, N.Y.: Syracuse Univ. Press, 1989). For a general analysis of women's changing position in Iran in the twentieth century, see the following: Farah Azari, *Women of Iran: The Conflict with Fundamentalist Islam* (London: Ithaca Press, 1983); William R. Darrow, "Women's Place and the Place of Women in the Iranian Revolution," in *Women, Religion, and Social Change,* ed. Yvonne Y. Haddad and Ellison B. Findly (New York: State Univ. of New York, 1985), 307–19; Haleh Esfandiari, *Reconstructed Lives: Women and Iran's Islamic Revolution* (Washington, D.C.: Woodrow Wilson Center, 1997); Adele Ferdows, "Women and the Islamic Revolution," *International Journal of Middle East Studies* 15, no. 2 (1983): 283–98; Homa Hoodfar, "The Women's Movement in Iran: Women at the Crossroad of Secularization and Islamization," *Women Living Under Muslim Laws,* The Women's Movement Series 1, no. 6 (1999): 12–18; Haideh Moghissi, "Women, Modernization, and Revolution in Iran," *The Review of Radical Political Economics* 23, no. 3/4 (1991): 205–33; Nesta Ramazani, "Women in Iran: The Revolutionary Ebb and Flow," *Middle East Journal* 47, no. 3 (1993): 409–28; Hamideh Sedghi, "Women, the State, and Development: Appraising Secular and Religious Gender Politics in Iran," in *The Gendered New World Order: Militarism, Development, and the Environment,* ed. Jennifer Turpin and Lois Ann Lorentzen (New York: Routledge, 1996), 113–26; and Hammed Shahidian, "National and International Aspects of Feminist Movements: The Example of the Iranian Revolution of 1978–79," *Critique: Journal for Critical Studies of the Middle East* 2 (1993): 33–53.

8. Janet Bauer, "Women, the Veil, and the Islamic Revolution in Iran," *Women in Anthropology: Symposium Papers 1979 and 1980,* Elizabeth J. Tudon (publication coordinator), Sacramento Anthropological Society (Sacramento, CA: California State Univ., 1983), 120–27; see also Anne H. Betteridge, "To Veil or Not to Veil: A Matter of Protest or Policy," in Nashat, ed., *Women and Revolution in Iran,* 109–28; Patricia Higgins, "Women in the Islamic Republic of Iran: Legal, Social, and Ideological Changes," *Signs: Journal of Women in Culture and Society* 10, no. 3 (1985): 477–94; Faegheh Shirazi-Mohajan, "The Politics of Clothing in the Middle East: The Case of Hijab in Post-Revolutionary Iran," *Critique: Journal for Critical Studies of the Middle East* 2 (1993): 54–63; Shirazi-Mohajan, "A Dramaturgical Approach to Hijab in Post-Revolutionary Iran," *Critique: Journal for Critical Studies of the Middle East* 2 (1995): 35–52; and "No to Veil!" *Women and Revolution,* Special Issue on Iran, 19 (1979): 1–2, 10.

2. Starry Nights

1. Louisa May Alcott, *Little Women,* 1868 (New York: Collier Books, 1962); Simone de Beauvoir, *The Second Sex,* trans. and ed. H. M. Parshley, 1952 (New York: Alfred A. Knopf, 1993); Charles Dickens, *Great Expectations,* 1861 (Oxford: Oxford Univ. Press, 1999); Anton Pavlovich Chekhov, *The Cherry Orchard,* 1936 (London: Eyre Methuen, 1978); and Fyodor Dostoyevsky, *Crime and Punishment,* trans. and annotated Richard Pevear and Larissa Volukhonsky, 1866 (New York: Vintage Books, 1993).

2. I experienced the same level of trust when I was conducting interviews with African American household workers for my doctoral dissertation. Again, because I did not have ties to the larger society or to the African American community, I contacted several people to inquire whether they could help me to secure contacts with African American household workers. This technique proved successful, and a couple of contacts led to others. People began introducing friends and relatives for me to interview. The women I interviewed were open and frank. Although they found it odd that a foreigner, especially an Iranian student, wanted to know about their work, they openly shared their work experiences with me. I believe the fact that I was a foreigner enabled them to open up to me easily; the usual racial and cultural barriers between whites and African Americans did not exist between us.

4. Ties That Bind: Mothers and Daughters

1. It must be noted that, while men entered arranged marriage blindly, not having met or known their wives, they nevertheless had the right to easy divorce. The religious and customary law gave absolute power to a man either to divorce a woman who was not approved or to marry a second wife if the financial situation allowed.

2. Nancy Chodorow, *The Reproduction of Mothering: Psychoanalysis and the Sociology of Gender* (Berkeley: Univ. of California Press, 1978), 39.

3. Ruth Wodak and Muriel Schultz, *The Language of Love and Guilt: Mother-Daughter Relationship from a Cross-Cultural Perspective* (Philadelphia, Pa.: John Benjamin Publishing, 1986), 4.

4. The relationship with the mother is the primary source of ego identity, security in the world, and feelings about oneself. Kathie Carlson argues that for many women this primary bond is damaged by a sense of hurt, anger, and longing. Kathie Carlson, *In Her Image: The Unhealed Daughter's Search for Her Mother* (Boston: Shambhala Publications, 1989), 35.

5. Lucy Rose Fischer suggests that it is possible for mothers to perceive their oldest daughters as mature at a relatively young age. Adult-like responsibilities are often thrust upon oldest daughters. Mothers who marry early may see their oldest daughter as being already grown up and something of a peer. Lucy Fischer, *Linked Lives: Adult Daughters and Their Mothers* (New York: Harper and Row Publishers, 1986), 33.

6. Fischer, *Linked Lives,* 35–36.

7. Ibid., 33.

8. Confiding in children happens most often with the oldest daughter and when there are problematic relations with the father. Thus, when there are blatant and ongoing problems between parents, daughters seem to become confidantes to their mothers. Witnesses of their parents' marital discord, daughters are drawn into an emotional alliance with their mothers. Fischer, *Linked Lives,* 29–30.

9. Friday, Nancy. *My Mother My Self: The Daughter's Search for Identity.* (New York: Dell Publishing, 1978), 170–71.

10. Ibid., 171.

11. In a traditional context, children are a guarantee against divorce and maltreatment. It is therefore crucial for the parents to form alliances with the children as protection against such mishaps.

12. Similarly, Friday also records the case of one woman, economically successful but single, who believed that the best present she could give her mother was her marriage.

13. Friday 1978, 358.

14. For an in-depth analysis of divorce laws and practices in Islam and in Iran, see Akbar Aghajanian, "Some Notes on Divorce in Iran," *Journal of Marriage and the Family* 48 (1986): 749–55; Homa Hoodfar, "Women and Personal Status Law: An Interview with Mehranguis Kar," *Middle East Report* 26, no. 1 (1996): 198; Ziba Mir-Hossaini, *Marriage on Trial: Islamic Family Law in Iran and Morocco* (London: I. B. Tauris, 1993); Jamshid Momeni, "Divorce in the Islamic Context: Emphasis on Shi'ite Islam," *Islamic Culture* 60, no. 2 (1986): 1–40; Vida Nassehy, "Female Role and Divorce in Iran," *International Journal of the Sociology of the Family* 21, no. 1 (1991): 53–65; and Behnaz Pakizegi, "Legal and Social Position of Iranian Women," in Lois Beck and Nikki Keddie, eds., *Women in the Muslim World* (Cambridge, Mass.: Harvard Univ. Press, 1978), 216–26.

15. Jessie Bernard has written about the same transformation in the West. The social changes such as improved household technology, increased job opportunities, and smaller families have led to a reexamination of and modifications to the traditional roles of the sexes. See Jessie Bernard, *The Future of Motherhood* (New York: Dial Press, 1974).

16. Fischer, *Linked Lives,* 24.

17. Ibid., 18.

18. Fischer notices the same tendency. Several of the daughters in her study reported that as children they perceived their fathers as being strict and fearsome. Years later, however, they realized that their fathers were not as frightening as they once saw them. Fischer, *Linked Lives*, 18; see also Friday 1978, 171.

19. This happened before the 1979 Revolution when, although rare, it was easier for single women to live by themselves.

20. Friday 1978, 30.

6. Fathers and Daughters: "I Have Yet to See a Man Like My Father"

1. Research shows that fathering is a salient activity and that fathers influence their children in important ways. See Kyle D. Pruett, *The Nurturing Father* (New York: Warner Books, 1987) and Bryan E. Robinson and Robert L. Barret, *The Developing Father: Emerging Roles in Contemporary Society* (New York: Guilford, 1986). In addition, Paul Amato shows that the father-child relationship is closely bound up with the well-being of both daughters and sons. According to Amato, regardless of the quality of the mother-child relationship, children's closeness to their fathers results in a higher degree of happiness and satisfaction. Furthermore, children who are closer to their fathers show fewer signs of distress. Paul Amato, "Father-Child Relations, Mother-Child Relations, and Offspring's Psychological Well-being in Early Adulthood," *Journal of Marriage and the Family* 56 (1994): 1031–42.

2. For a historical account of women's changing roles throughout the twentieth century in Iran, see Janet Afary, "On the Origins of Feminism in Early 20th Century Iran," *Journal of Women's History* 1, no. 2 (1984): 65–87. Mahnaz Afkhami and Erika Friedl, eds., *In the Eye of the Storm: Women in Post-Revolutionary Iran* (Syracuse, N.Y.: Syracuse Univ. Press, 1994); Haleh Afshar, *Islam and Feminism: An Iranian Case Study,* Women's Studies at York Series (New York: St. Martin's, 1998); Shahla Haeri, "Of Feminism and Fundamentalism in Iran and Pakistan," *Contentions* 4, no. 3 (1995): 129–49; Haeri, "Women, Law, and Social Change in Iran," in *Women in Contemporary Muslim Societies,* ed. Jane I. Smith (Lewisburg, Pa.: Bucknell Univ. Press, 1980), 209–34; Guity Nashat, "Women in Pre-Revolutionary Iran: A Historical Overview," in *Women and Revolution in Iran,* ed. Guity Nashat (Boulder, Colo.: Westview, 1983), 5–36; Eliz Sansarian, *The Women's Rights Movement in Iran: Mutiny, Appeasement, and Repression from 1900 to Khomeini 1982* (New York: Praeger, 1983); Azar Tabari, "The Women's Movement in Iran: A Hopeful Prognosis," *Feminist Studies* 12, no. 2 (1986): 342–60; Azar Tabari and Nahid Yeganeh, eds. *In the Shadow of Islam: The Women's Movement in Iran* (London: Zed Press, 1982); and Gholamreza Vatandoust, "The Status of Iranian Women During the Pahlavi Regime," in *Women and the Family in Iran, ed.* Asghar Fathi (Leiden: J. Bridl, 1985); 107–30.

3. Research shows that many children of divorced parents continue to think of their fathers as key figures in their lives, even when the fathers have little contact with them. Judith S. Wallerstein and Sandra Blakeslee, *Second Chance: Men, Women, and Children a Decade after Divorce* (New York: Ticknor and Fields, 1989).

7. Marriage and Courtship: "I Wasn't Looking for a Husband"

1. At traditional gatherings at which the two families meet, it is customary for the families to ask a series of questions about each other. These questions are usually about family background, the economic standing and job prospects of the future husband, the family's place of residence, etc.

2. "Mehr" is a certain amount of money and gold negotiated by the two families to be presented to the bride. The Mehr is, however, seldom exchanged. In actuality, it is supposed to be a protection mechanism against divorce. If cashed it could function as alimony. See also Bagher Saroukhani, "Dower (mahriyeh): A Tradition of Mate Selection in Iran," *International Journal of Sociology of the Family* 9 (1985): 17–26.

3. According to Islamic law, the mother has the right to children's custody up to the age of two years for male children and seven years for female children. After these ages, the children will automatically go to the father. Many women know they will lose their children to their husband upon divorce. In this context, even if women's families are willing to support them and their children and take them in, the women remain afraid of losing their children to a former husband, in-laws, or an uncaring stepmother.

8. Women's Lives, Women's Words: "In Those Days All the Girls Worked"

1. For an extended analysis of women's participation in the labor force in Iran, consult the following sources: Haleh Afshar, "Women and Work in Iran," *Political Studies* 45, no. 5 (1997): 755–67; Parvin Ghorayshi, "Women, Paid-Work, and the Family in the Islamic Republic of Iran," *Journal of Comparative Family Studies* 27 (1996): 453–66; Azadeh Kian, "Gendered Occupation and Women's Status in Post-Revolutionary Iran," *Middle Eastern Studies* 31 (1995): 407–21; Valentine Moghadam, "Women's Employment Issues in Contemporary Iran: Problems and Prospects in the 1990s," *Iranian Studies* 28 (1995): 175–202; and Sally Weiskopf-Bock, "The Working Iranian Mother," in *Women and the Family in Iran,* ed. Asghar Fathi (Leiden: J. Brill, 1985), 187–94.

2. Research shows that involvement and attention from the father are positively associated with children's intellectual development. This is particularly true when fathers show interest in their children's academic development, assist with their homework, and have high educational expectations for their children. See Amato, "Father-Child Relations." In addition, John Snarey contends that paternal involvement during childhood positively affects adult daughters' and sons' educational and occupational mobility. Snarey, *How Fathers Care for the Next Generation,* (Cambridge, Mass.: Harvard Univ. Press, 1993).

3. Research shows it is common to assign more household chores to girls than to boys. Daughters perform more housework both during the week and on the weekends. Jacqueline Goodnow, "Children's Household Work: Its Nature and Functions," *Psychological Bulletin* 103 (1988): 5–26; Lynn K. White and David B. Brinkerhoff, "Children's Work in the Family: Its Significance and Meaning," *Journal of Marriage and the Family* 43 (1981): 789–98.

4. Research in the United States suggests that, although family life has changed, at least one element has remained quite stable: the division of household labor. Even when both husband and wife are working full-time, women still continue to perform most of the housework. Sarah F. Berk, *The Gender Factory: The Appointment of Work in American Households* (New York: Plenum, 1985); Joseph H. Pleck, *Working Wives, Working Husbands* (Beverly Hills, Calif.: Sage, 1985).

5. Compared with mothers, fathers still do relatively little childcare. Sarah F. Berk, *The Gender Factory.* Further research indicates that most of men's time spent in childcare happens when mothers are absent. A. A. Brayfield, "Juggling Jobs and Kids: The Impact of Employment Schedules on Fathers' Caring for Children" (manuscript, 1993).

6. The majority of middle- and upper-class women born around the turn of the century in urban centers did not engage in paid employment. Their fathers and husbands were the sole economic providers of the family. A generation later, a small number of women entered the labor force in predominantly teaching or government-related positions. The trend toward women's increased participation in the labor force continued over time. Husbands' reluctance to spend their wives' salaries on household expenses and resulting encouragement to wives to spend it on what they pleased may have its origin in the Islamic law that allows women to own, to inherit (although half of the men's share), and to dispose of their property as they wish. Some men may have believed in this law, leaving their wives free to practice their right and to dispose of their income and property as they pleased. Needless to say, abuses sometimes occur. There certainly have been a multitude of women whose brothers and fathers never gave them their fair share and many whose husbands took control of the wife's property, taking advantage of their capital and violating women's control over their property. But it is also significant to reiterate the fact that the Islamic law regarding property respects women's right to own property. The tendency for some women to spend their money as they please may reflect this religious/cultural practice, which holds men responsible for the family maintenance while women are seen as independent property owners. While marrying a rich wife could certainly be an advantage for a man, religious and cultural precepts have allowed some women to have a measure of control over their property.

7. Research shows that, regardless of women's gainful employment, mothers continue to do far more housework than do fathers. Myra M. Ferree, "Beyond Separate Spheres: Feminism and Family Research," *Journal of Marriage and the Family* 52 (1987): 886–94. See also Beth Manke, L. Brenda Seery, C. Ann Crouter, and Susan M. McHale, "The Three Corners of Domestic Labor: Mothers', Fathers', and Children's Weekday and Weekend Housework," *Journal of Marriage and the Family* 56 (1994): 657–68.

8. Studies researching the impact of the division of household chores show that sharing housework decreases wives' depression and increases their marital and personal well-being. Catherine E. Ross, John Mirrowsky, and Joan Huber, "Dividing Work, Sharing Work, and in-Between," *American Sociological Review* 48 (1987): 809–23; Rosalind C. Barnett and Grace K. Baruch, "Determinants of Fathers' Participation in Family Work," *Journal of Marriage and the Family* 49 (1987): 29–40.

9. Research shows that, although the majority of women perform more household tasks than do

men, only a minority of women view the division of labor in their families as being unfair. Linda Thompson and Alexis Walker, "Gender in Families: Women and Men in Marriage, Work, and Parenthood," *Journal of Marriage and the Family* 51 (1989): 845–71.

10. Research in the United States shows that fathers still spend relatively little time in child care. Furthermore, they rarely take sole responsibility for their children. Michael E. Lamb, "The Emergent American Father," in *The Father's Role: Cross-Cultural Perspectives,* ed. Michael E. Lamb (Hillsdale, N.J.: Lawrence Erlbaum, 1987), 3–26; Joseph H. Pleck, *Working Wives, Working Husbands* (Beverly Hills, Calif.: Sage Publications, 1985). Even when mothers are employed full-time, they spend twice as much time on housework and childcare as do fathers. Arlie Hochschild, *The Second Shift* (New York: Avon, 1989).

Bibliography

Abrahamian, Ervand. *Iran Between Two Revolutions.* Princeton, N.J.: Princeton Univ. Press, 1982.

Afary, Janet. "The Debate on Women's Liberation in the Iranian Constitutional Revolution, 1906–1911." In *Expanding the Boundaries of Women's History: Essays on Women in the Third World,* edited by Cheryl Johnson-Odim and Margaret Strobel, 101–21. Bloomington: Indiana Univ. Press, 1993.

———. "On the Origins of Feminism in Early 20th Century Iran." *Journal of Women's History* 1, no. 2 (1984): 65–87.

Afkhami, Mahnaz, and Erika Friedl, eds. *In the Eye of the Storm: Women in Post-Revolutionary Iran.* Syracuse, N.Y.: Syracuse Univ. Press, 1994.

Afshar, Haleh. *Islam and Feminism: An Iranian Case Study.* Women's Studies at York Series. New York: St. Martin's, 1998.

———. "Women, Marriage, and the State in Iran." In *Women, State, and Ideology,* edited by Haleh Afshar, 70–86. Basingstoke: Macmillan, 1987.

———. "Women and Work in Iran." *Political Studies* 45, no. 5 (1997): 755–67.

Aghajanian, Akbar. "Family Planning and Contraceptive Use in Iran, 1967–1992." *International Family Planning Perspectives* 20, no. 2 (June 1994): 66–69.

———. "Some Notes on Divorce in Iran." *Journal of Marriage and the Family* 48 (1986): 749–55.

Amato, R. Paul. "Father-Child Relations, Mother-Child Relations, and Offspring's Psychological Well-being in Early Adulthood." *Journal of Marriage and the Family* 56 (1994): 1031–42.

Asgar, Fathi. *Women and the Family in Iran.* Leiden: E. J. Brill, 1985.

Azari, Farah. *Women of Iran: The Conflict with Fundamentalist Islam.* London: Ithaca Press, 1983.

Bamdad, Badr al-Moluk. *From Darkness into Light: Women's Emancipation in Iran.* Translated by F. R. C. Bagely. Hicksville, N.Y.: Exposition Press, 1977.

Barnett, Rosalind Chait, and Grace K. Baruch. "Determinants of Fathers' Participation in Family Work." *Journal of Marriage and the Family* 49 (1987): 29–40.

Bauer, Janet. "Demographic Change, Women, and the Family in a Migrant Neighborhood in Tehran." In *Women and the Family in Iran,* edited by Asghar Fathi, 158–86. Leiden: E. J. Brill, 1985.

———. "Women, the Veil, and the Islamic Revolution in Iran." *Women in Anthropology: Symposium Papers 1979 and 1980.* Elizabeth J. Tudon (publication coordinator), 120–27. Sacramento Anthropological Society. Sacramento, Calif.: California State Univ., 1983.

Bayat-Phillip, Mangol. "Women and Revolution in Iran, 1905–1911." In *Women in the Muslim World,* edited by Lois Beck and Nikki Keddie, 295–308. Cambridge, Mass.: Harvard Univ. Press, 1978.

Berk, Sarah Fenstermaker. *The Gender Factory: The Appointment of Work in American Households.* New York: Plenum, 1985.

Bernard, Jessie. *The Future of Motherhood.* New York: Dial Press, 1974.

Betteridge, Anne H. "To Veil or Not to Veil: A Matter of Protest or Policy." In *Women and Revolution in Iran,* edited by Guity Nasaht, 109–28. Boulder, Colo.: Westview, 1983.

Brayfield, April A. "Juggling Jobs and Kids: The Impact of Employment Schedules on Fathers Caring for Children." *Journal of Marriage and the Family* 57 (1995): 321–32.

Carlson, Kathie. *In Her Image: The Unhealed Daughter's Search for Her Mother.* Boston: Shambhala Publications, 1989.

Chodorow, Nancy. *The Reproduction of Mothering: Psychoanalysis and the Sociology of Gender.* Berkeley: Univ. of California Press, 1978.

Darrow, William R. "Women's Place and the Place of Women in the Iranian Revolution." In *Women, Religion, and Social Change,* edited by Yvonne Y. Haddad and Ellison B. Findly, 307–19. New York: State Univ. of New York, 1985.

Esfandiari, Haleh. *Reconstructed Lives: Women and Iran's Islamic Revolution.* Washington, D.C.: Woodrow Wilson Center, 1997.

Ferdows, Adele. "Women and the Islamic Revolution." *International Journal of Middle East Studies* 15, no 2 (1983): 283–98.

Fernea, Elizabeth W. *In Search of Islamic Feminism: One Woman's Global Journey.* London: Anchor Books Doubleday, 1998.

Fernea, Elizabeth W., and Robert A. Fernea. *The Arab World: Personal Encounters.* London: Anchor Books Doubleday, 1985.

Ferree, Myra M. "Beyond Separate Spheres: Feminism and Family Research." *Journal of Marriage and the Family* 52 (1987): 886–94.

Fischer, Lucy Rose. *Linked Lives: Adult Daughters and Their Mothers.* New York: Harper and Row Publishers, 1986.

Friday, Nancy. *My Mother My Self: The Daughter's Search for Identity.* New York: Dell Publishing. 1978.

Ghorayshi, Parvin. "Women, Paid-Work, and the Family in the Islamic Republic of Iran." *Journal of Comparative Family Studies* 27 (1996): 453–66.

Goodnow, J. "Children's Household Work: Its Nature and Functions." *Psychological Bulletin* 103 (1988): 5–26.

Haeri, Shahla. *Law of Desire: Temporary Marriage in Shi'i Iran.* Syracuse, N.Y.: Syracuse Univ. Press, 1989.

———. "Of Feminism and Fundamentalism in Iran and Pakistan." *Contentions* 4, no. 3 (1995): 129–49.

———. "Women, Law, and Social Change in Iran." In *Women in Contemporary Muslim Societies,* edited by Jane I. Smith, 209–34. Lewisburg, Pa.: Bucknell Univ. Press, 1980.

Higgins, Patricia. "Women in the Islamic Republic of Iran: Legal, Social, and Ideological Changes." *Signs: Journal of Women in Culture and Society* 10, no. 3 (1985): 477–94.

Hochschild, Arlie. *The Second Shift.* New York: Avon, 1989.

Hoodfar, Homa. "Bargaining with Fundamentalism: Women and the Politics of Population Control in Iran." *Reproductive Health Matters* 8 (1996): 30–39.

———. "Population Policy and Gender Equity in Post-Revolutionary Iran." In *Family, Gender, and Population in the Middle East: Policy in Context,* edited by Carla Makhlouf Obermeyer, 105–35. Cairo: American Univ. in Cairo Press, 1995.

———. "The Women's Movement in Iran: Women at the Crossroad of Secularization and Islamization." *Women Living Under Muslim Laws* The Women's Movement Series 1, no. 6 (1999): 12–18.

———. "Women and Personal Status Law: An Interview with Mehranguis Kar." *Middle East Report* 26, no. 1 (1996): 36–38.

Kian, Azadeh. "Gendered Occupation and Women's Status in Post-Revolutionary Iran." *Middle Eastern Studies* 31 (1995): 407–21.

Lamb, Michael E. "The Emergent American Father." In *The Father's Role: Applied Perspectives,* edited by M. E. Lamb, 3–26. Hillsdale, N.J.: Lawrence Erlbaum, 1987.

Manke, Beth, L. Brenda Seery, C. Ann Crouter, and Susan M. McHale. "The Three Corners of Domestic Labor: Mothers', Fathers', and Children's Weekday and Weekend Housework." *Journal of Marriage and the Family* 56 (1994): 657–68.

Mir-Hossaini, Ziba. *Marriage on Trial: Islamic Family Law in Iran and Morocco.* London: I. B. Tauris, 1993.

Moghadam, Valentine. "Women's Employment Issues in Contemporary Iran: Problems and Prospects in the 1990s." *Iranian Studies* 28 (1995): 175–202.

Moghissi, Haideh. "Women, Modernization, and Revolution in Iran." *The Review of Radical Political Economics* 23, no. 3/4 (1991): 205–33.

Momeni, Jamshid. "Divorce in the Islamic Context: Emphasis on Shi'ite Islam." *Islamic Culture* 60, no. 2 (1986): 1–40.

Mossavar-Rahmani, Yasmin L. "Family Planning in Post-Revolutionary Iran." In *Women and Revolution in Iran,* edited by Guity Nashat, 253–62. Boulder, Colo.: Westview, 1983.

Nashat, Guity. "Women in Pre-Revolutionary Iran: A Historical Overview." In *Women and Revolution in Iran,* edited by Guity Nashat, 5–35. Boulder, Colo.: Westview, 1983.

Nassehy, Vida. "Female Role and Divorce in Iran." *International Journal of the Sociology of the Family* 21, no. 1 (1991): 53–65.

"No to Veil!" *Women and Revolution.* Special Issue on Iran, 19 (1979): 1–2, 10.

Obermeyer, Carla Makhlouf. "Reproductive Choice in Islam: Gender and State in Iran and Tunisia." *Studies in Family Planning* 25, no. 1 (Jan./Feb. 1994): 41–51.

Pakizegi, Behnaz. "Legal and Social Position of Iranian Women." In *Women in the Muslim World,* edited by Lois Beck and Nikki Keddie, 216–26. Cambridge, Mass.: Harvard Univ. Press, 1978.

Pleck, Joseph H. *Working Wives, Working Husbands.* Beverly Hills, Calif.: Sage Publications, 1985.

Pruett, Kyle D. *The Nurturing Father.* New York: Warner Books, 1987.

Ramazani, Nesta. "Women in Iran: The Revolutionary Ebb and Flow." *Middle East Journal* 47, no. 3 (1993): 409–28.

Robinson, Bryan E., and Robert L. Barret. *The Developing Father: Emerging Roles in Contemporary Society.* New York: Guilford, 1986.

Ross, Catherine E., John Mirrowsky, and Joan Huber. "Dividing Work, Sharing Work, and In-Between." *American Sociological Review* 48 (1983): 809–23.

Sansarian, Eliz. *The Women's Rights Movement in Iran: Mutiny, Appeasement, and Repression from 1900 to Khomeini 1982.* New York: Praeger, 1983.

Saroukhani, Bagher. "Dower (mahriyeh): A Tradition of Mate Selection in Iran." *International Journal of Sociology of the Family* 9 (1985): 17–26.

Sedghi, Hamideh. "Women, the State, and Development: Appraising Secular and Religious Gender Politics in Iran." In *The Gendered New World Order: Militarism, Development, and the Environment,* edited by Jennifer Turpin and Lois Ann Lorentzen, 113–26. New York: Routledge, 1996.

Shahidian, Hammed. "National and International Aspects of Feminist Movements: The Example of the Iranian Revolution of 1978–79." *Critique: Journal for Critical Studies of the Middle East* 2 (1993): 33–53.

Shirazi-Mohajan, Faegheh. "A Dramaturgical Approach to Hijab in Post-Revolutionary Iran." *Critique: Journal for Critical Studies of the Middle East* 7 (1995): 35–52.

———. "The Politics of Clothing in the Middle East: The Case of Hijab in Post-Revolutionary Iran." *Critique: Journal for Critical Studies of the Middle East* 2 (1993): 54–63.

Snarey, John. *How Fathers Care for the Next Generation: A Four-Decade Study.* Cambridge, Mass.: Harvard Univ. Press, 1993.

Tabari, Azar. "The Women's Movement in Iran: A Hopeful Prognosis." *Feminist Studies* 12, no. 2 (1986): 342–60.

Tabari, Azar, and Nahid Yeganeh, eds. *In the Shadow of Islam: The Women's Movement in Iran.* London: Zed Press, 1982.

Tabataba'i, Allameh, and Seyyed Hossein Nasr. "Mut'ah or Temporary Marriage." In *Shi'ism: Doctrines, Thought, and Spirituality,* edited by Seyyed Hossein Nasr et al., 213–16. Albany, N.Y.: State Univ. of New York, 1988.

Thompson, Linda, and Alexis J. Walker. "Gender in Families: Women and Men in Marriage, Work, and Parenthood." *Journal of Marriage and the Family* 51 (1989): 845–71.

Touba, Jacquiline Rudolph. "The Effects of the Iranian Revolution on Women and the Family in Iran: Some Preliminary Observations." In *Women and the Family in Iran,* edited by Asghar Fathi, 131–50. Leiden: E. J. Brill, 1985.

Tucker, E. Judith. *Arab Women: Old Boundaries, New Frontiers.* Bloomington and Indianapolis: Indiana Univ. Press, 1983.

Vatandoust, Gholamreza. "The Status of Iranian Women During the Pahlavi Regime." In *Women and the Family in Iran,* edited by Asghar Fathi, 107–30. Leiden: E. J. Brill, 1985.

Wallerstein, Judith S., and Sandra Blakeslee. *Second Chance: Men, Women, and Children a Decade after Divorce.* New York: Ticknor and Fields, 1989.

Weiskopf-Bock, Sally. "The Working Iranian Mother." In *Women and the Family in Iran,* edited by Asghar Fathi, 187–94. Leiden: E. J. Brill, 1985.

White, Lynn K., and Daniel B. Brinkerhoff. "Children's Work in the Family: Its Significance and Meaning." *Journal of Marriage and the Family* 43 (1981): 789–98.

Wodak, Ruth, and Muriel Schultz. *The Language of Love and Guilt: Mother-Daughter Relationship from a Cross-Cultural Perspective.* Philadelphia, Pa.: John Benjamin Publishing, 1986.

Zipes, Jack. *Arabian Nights: The Marvels and Wonders of the Thousand and One Nights.* Adapted by Jack Zipes. New York: Signet Classics, 1991.